THE CHANG
FACE OF SP
EDUCATIONAL
NEEDS

Mar

Tel:

The Changing Face of Special Educational Needs shows teachers, Special Educational Needs Coordinators (SENCOs) and students in teacher training how to respond to the rapidly changing context of special education. This highly practical and accessible text unlocks the often confusing field of special education provision in schools today by:

- summarising and clarifying new policy directions as they emerge, in light of recent coalition government policies on education, SEN and disability;
- suggesting clear, practical activities to bring the theory to life, helping practitioners to review and reflect on their work;
- encouraging critical reflection about existing systems within the school context, considering whether these will remain appropriate and 'fit for purpose';
- giving opportunities for teachers, SENCOs and senior leaders to contextualise the new changes in terms of the implications for practice in their own school.

Packed with activities, case studies and points for reflection, this timely book will help the teacher, SENCO, senior leader or adviser to make sense of the rapid pace of change of policy and terminology related to SEN. It will help practitioners in a positive and supportive way, emphasising the exciting opportunities that these changes will provide for developing new, innovative and creative working practices.

This book will also be essential reading for all SENCOs completing the National Award for SEN Coordination.

Al   ins is Course Director of the National Award for SEN Coordination at   Christ Church University, where she developed, leads and teaches the new   training programme for SENCOs.

THE CHANGING FACE OF SPECIAL EDUCATIONAL NEEDS

Impact and implications for SENCOs and their schools

Alison Ekins

Routledge
Taylor & Francis Group

LONDON AND NEW YORK

First published 2012
by Routledge
2 Park Square, Milton Park, Abingdon, Oxon OX14 4RN

Simultaneously published in the USA and Canada
by Routledge
711 Third Avenue, New York, NY 10017

Routledge is an imprint of the Taylor & Francis Group, an informa business

British Library Cataloguing in Publication Data
A catalogue record for this book is available from the British Library

Library of Congress Cataloging in Publication Data
Ekins, Alison.
  The changing face of special educational needs: impact and implications
  for SENCOS and their schools/by Alison Ekins.
    p. cm.
  Includes bibliographical references and index.
  1. Special education.   2. Inclusive education.   I. Title.
  LC3965.E4 2012
  371.9 – dc22   2011015596

ISBN: 978-0-415-67614-4 (hbk)
ISBN: 978-0-415-67615-1 (pbk)
ISBN: 978-0-203-69812-9 (ebk)

Typeset in Times New Roman by
Florence Production Ltd, Stoodleigh, Devon

MIX
Paper from
responsible sources
FSC® C004839
www.fsc.org

Printed and bound in Great Britain by
TJ International Ltd, Padstow, Cornwall

CONTENTS

ACKNOWLEDGEMENTS

I would like to thank my family for their ongoing support, without which none of this would have been possible!

I would also like to thank colleagues who have supported me in developing ideas, including providing me with the most up-to-date reflections from their different perspectives on the changes that we are embarking on. In particular, I would therefore like to acknowledge and thank, Tony Booth, Sonia Blandford and Kevin Williams.

Most importantly, I would like to thank the many SENCOs that I work with, and to acknowledge the tremendous work that they put in, working to change and improve systems for pupils with SEN and/or disabilities and their families. I hope that this book will provide some support to them as they continue in their journey to develop meaningful practices that inclusively support the needs of all pupils.

RE-EXAMINING PRACTICES IN A TIME OF CHANGE

THIS CHAPTER:

▪ contextualises the current period of rapid change within the Education and Special Educational Needs (SEN) systems;

▪ identifies key themes emerging from recent research and government documents relating to the need for change within the SEN system;

▪ considers the need for a values-based approach to change and development;

▪ summarises key principles for effective school development;

▪ introduces a framework for developing thinking and practice.

> We need to act urgently to ensure we do not let a generation of children leave school ill-equipped to lead an independent life and make a contribution to society.
>
> (Lamb, 2009: 2)

This book reflects on the changing context for education and special educational needs (SEN), at a time when recent systems have been identified as failing large numbers of pupils with SEN and/or disabilities:

> All children deserve a good education, with staff in schools giving them the confidence, self belief and teaching that they need to fulfil their potential. To date, the education system has failed to address barriers to learning and does not show the same unremitting commitment to every child's progress that is seen in the best schools.
>
> (DfE, 2011: 65)

While the sentiment in the opening sentence from the DfE (2011) is to be admired, this book critically examines the direction and potential impact of current change, helping practitioners explore ways that all children can receive the 'good', or better than good education that they deserve.

To do this involves posing challenging questions regarding the purpose of education; the definition of a 'good education'; what 'good education' will look like; and whether it will look the same for all children. In the context of changing policy directions and practices within the education and SEN systems, how far these challenging questions are actually acknowledged and addressed will be considered throughout the chapters in the book, and again specifically in the last chapter.

THE CURRENT PERIOD OF RAPID CHANGE

In England, we are in a time of unprecedented change brought about by the effects and impact of global economic recession, change of government and sweeping reforms of the education system and services to support children and families.

Since the election of the coalition government, we have seen the introduction of new policies and governmental priorities that promise radical reform of services to support the needs of children, focused on providing better outcomes for all. This has included the publication of the recent Green Paper *Support and Aspiration: A new approach to special educational needs* (DfE, 2011), which, while only a consultation document, still sets out the vision and direction of future policies. This is said to set out an 'ambitious vision for reform . . . [including] wide ranging proposals to improve outcomes for children and young people who are disabled or have SEN, minimise the adversarial nature of the system for families and maximise value for money' (DfE, 2011: 13).

We therefore find ourselves in a 'changing landscape' (Hallett and Hallett, 2010: 9) in relation to special educational needs, the role of the SENCO and also the development of the education system more widely.

The 'Case for Change' (DfE, 2010b) within both the education and special educational needs systems is clear. While new policies are certainly politically motivated, as a result of the changing government and the impact of the global economic recession, there is also a fundamental underlying need for change within both the education and special educational needs systems.

As many have noted (Warnock, 2005; House of Commons Select Committee, 2006; Lamb, 2009; Alexander, 2010), the existing system in place to support pupils with SEN within the education system is based on an outdated model of society, which is now not 'fit for purpose' (House of Commons, 2006: 12). It is noted that: 'Nearly everything about the construction of our current social system is based on separation and segregation. It is not a system which is well suited to the delivery of equality, participation and inclusion' (Rix *et al.*, 2010: 4).

A radical overhaul of the system (Lamb, 2009; DfE, 2011) is therefore required. For positive change to occur, which will impact meaningfully on pupils with SEN and/or disabilities and their families, we do need to consider fresh new approaches to conceptualising and responding to the complex concepts of special educational needs and disability. As Rix (2010) notes:

> Our chances of achieving structures and procedures that are responsive to individuals means we must not be wedded to any aspects of the system as it presently stands. We must be prepared to adapt to the circumstances, in a way that takes account of its ongoing impact on those affected. To develop in this way requires a great deal of flexibility. Our systems need to be capable of adapting and continuing to be adaptive without diminishing their cohesiveness or accountability.
>
> (Rix *et al.*, 2010: 4)

It is clear therefore that 'change is necessary' (Rix *et al.*, 2010: 4). While the current government promotes the new policies and proposals as providing a 'radical reform' of education and special educational needs systems (DfE, 2010a; DfE, 2011), this book will support practitioners to critically examine exactly how 'radical' these changes are, and how meaningful and effective they will be in terms of improving outcomes and life chances for pupils with SEN and/or disabilities. As Lamb (2009) notes:

We have a unique opportunity now to make a real and lasting change for future generations of children. This will only be realized if everyone within the system works towards these ends. The cultural change required will not be straightforward to implement – or always immediate – but should deliver greater ambition for our most vulnerable children and much greater engagement with their parents.

At this time, it is therefore essential that practitioners working in schools take time to critically consider the 'unique opportunities' that they have to change and develop existing practices to ensure meaningful impact for the pupils that they serve.

KEY THEMES SHAPING THE DEVELOPMENT OF NEW SYSTEMS

In recent years, we have seen a proliferation of reports and reviews about aspects of the special educational needs system within England (House of Commons, 2006; Bercow, 2008; Lamb, 2009). All identify the many flaws and failings of the current system, and many identify similar themes and key issues that need to be addressed in order to improve the way that the SEN system supports parents of and pupils with SEN and/or disabilities, identifying a number of common themes:

- communication with parents;
- parental confidence in the system;
- early identification of needs;
- services that work around the family;
- joint work across professional boundaries;
- greater equity in access to additional provision;
- the quality of training for staff, particularly for staff educating children and young people with the most complex needs.

(OFSTED, 2010: 17)

These themes have been reflected strongly within the OFSTED Review (2010), the recent DfE (2010a) White Paper, *The Importance of Teaching* and DfE (2011) Green Paper on SEN, *Support and Aspiration: A new approach to special educational needs*.

Within the OFSTED (2010) review of SEN and Disability, a number of specific recommendations for change were proposed, including the following:

- Schools should not be the only organisations held to account legally for the outcomes of children and young people with special educational needs and disabilities. All the services involved in any common assessment should be bound equally by its terms.
- The Code of Practice for Special Educational Needs and its statutory basis should be reviewed to reflect these recommendations across relevant departments.
- Any further changes to legislation or guidance should not simply add to the current arrangements but, rather, should simplify them and improve their consistency across different services and for children of different ages and levels of need.

(OFSTED, 2010: 14)

Throughout this book (and particularly in Chapters 2 and 3) the range of recommendations resulting from recent reviews and reports on the failings of the SEN system are critically reviewed and evaluated to determine how far the expectations and call for change has been answered within the recent policies to emerge from the coalition government.

This is an important time for the development of systems and processes to support all pupils, and particularly those with SEN and/or disabilities. These changes will have an impact on ways that practitioners can respond to meeting the needs of pupils with SEN and/or disabilities in their classrooms. They will have an impact on the way that pupils with SEN and their parents have statutory entitlements and equitable rights to meaningful learning experiences. Yet, the recent consultation process (10 September 2010–15 October 2010), leading to the publication of the Green Paper in March 2011, only received around 1,800 responses, 40 per cent of which are noted to have come from parents (DfE, 2011).

As there are currently 'just over one in five pupils – 1.7 million school-age children in England identified as having special educational needs' (OFSTED, 2010: 5) such a response rate seems disappointingly low.

It is essential that school-based practitioners, higher education colleagues, advisers, professionals from education, health and social care working with vulnerable pupils and families with SEN and/or disabilities, and, of course, parents and pupils themselves actively engage in detailed critical review and reflection about the reality of the situation for pupils with SEN and/or disabilities, and ways that it can be radically reformed in order to offer better outcomes for all.

The responses to the initial consultation did, however, identify some clear themes, which, while not statutory at the point of writing, will inform the development of future statutory policy documents. These include acknowledgement that:

▨ The system for supporting children, young people and families is overly complex, bureaucratic and adversarial.

▨ Parents want better information on the services available and the choice of schools.

▨ Better training is needed for school staff to recognise children's needs and work better with children and their parents.

▨ Education, health and social care services need to work better together to identify and deliver on children's needs.

(DfE, 2011: 26)

There is a call for the development of 'new and innovative ways of improving outcomes for disabled children and children with SEN' (DfE, 2011: 75) and a commitment to ensuring that 'there are more equitable opportunities to access high quality provision, regardless of need or location' (DfE, 2011: 76).

The purpose of this book is therefore to support practitioners to critically examine how fully and effectively new and innovative approaches are being developed, both through policy statements and through the development of practices in schools.

TERMINOLOGY

Before proceeding, it is important to reflect on the use of terminology throughout the book. This was a difficult issue to address. As the discussions in Chapters 3 and 7 highlight, the term 'SEN' is a complex and ambiguous one. Ideally, at this point of change and development within the education system, I would have liked to have seen the removal of this confused terminology, with a more appropriate and meaningful term being introduced to support discussions about and identification of pupils with complex special educational needs, along an inclusive continuum of support needs that identifies that any and all pupils have different learning needs and requirements. However, for now, SEN remains the term, or label, that is consistently used within educational discussions.

Linked to the complex issue of SEN, however, is also the concept of disability, which, in its own right is a complex and difficult label, meaning different things to different people. There is therefore 'increasing confusion between SEN and disability. While there is considerable overlap, it is not the case that all children with disabilities are defined as having SEN or that all children with SEN are defined as having a disability' (House of Commons, 2006: 16).

Having acknowledged the problems and tensions that the terms 'SEN' and 'disability' present, as both continue to be established terms, for ease of purpose, the term 'SEN and/or disabilities' will be used throughout the book.

A VALUES-BASED APPROACH TO CHANGE AND DEVELOPMENT

This book is specifically written to support practitioners to understand and actively engage, through critical reflection, in the changes that are taking place within the SEN system in particular.

However, SEN practices do not develop in isolation. They should not be considered as something that develops separately from policies and practices to support pupils in education generally. For too long, policies around SEN have been sidelined and not considered within the bigger picture of educational trends and patterns impacting on education more widely. Thus, it is acknowledged that:

> The SEN system often gets discussed as if it is a separate system that operates outside the broader education sector. It is widely recognized that this is not the case . . . SEN policy needs to be considered in a broader educational context.
>
> (House of Commons, 2006: 18)

Tensions between competing policy drives have therefore been exacerbated, where SEN is seen as separate to and competing with broader educational policy and practice, as evidenced in the 'unwillingness of successful mainstream schools (selective and non selective) to take their fair share of SEN pupils' (House of Commons, 2006: 47).

Thus it is identified that:

> the government should give careful consideration to the impact that key drivers such as league tables are having on admissions – particularly to the most successful non-selective state schools. There is strong evidence that the existing presentation of performance data in league tables does not reflect well on many children with SEN and consequently acts as a disincentive for some schools to accept them. This cannot continue.
>
> (House of Commons, 2006: 47)

This was apparent within the previous government's at times competing policies around SEN and inclusion, and the rapid driving up of standards. Without clear attention being paid to how the two policy drives could comfortably sit beside each other, they were often viewed as competing agendas, incompatible and unrealistic. As the House of Commons Select Committee Report at the time acknowledged that separate and confusing policies about SEN, sometimes linked to wider inclusion agendas, and the 'raising attainment agenda sit very uncomfortably together at present' (House of Commons, 2006: 66).There is therefore a real need for discussions and policies about special educational needs to be 'brought into the mainstream education policy agenda' (House of Commons, 2006: 7) rather than developed separately and in isolation from wider policies.

Policy developments also need to fully reflect the experiences of pupils, and there are some concerns, as Parry *et al.* (2010) note that increasingly an 'emerging gap has developed between policy intentions and the real experiences of young people "on the margins" (Milbourne, 2009; Reay, 2008; Sheppard *et al.*, 2008)' (Parry *et al.*, 2010: 1).

To be able to understand the impact of changes to practice in schools on the experiences of the pupil, it is therefore also important to consider inclusive principles: the whole experience of the child:

■ What does the child with SEN and/or disabilities experience in school?
■ Are they fully included within the teaching and learning opportunities experienced by their peers?
■ How are pupils with SEN and/or disabilities perceived by their teachers and other staff within the school setting? Are they the 'responsibility' of another member of staff, the SENCO or a teaching assistant? Or are they seen to be fully included, and the full responsibility of the class teacher?
■ What about systems and processes to support pupils with SEN and/or disabilities? Are these separate and different systems and processes to those which support other pupils? Or are systems set up inclusively to remove the focus on differences between pupils with SEN and/or disabilities and other peers?

These, and other key challenging questions, run throughout the chapters in this book, with commentary and activities designed to support the practitioner to actively question and reconsider existing practice, in order to enable effective development of thinking, understanding and practice within the school context. It is acknowledged therefore that educational issues are often 'complex and contentious and often involve passionately held beliefs and values' (Barton, 2010: 91).

This book is about supporting practitioners to more fully understand and engage with those contentious or emotive issues. The book aims to help practitioners to reconnect and engage with the principles and values that underpin our system and the changes that are being introduced. It is about supporting practitioners to reflect on and question taken-for-granted assumptions, practices and expectations.

In a time of significant educational change, with the introduction of new policy directions introduced by the coalition government, there is therefore a need to stop and critically consider the implications of this changing context for pupils with SEN and/or disabilities. We must ensure that, throughout changing policy directives, the focus remains on the child: the experiences and opportunities that the changing contexts provide for pupils with SEN and/or disabilities and their families. Indeed, it is interesting that within the recent Green Paper on SEN (DfE, 2011) while there is a very clear focus on changing SEN systems to support the needs of parents and families of pupils with SEN and/or disabilities, the voice of the child, the pupil with SEN and/or disabilities is not so clear.

Throughout the education system, we will come across competing values and principles. This is particularly noticeable in the current period of change as a result of a new government, and the new priorities that they are emphasising within the emerging policies. Education policies are, therefore, not just developed to respond to the fundamental rights and needs of individual pupils with SEN and/or disabilities. Instead, they are developed within the context of a much broader political agenda, following the principles of the elected government. As Barton (2010) identified: 'Government priorities and decisions, and the values informing them, are all part of the public manifestation of the intentions and vision they hold with regard to the form of society they wish to see develop and continue' (Barton, 2010: 91).

Yet, we must acknowledge that education, including special education, is not just a matter of curriculum delivery. Instead, it is about a deep connection with values and principles.

While, for many of us, we will not have direct impact on the development of the actual policies emerging from government, as practitioners, it is our responsibility to interpret those policies within the context of the pupils with whom we are working. The current government seems to be providing more opportunities for schools to do this, through their emphasis on reducing bureaucracy, reduced prescription from government and an increased focus on the development of innovative and creative approaches to respond more directly to individualised contexts (DfE, 2010a; DfE, 2011). The new coalition government has therefore expressed an interest in introducing 'new and innovative ways of improving outcomes for disabled children and children with SEN. We support the move to a more integrated education system' (DfE, 2011: 75).

Real, meaningful, radical reform will not be achieved by 'tinkering at the edges' of the system. Nor will it be achieved through the introduction or implementation of prescriptive 'one size fits all' models of practice. Rather, change will only be effectively secured through detailed discussions based on consideration of 'enhanced rights and a cultural shift in the way in which schools, local authorities and other professionals work with parents and children' (Lamb, 2009: 1).

It is this 'cultural shift' that this book is concerned with, supporting practitioners to engage with greater understanding with the widespread cultural changes that are required in order to improve the outcomes, experiences and participation of pupils with SEN and/or disabilities throughout the education system.

KEY PRINCIPLES FOR EFFECTIVE SCHOOL DEVELOPMENT

This book is about meaningful whole school development within a time of change. It is not a book that is only intended for the SENCO or SEN specialist teacher. Rather, this book reflects the principle that for SEN systems to change to enable improvements in practice for all pupils with SEN and/or disabilities and their parents and families, all staff – teachers and support staff – need to be actively involved in regular reviews of practice in their school setting. It is widely acknowledged that 'All teachers are teachers of SEN' (DES, 1999; DfES, 2004; House of Commons, 2006; Lamb, 2009) but yet this is still often not the established day-to-day practice within our schools. Often the coordination and planning for pupils with SEN and/or disabilities falls to one identified member of staff within the school – the SENCO, and the day-to-day individual support for pupils with high levels of complex needs often falls to the unqualified teaching assistant or learning support assistant.

Such practices must be challenged, in order to establish an approach to critically reconsidering and examining existing practices and to develop a whole school approach to meeting the needs of pupils with SEN and/or disabilities, which is fully embedded within an approach to whole school development.

Much has been written about principles of effective school development, traditionally separated into the fields of 'school effectiveness' and 'school improvement' (see, for example: Stoll and Fink, 1989; Slee *et al.*, 1998; MacBeath, 1999; Hopkins, 2007; MacBeath *et al.*, 2007), and while it is not the intention here to present the various discussions in detail, it is essential to emphasise the importance of a whole school approach to school development. The term 'school development' rather than 'school improvement' is used here to signify understanding that 'schools are complex social contexts where any initiatives to change practice must be seen as a developmental process' (Ekins and Grimes, 2009: 7). Not all schools develop practice in the same way, and the way that they do develop practice is highly dependent on underlying aspects of the embedded culture and ways that staff work together (Ekins, 2010b). Change is therefore a developmental process, rather than a simple process of 'improvement' or 'developing effectiveness'.

Many different models have been produced to support effective whole school development, or improvement, processes, including the implementation of the School Improvement Cycle (DfES, 2005); termly school improvement cycles (DCSF, 2009) and also other approaches including the Index for Inclusion (Booth and Ainscow, 2002).

Since the beginning of the twenty-first century the Index for Inclusion has provided a whole school resource and tool to explore and re-examine aspects of practice. This model has been built on the importance of the inter-relationship between inclusive cultures; inclusive policies and inclusive practices; with the emphasis on inclusive cultures providing the foundation on which the others – policies and practices – are built.

As we enter into this period of change and development within the education system, the Index for Inclusion has been revised, to incorporate a fourth dimension and reflect the developing understanding by the authors of the impact of curriculum on the production of meaningful learning experiences for all pupils.

Building on the work of Booth and Ainscow (2002) through their focus on the need to 'remove barriers to learning and participation for all' (Booth and Ainscow, 2002: 4), and the need to not only focus on the policies and practices within a school, but to pay close attention to the underlying cultures within the school, the key principles underpinning the approach to school development within this book include:

▪ collaboration
▪ shared vision/principles
▪ collective responsibility
▪ shared ownership.

While they have been presented above as separate bullet points, it is important to note that the links between each principle are often blurred and messy; it is not always easy to define where we move from one principle into another. They are not linear or hierarchical. Rather, they work together to underpin a values-based approach to school development, which is based on an intrinsic understanding of the need for all staff to work together and be part of the whole school development process. Therefore, while it is acknowledged that at times, there may be the need for an identified individual to take the lead in introducing or implementing a change of development in practice within the school context, for that change or development to become effective and embedded within whole school practice, it needs to be shared and understood by all staff, who show commitment to engaging in the change, and who recognise their responsibilities and duties in respect of the change.

High levels of reflective dialogue and collaboration between staff members are therefore required in order to effect meaningful whole school change and development. Staff need to be provided with an environment and culture where reflective questioning of existing practice is encouraged, where there are opportunities for different staff members to put forward new and innovative ideas about ways to develop and improve practice, and where outdated practices that are not impacting directly on practice and improved outcomes for pupils are identified and re-examined.

These principles would seem to fit within the notion of 'communities of practice' (Lave and Wenger, 1998; Sergiovanni, 2001; Ainscow *et al.*, 2006; Howes *et al.*, 2009), which has gained emphasis within educational discussions. A 'community of practice' is defined as 'one where teachers participate in decision making, have a shared sense of purpose, engage in collaborative work and accept joint responsibility for the outcomes' (Harris, 2006: ix).

Durrant and Holden (2006) note that there is a difference between 'shared leadership of change (as opposed to simply shared implementation)' (Durrant and Holden, 2006: 9). This is an important point. To what extent do opportunities currently exist within our schools to encourage shared leadership of change, rather than the simpler shared implementation?

With the current government focus on lessening the tight prescription and controls from Whitehall that we saw through the Labour government (with increased prescription about which interventions and teaching approaches to use), there is a promise of greater opportunity to develop individualised innovative approaches to respond to the needs of pupils within particular school contexts (DfE, 2010a; DfE, 2011). This may therefore provide the platform for enhanced opportunities to really engage in shared leadership of change, through the key principles of:

- collaboration
- shared vision/principles
- collective responsibility
- shared ownership.

However, meaningful school development is not just about teachers working together (although this is, admittedly, a key component). For real change to occur that is relevant to the pupils and families that the school is serving, all stakeholders, including the pupils and families themselves, need to be encouraged to engage in critical review and decision making about how practices need to develop to enable improved outcomes for all pupils. This will, especially, include involving pupils with SEN and/or disabilities in a whole 'school improvement cycle of analysis, action, evaluation and review' (DfE, 2010c: 4).

This is likely to look different for each school, as it needs to reflect the particular and individual context within which the school is operating: including factors impacting on and significant within the local community, the relationship between parents and school staff and individual circumstances impacting on the school.

These principles are also reflected in the *Achievement for All* approach, which has recently been highlighted (Lamb, 2009; DCSF, 2010b; DfE, 2011) as an effective way to raise outcomes for pupils with SEN. *Achievement for All* has three main aims:

■ to improve the attainment and progress of children with SEN and disabilities;
■ to improve the engagement of their parents with the school;
■ to improve the wider outcomes for this group.

(Lamb, 2009: 23)

These aims, however, are achieved within a whole school approach that considers and develops underlying cultures and practices within the whole school context, rather than through an approach that simply implements strategies for pupils with SEN. The focus is on finding ways to improve the access, aspirations and achievement of all pupils, particularly those with SEN and/or disabilities. This is achieved through developing understanding of the importance of a cultural shift within the school; moving away from an approach where the SENCO is the sole supporter of pupils with SEN, to one in which all staff share responsibility and work proactively and collaboratively to improve outcomes for all pupils, including those with SEN and/or disabilities. Thus:

Achievement for All provides a framework for leaders to help drive school improvement. [It] takes a whole school approach to school improvement, focusing on improving teaching and learning for all children and young people, particularly the 20% of the school population identified as [having] special educational needs and/or disabilities.

(National College, 2010a: 1)

Achievement for All is therefore an approach that emphasises long-term sustainable impact over short-term quick fix solutions, which rarely significantly impact on the longer term needs and experiences of the individual. It is about changing the culture of expectations and practices across a whole school community, to include raising the aspirations of pupils and parents themselves.

The approach is based on principles that are very similar to those identified in the discussions above as central to meaningful whole school development:

■ Shared vision – a core set of values and beliefs, shared by all staff, that all children and young people have the right to opportunities to develop their learning.
■ Commitment – to creating an ethos and culture of achievement across the whole school, a determination to secure the best provision for vulnerable children and young people and to provide effective professional development for staff.
■ Collaboration – with parents, children and young people and others within and beyond the school, including other schools, to develop and share best practice.
■ Communication – with and between children and young people, their parents, staff, other schools and other agencies.

(National College, 2010a: 1)

These principles, moving SEN understanding, development and practices away from the sideline and into a whole school approach that supports cultural shifts in thinking and practice are at the heart of the approach supported within this book. This book therefore carefully considers the principles underpinning effective whole school development, supporting practitioners to engage with the ideas through values-based reflection, emphasising that change will not occur through one person alone, but through the development of a culture and community of practice built onon principles of shared leadership. In this way, it is understood that: 'Inclusive, systemic education reform calls for reflective collaboration among all stakeholders' (Bentley, 2010: 265).

Changing and reforming our education and SEN systems is therefore not just about the simple implementation of specific strategies. It must be understood, instead, that it will involve a values-based approach to critical review and reflection that will, at times, be challenging and difficult.

A FRAMEWORK FOR DEVELOPING PRACTICE

Reviewing existing knowledge, understanding and practices is an essential starting point to any meaningful change or development in practice. All too often, changes in practice are made without clearly examining and understanding how effective the initial practice was, and changes are imposed regardless of whether it was actually necessary. At other times, practices become so deeply embedded within the culture of practice, in a school, or indeed within the education system, that the practice or principle is accepted without question.

This book supports an approach to the development of practice that is based on prioritising time for critical review and reflection before meaningful action planning occurs to impact positively on practice and systems within the whole school context.

In my recent work with SENCOs engaged on the new statutory National Award for SEN Coordination course, and in my approach to working directly with schools in advisory and consultancy capacities, I have therefore developed a framework to support the development of critical and reflective thinking, which is focused on impact and leads to meaningful action planning to promote positive impact within the school context. This has become a powerful tool in supporting whole school transformation, with individuals and whole staff engaging in a dynamic process of:

- review
- reflection
- action
- impact.

Within my teaching and advisory work with schools, these linked and dynamic processes have evolved into the framework for thinking and action shown in Figure 1.1.

This model is a powerful tool to support the development of meaningful review and reflection about existing practices, which then ultimately leads to relevant action planning and impact on the development of practices leading to improved outcomes for all pupils, including those with SEN and/or disabilities within the school context.

In a time of significant change and development within the political and educational contexts, it is therefore important to support an approach that emphasises the need to reconnect with values, through critical and meaningful review and reflection about the

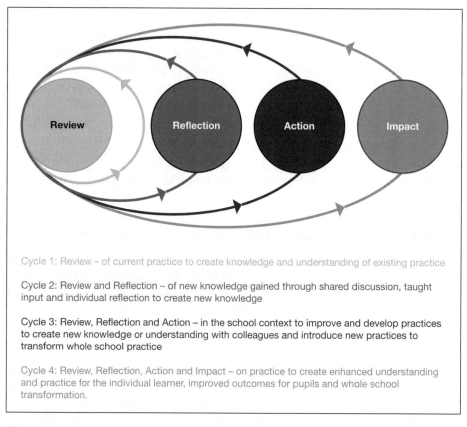

Cycle 1: Review – of current practice to create knowledge and understanding of existing practice

Cycle 2: Review and Reflection – of new knowledge gained through shared discussion, taught input and individual reflection to create new knowledge

Cycle 3: Review, Reflection and Action – in the school context to improve and develop practices to create new knowledge or understanding with colleagues and introduce new practices to transform whole school practice

Cycle 4: Review, Reflection, Action and Impact – on practice to create enhanced understanding and practice for the individual learner, improved outcomes for pupils and whole school transformation.

■ **Figure 1.1** Impact focused development of practice in schools

appropriateness of existing practices compared with new developments that will emerge. When thinking about how to most effectively present the discussions in this book so as to enable practitioners to engage in the same sort of process, I have therefore decided to explicitly use the same principles to structure each chapter.

Throughout all chapters a range of activities have been planned to support readers to directly engage with the review, reflection, action and impact cycle. While it is possible, and useful, to engage in and undertake these activities by yourself, to critically review and reflect on your own practices and consider ways to change and develop it to enhance outcomes for the pupils with whom you work, the importance of collaborative, whole school strategic review and reflection is emphasised. Thus, you are encouraged to engage as fully as possible with the discussions throughout the book, to stimulate wider whole school review and reflection, leading to shared commitment to action planning for changes to be made, and a collective evaluation of the impact of the changes that have been made.

Within each chapter, you will be supported to initially review your existing know-ledge about key systems or concepts, and to reconsider practices that currently exist in your school. This is a central part of the approach that I have developed. It is important that practitioners feel that their expertise and knowledge is valued and used as a way to develop practices, rather than ignored. The approach is empowering, aimed at supporting all staff to consider their own personal skills and knowledge relating to different concepts and aspects of practice. In this way, the approach that I have developed and will use throughout the book, explicitly acknowledges that practitioners are not 'empty vessels' waiting to be filled. Neither are teachers simple 'technicians' or 'deliverers' of a prescribed curriculum. Rather, the focus is on empowering teachers and practitioners to feel able to lead change and development within their school contexts in meaningful ways. In this way, the approach seeks to 'nurture the expert within' (Dadds, 2001: 50).

This is an important starting point of any meaningful change that the practitioner will feel real commitment and ownership towards.

Drawing on the work of Ainscow *et al.* (2006), I use the concept of 'principled interruptions' to encourage practitioners to 'make the familiar unfamiliar' (Delamont and Atkinson, 1995). This is a powerful strategy and technique, and in the specifically designed review questions at the start of each chapter, the reader will be supported to question existing practices in ways that they may not have previously considered. The focus is on moving beyond acceptance of existing practices and assumptions: 'this is the way we always do it/think about it here' into an approach where those established practices are actually critically re-examined to expose any inconsistencies in approach. For example, the traditional deployment of support staff to work with individual identified pupils with SEN; or the established use of setting as a practice to best meet the needs of all pupils may be critically re-examined to ensure that the established practice really is the most effective in producing improved outcomes for all pupils, and particularly those with SEN and/or disabilities.

This strategy is often overlooked in the busy context of the school or classroom, where the focus can be on the 'here and now'. This book emphasises that, when time can be prioritised for the effective review and re-examination of practice through the use of 'principled interruptions', the impact on whole school practice can be significant.

Building on the review process at the start of each chapter, a range of strategies are used to support the reader to engage in creating new knowledge and understanding of systems, processes, practices and assumptions through the process of critical reflection. Within this section of each chapter, new knowledge (in the form of up-to-date information about current changes occurring within the education and SEN systems) is presented, with opportunities to critically reflect on the implications of those changes for the development of practice across the education system, and within your own particular school setting.

Again, a critical approach is taken to exposing embedded assumptions, values and tensions that may occur within and between different policy documents shaping the future of education and the way that pupils with SEN are supported.

There is significant value at this stage of the process, as there is throughout, in discussing some of the questions that arise with others. Discussion – the articulation and expression of different assumptions and beliefs about practices with colleagues – will enable deeper understanding and critical reflection to occur. In this, I draw on Schön's (1983) concept of Reflection in Action and Reflection on Action. However, I see this as occurring not as an individual activity, but instead as part of a collaborative learning process. Through collaboration and discussion assumptions, meanings and understandings are negotiated, re-examined and applied in new ways to different contexts to enhance meaning and practice.

At this stage, as a result of the process of review leading to reflection, new knowledge is therefore individually created, and it is this deeper understanding that will enable more effective action planning to suit the needs of the school, and the pupils that it serves. Within each chapter, readers are therefore encouraged at this stage to consider a range of action planning strategies, and to identify the specific ways that they will develop practices that are relevant and will be meaningful to the school.

The approach that I have developed acknowledges, however, that this should not be the end of the cycle of whole school development. Practitioners have become familiar, through the School Improvement Cycle (DfES, 2005) of the need to continually monitor, review and evaluate the adoption of systems and processes. However, in a busy school context, often overloaded with new initiatives coming on board before the full implementation of previous planned actions, this aspect of the cycle can be forgotten or missed. In the approach that I have developed there is, therefore, a need to very specifically focus on this aspect of developing practice. New practices and systems are not effective if they do not positively address the specific needs of the pupils for whom they are developed. Keeping a close focus on impact (and this is not just in terms of attainment levels, but can also include wider outcomes such as positive engagement, rising aspirations and increased involvement of parents) is therefore essential. To do this, however, requires a clear understanding and articulation of what impact is hoped for and expected. Again, this is an issue that is often overlooked, with not enough time to planning what level of impact should be achieved measured against the level and cost of resources going in to support the change in practice. Without such clear articulation, there can be an assumption that any change is positive, when, in reality, the change may not have had the positive and meaningful impact on outcomes that is needed or should be expected.

The review, reflection, action, impact cycle is a powerful tool for supporting whole school transformation of practice and assumptions. While I have used it here as a way to structure the discussions within each chapter, it is important that the model is rooted in practice. It was developed and has been used initially in practice to support practitioners in the very real task of re-evaluating existing practices to identify where changes need to occur and how this can happen. I would therefore encourage you, as you engage with the discussions, to use the activities presented to start the development of a journey within your school setting: one that is focused on the central principles of review, reflection, action and impact.

Collaboration is essential as part of the process. Meaningful development of practice rarely occurs if it is led solely by one person. Rather, there needs to be understanding of the importance of shared ownership established through collective discussion, under-standing and prioritisation of the changes in practice, systems or assumptions that are needed. All of the activities throughout the book can therefore be used to stimulate collaborative discussions as part of whole staff training and whole school development.

FINALLY

One of the respondents from the initial SEN and Disability consultation (DfE, 2011) identified:

> If I want to go somewhere I've never been before in my car – I get a map. A good map shows all the routes and the landscapes and the options. Where is the map for families to use if their child is identified with SEN? Here is our chance to create a map – one that all people can understand – using common language and well explained assessments.
>
> (DfE, 2011: 27)

Using the process that I have evolved to use through the book, it is hoped that you will be empowered to develop a clear map of SEN provision and practice, which is based on your critical review of existing practice, informed understanding of new approaches and thinking, and clear action planning that has had a direct impact to improve and develop practices within your school context.

Reflective activity 1.1

- What does the current 'map' of SEN provision look like?
- Where do you and your colleagues go for support and guidance about SEN procedure and practice?
- Where do parents go for support and guidance?
- Is the current guidance clear?
- Does it provide a useful 'map' of SEN procedure and system?
- What does the 'map' of SEN provision and practice look like in your school context?
- Would all colleagues draw the same 'map', or would there be differences?
- Would parents be able to identify/draw the same 'map'?
- What does this tell us about how well things are currently working?

Once you have finished the book, and have engaged in and had time to evaluate the impact of some of the reflections and action planning that you have completed, draw a new 'map' of SEN practice and provision. Return to this initial map and compare how practices have changed and developed as a result.

By the end of the book, it is hoped that the reader will have gained more under-standing of the developing map of SEN provision and practice nationally, as well as reflective prompts to enable you to develop your own map of SEN provision and practice within the context of your own school.

THE CHANGING POLICY CONTEXT

THIS CHAPTER:

- critically reviews recent policy drivers;
- reflects on a changing policy context;
- considers the emphasis on diversity of provision through the development of new Academies and Free Schools;
- examines the positioning of inclusion and inclusive education within current education discourse;
- critically considers the impact of these on practice and on outcomes for pupils with SEN and/or disabilities.

REVIEW

Before critically examining the changing policy context and the impact that this will have on the school, practitioner and pupil with SEN and/or disabilities, it is first important to review existing knowledge of education and SEN policy trends in recent years.

The changing policy context: review of existing knowledge

- What have been the principles underpinning the recent policy context?
- How has this impacted on practice in your school?
- What impact has this had on pupils in your school and on outcomes for pupils with SEN and/or disabilities?
- What have been recent policy priorities in relation to SEN and disability?
- How have these related to wider education policies?
- Have any tensions been created?
- What is the relation between policy and practice?
- Which aspects of policy have impacted positively on practice?
- Which have produced tensions, and how have these been resolved?

REFLECTION

In response to the question above, you may have identified a number of key themes underpinning recent government policy and guidance. Through the Labour government, this included the raising of standards, through a focus on directed strategies (National Strategies) and a focus on wider outcomes for pupils, through *Every Child Matters*. There was also an uncomfortable positioning of inclusion and standards within government documents, with different documents variously emphasising the importance of one or other approach. As Norwich identifies: '[t]he tension between the push for externally visible standards and providing inclusively and flexibly for pupils with SEN has been recognized since the implementation of the 1988 Act (Weddell, 1988)' (Norwich, 2010: 38).

A confused definition of inclusion and inclusive education also emerged through the raft of Labour government documents, which variously linked inclusion specifically with the placement and provision of pupils with SEN, and more generally within a rights-based approach to social inclusion (House of Commons, 2006; Ainscow *et al.*, 2006). Thus, OFSTED (2010) found that local authorities and providers: 'felt that some government policies worked against others' (OFSTED, 2010: 59).

Reflective activity 2.1

■   How have these key features of recent policy impacted on the development of practice in your school setting:

 –   Standards
 –   Widening outcomes: *Every Child Matters*
 –   Tension between standards and inclusion
 –   Confused definition of inclusion.

A CHANGING POLICY CONTEXT

Reflective activity 2.2

■   What key themes have you already noticed emerging in coalition government policy and education discourse?
■   What impact will these have on:

 –   The education system?
 –   Your school?
 –   Your own practice?
 –   Pupils?

continued overleaf . . .

Appendix 1 provides a summary of the key issues identified by the DfE White Paper (DfE, 2010a), which sets out the policy direction for the coalition government while they are in power.

Spend some time reflecting on the issues that are identified.

■ What are the main issues that may impact on your particular school and your own practice?

■ What would you identify as positive policy directions?

■ Are there any that create tensions, or uncertainty?

■ How could these tensions or uncertainties be resolved or addressed?

■ What impact may these changes have on:

 – the profession as a whole
 – practice in your school
 – yourself as a practitioner
 – the day-to-day experiences and outcomes for pupils with SEN.

Within new government policy, there is a commitment to significant educational reform, with a focus on and an acknowledgement that 'England's school's can be better' (DfE, 2010b: 2). Current discussions continue to focus (as the previous Labour government's did) on the concerning gap between high and low performing pupils, and the 'gap between the rich and the poor' (DfE, 2010b: 2). It is therefore noted that England has 'one of the highest gaps between high and low performing pupils, and a strong relationship between social background and performance' (DfE, 2010b: 2). Coalition government policy challenges this trend, stating that: 'for a very long time in this country, the "long tail of underachievement" has been tolerated; sometimes it has been seen as an inevitable consequence of a system which does a very good job for some' (DfE, 2010b: 2).

This focus on the gap between different groups of pupils will therefore continue to be prioritised within emerging policies, although there has been a significant change in terminology and focus away from 'narrowing the gap' (DCSF, 2010a) and instead emphasising the need to 'close the gap' (DfE, 2010b).

While the changing policy context is rooted in fundamental differences in political ideology, from the recent Labour government to the newly elected Conservative driven coalition government, we cannot escape the fact that the global economic recession also directly impacts on the direction of policy. Thus, throughout coalition government documents there are explicit references to the impact of an uncertain economic future on the development and direction of new practices within the education system. It is noted that:

■ The context for reform in England is challenging. We face a record level of national debt, and the need to tackle it means that while school funding will grow lightly in real terms, it cannot grow faster. Meanwhile, pupil numbers are projected to rise from 2010 onwards, following a decade of decline (DfE, 2010a: 5).

■ The challenge today is to use resources in the most efficient way possible. The current financial climate does not allow any government to be careless with resources (DfE, 2011: 15).

■   The link between greater achievement for pupils with SEN and 'higher productivity gains and growth for the economy' (DfE, 2011: 23) is also noted.

It is therefore important that a close focus is maintained on ensuring that the new measures really do work in the best interests of the child rather than being based on centralised cost-cutting efforts.

REDUCING LINKS TO CENTRALISED GOVERNMENT DECISION MAKING

A clear, new focus in the coalition government rhetoric is based on new freedoms from top-down governmental prescription and bureaucracy. The new policy reforms, which aim to 'make England's schools better', include a raft of measures to reduce bureaucratic burdens on schools, and place more emphasis and attention on improving positive outcomes for pupils. There is therefore an aim to reduce bureaucracy, with recognition that 'headteachers have been overwhelmed with top-down initiatives rather than having the freedom to drive improvements' (DfE, 2011: 9). Therefore, 'rather than directing change from Whitehall, we want to make it easier for professionals and services to work together, and we want to create the conditions that encourage innovative and collaborative ways of providing better support for children, young people and families' (DfE, 2011: 11).

Already, this is being evidenced in the removal of previous key policy guidance. Thus, while the principles behind *Every Child Matters* are being retained by the government, new government guidance and policy has made it clear that these principles for practice do not need to be set out in a prescriptive way:

> The majority of the important work that schools do is not as a result of government prescription – for example intervening early and offering additional support to pupils who need it, protecting pupils from harm, and working with their local communities. Good schools play a vital role as promoters of health and wellbeing in the local community and have always had good pastoral systems. They understand well the connections between pupils' physical and mental health, their safety, and their educational achievement. They create an ethos focused on achievement for all, where additional support is offered early to those who need it, and where the right connections are made to health, social care and other professionals who can help pupils overcome whatever barriers to learning are in their way. Good schools work with parents, community organisations and local agencies to create a healthy, safe and respectful environment in school, after school, and on the way to and from school. Good teachers instil an ethos where aspiration is the best reason for children to avoid harmful behaviour.
>
> (DfE, 2010a: 28)

It is interesting to note that the phrases used throughout this statement reflect the five outcomes of the previous *Every Child Matters* document:

■   Being Healthy
■   Staying Safe
■   Enjoy and Achieve
■   Economic Well being
■   Positive Contribution.

as well as underlying principles for multi-agency working but yet without actually making direct reference to *Every Child Matters*.

Reflective activity 2.3

■ How have these principles become embedded in best practice in your school setting?
■ What impact can be evidenced?
■ Which areas still need to be developed?
■ Why is this?
■ How could this be achieved?
■ Do you think that this can be achieved without the over-arching *Every Child Matters* document?

Reform of the National Curriculum is also proposed, in order to create 'curriculum coherence' (DfE, 2010b: 15), with a reduction in the prescription that became common through the former Labour government approach to the National Curriculum, National Literacy Strategy and National Numeracy Strategy with its scripts for lesson delivery. Instead the focus is on enabling teachers to exercise their 'professional judgement' (DfE, 2010b: 17). Thus, it is suggested that 'The National Curriculum should set out only the essential knowledge and understanding that all children should acquire and leave teachers to decide how to teach this most effectively' (DfE, 2010a: 40), with the vision to enable schools and teachers to take 'greater control over what is taught in schools, innovating in how they teach and developing new approaches to learning' (DfE, 2010a: 40).

This reduction of tight control on schools will also happen at local levels, with a commitment expressed by the government to: 'remove the duty on schools and colleges to cooperate with children's Trusts and abolish the requirement for local authorities to produce a Children and Young People's Plan' (DfE, 2010a: 29).

There is recognition expressed that 'Government can leave schools and local authorities to make decisions for themselves in all of these areas – because central government is not as well placed as local people to make decisions' (DfE, 2010a: 29).

Thus, there is to be a shift in focus of school improvement processes. Over recent years these have become increasingly prescribed by government, with the establishment of School Improvement Partners for all schools. The processes that have evolved and developed have arguably focused more on enforcing compliance with government priorities (DfE, 2010a, 2010b) than on meaningful school improvement and development.

The requirement for each school to have an identified School Improvement Partner, and to complete a centralised, standardised self-evaluation form (the SEF) has therefore been removed, opening up possibilities for schools to engage more effectively with a wider range of objective outsiders in a critical friend role to support the development of their own school priorities and action planning. Thus:

> We will expect schools to set their own improvement priorities. As long as schools provide a good education, we will not mandate specific approaches. Schools will

determine what targets to set for themselves, choose what forms of external support they want and determine how to evaluate themselves.

(DfE, 2010a: 74)

There is also clear commitment stated of the move towards enabling schools to become 'autonomous institutions collaborating with each other on terms set by teachers, not bureaucrats' (DfE, 2010a: 12) and on providing the context to enable 'every school to be able to shape its own character, frame its own ethos and develop its own specialisms, free of either central or local bureaucratic constraint' (DfE, 2010a: 11).

This is therefore a potentially exciting time for education and schools. After a prolonged period of top-down prescription about everything from curriculum, to teaching strategy, to school improvement measures, the new emphasis in emerging policy suggests that schools will now increasingly find themselves able to innovate and determine their own direction of travel.

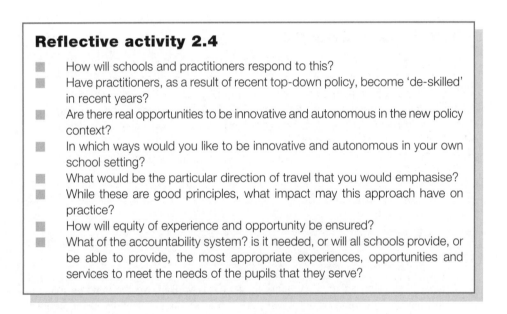

Reflective activity 2.4

■   How will schools and practitioners respond to this?
■   Have practitioners, as a result of recent top-down policy, become 'de-skilled' in recent years?
■   Are there real opportunities to be innovative and autonomous in the new policy context?
■   In which ways would you like to be innovative and autonomous in your own school setting?
■   What would be the particular direction of travel that you would emphasise?
■   While these are good principles, what impact may this approach have on practice?
■   How will equity of experience and opportunity be ensured?
■   What of the accountability system? is it needed, or will all schools provide, or be able to provide, the most appropriate experiences, opportunities and services to meet the needs of the pupils that they serve?

DIVERSITY OF PROVISION THROUGH THE DEVELOPMENT OF NEW ACADEMIES AND FREE SCHOOLS

One of the key policy drivers of the coalition government is the commitment to increase the number of schools becoming Academies: to include both mainstream and special Academies, and to introduce new Free Schools into the educational arena. Emerging government policies therefore set out clear intentions to enable professionals to develop new and innovative practices are particularly evidenced in the coalition government commitment to increasing the number of Academies and Free Schools, which are free of top-down governmental or local authority control:

By injecting greater autonomy into the school system, we aim to create a school system that is able to offer a range of high quality specialist provision for children with SEN; to innovate and pioneer new education pathways and curricula; and to offer parents a genuine choice of school for their child and to respond effectively to parents' choices.

(DfE, 2011: 51)

There is therefore a clear focus on the development of Academies across our education system, and this will include Special Academies that will develop the role and expertise of traditional local authority special schools. For the coalition government, this move towards Academies and Free Schools supports their belief that: 'real choice for parents requires a diverse and dynamic school system that offers a wide range of high quality provision and that has the autonomy and flexibility to respond effectively to parental choice' (DfE, 2011: 51).

Reflective activity 2.5

■ What impact do Academies have on providing real choice to parents?
■ Will it provide greater choice for some parents, or for all parents?
■ What will be the impact on choice for pupils with SEN and/or disabilities?
■ How else can the education system become more diverse and dynamic?
■ What can your individual school setting do to embed theses principles into the way that you support pupils with SEN and/or disabilities?
■ How will inclusive and equitable entitlements for all pupils be retained and protected?

Academies are provided as examples of what innovation and autonomy can achieve, with the emphasis on ways that Academies:

have been securing improvements in standards well above the national average, turning around some of the worst-performing secondary schools in the country. Schools which had become sink schools with chronically low aspirations, poor behaviour and a culture of failure are now centres of excellence.

(DfE, 2010a: 51)

There is, therefore, a move towards encouraging collaboration between successful Academies and less successful schools, with interest in chains of Academies, or federations of schools led by strong school leaders (DfE, 2010b), and a commitment to:

ensure that the very lowest performing schools, attaining poorly and in an Ofsted category or not improving, are partnered with a strong sponsor or outstanding school and converted to become Academies to effect educational transformation.

(DfE, 2010a: 56)

Reflective activity 2.6

■   How is this 'educational transformation' possible?

■   What are the significant factors in making Academies so successful?

■   Are all Academies similarly successful?

■   If you currently work in an Academy where standards have been significantly improved, spend time reflecting on how this has been achieved: what were the significant factors, and were these specific to your own school, or could they be shared and replicated in other schools?

■   If you work in a maintained school, would there be any benefits in exploring ways to link or collaborate with Academies in your area to find out more about their individual style of school development?

The DfE (2010a) identify the following as key features explaining why Academies are so successful in securing significant improvements:

■   They have the opportunity to set their own direction.

■   Headteachers have more freedoms to:

  –   innovate with the curriculum;
  –   insist on tougher discipline;
  –   pay staff more;
  –   extend school hours;
  –   develop a personal approach to every pupil.

■   How important do you think these features are/were to the educational transformation of your own school setting?

■   How could you embed those principles or practices into your own context?

While it could be assumed that the success of Academies is that they are able to set their own admission criteria, it was heartening that through the Academies Act (2010) there has been a statutory requirement for Academies, as well as the new Free Schools, to meet the same duties and obligations as maintained schools in respect of SEN legislation. Academies therefore have a statutory duty to accept a pupil with a statement if that is the choice of the parent, and it is named on the statement.

There is therefore a need to ensure a focus on identifying and sharing case studies of best practice, where the needs of pupils with SEN and/or disabilities are being well served and positive outcomes are being significantly improved; as well as identifying examples where pupils with SEN and/or disabilities are being failed by the new system. This will be particularly important through the introduction and establishment of Special Academies: Special Schools that take on Academy status, where the government intends to:

> Open up the alternative provision market to new providers and diversify existing provision by legislating to allow PRUs to become new Academies, encouraging Free Schools that offer alternative provision, and supporting more voluntary sector providers alongside Free Schools. Alternative provision Free Schools in particular will be a route for new voluntary and private sector organizations to offer high-quality education for disruptive and excluded children and others without a mainstream school place.
>
> (DfE, 2010a: 38)

Reflective activity 2.7

▨　Do all pupils with SEN have equitable rights to access all school settings, or are there still perverse incentives for Academies not to include the widest range of pupils?

▨　What are current experiences?

▨　How are the statutory entitlements and the rights to equitable learning experiences going to be preserved and protected for all pupils with SEN and/or disabilities?

▨　What will happen to pupils who are excluded from the 'mainstream'? Will we end up with a two-tier educational system where pupils with complex needs are removed from 'mainstream' education, and always educated separately?

VOLUNTARY ORGANISATIONS

Emerging government policy is focusing on the increased role that they envisage for voluntary organisations to work with schools and professionals to support meeting the needs of pupils with SEN and/or disabilities (DfE, 2010a; DfE, 2011).

While we may be cynical that this is just another example of a measure to cut costs across all services, it does certainly fit with the Conservative focus on the 'Big Society'.

Voluntary organisations are therefore considering ways to reposition themselves within this new policy context to be able to provide the most effective support for pupils with SEN and/or disabilities and their families.

KIDS, a charity that currently supports over 7,000 disabled children, young people and their families across 50 per cent of the local authorities in England, is therefore already starting to consider the implications of the new proposals on the strategic development of their practices. In particular, the following will be key areas where voluntary organisations may take an increased role in providing support and services to pupils with SEN and/or disabilities and their families:

▨　assessment processes;

▨　key working to support families in coordinating services and managing budgets.

Williams (2011) has therefore identified a number of perceived benefits to practice and support for pupils with SEN and/or disability and their families from developing the use of voluntary organisations including:

1　Independent of Local Authorities, schools and the NHS.
2　Cheaper?
3　Long experience of working across the statutory services.
4　Parents typically view voluntary organisations in a more positive light than some statutory services.

(Williams, 2011)

As well as some areas of tension that still need to be explored:

1   Cheaper: possibly not cheaper, as a competitive market-place economy may evolve?
2   Easier to cut?
3   Capacity?
4   Once the voluntary sector 'gatekeeps' – will we be seen any differently to statutory services?
5   Voluntary sector today – private sector tomorrow?

(Williams, 2011)

The issue of developing the involvement of voluntary organisations in processes and systems that have traditionally been monitored and accountable for through local authority or government systems will not be simple. From both the voluntary organisation perspective, and the school perspective there will be the need to engage in critical reflection about how systems will change and develop, and how to manage that transition in order to ensure that positive outcomes for the pupil with SEN and/or disabilities and their families remain at the heart of the process. As Williams (2011) notes:

Schools have been, and are, the most important organisation in the life of a disabled child from 4–18. Voluntary organisations have tended to wrap our services around schools – with early years, transition and school holiday support. It's time for a strategic alliance between schools and their local disabled children's voluntary organisations.

Reflective activity 2.8

■   How can this 'strategic alliance' be achieved?
■   What will be the benefits of working in new ways with voluntary organisations?
■   What experiences do you currently have of working with voluntary organisations?
■   What can voluntary organisations offer to schools and practitioners in terms of helping them to improve practices to support pupils with SEN and/or disabilities?
■   What may be the potential tensions or difficulties of relying on voluntary organisations to provide the support that is necessary for assessment processes and keyworking services for supporting parents to coordinate provision and manage personal budgets?
■   How can these be positively addressed?

THE POSITIONING OF INCLUSION AND INCLUSIVE EDUCATION WITHIN CURRENT EDUCATION DISCOURSE

The definition of inclusion within Labour government policy was confused. Variously, inclusion was positioned as referring to a narrow definition relating to the placement of pupils (often with an emphasis on enabling more pupils with complex needs to access local mainstream school settings); but also to a broader definition of enhancing social inclusion and wider equitable rights across society. This has produced a situation where:

> The word alone invokes a great deal of strong feeling and antagonism. Polar opposite views have been represented to the Committee: from fervent advocates of inclusion who regard it as a human rights issue that all children should be included in mainstream schools; to those who see inclusion policy as the root of all problems in SEN, such as a hesitance on the part of local authorities to issue statements and the closure of special schools that parents have fought hard to keep open.
> (House of Commons, 2006: 22)

This, when then added to the problematic tensions created by a policy context that emphasised the driving up of standards through a range of performance measures that encouraged comparison and competition between schools, but that did not reflect school's increasing successes including pupils who may not 'perform well' on league table data, produced a confusing picture of the value placed on inclusion.

Within new coalition government policy a theme that emerges is the notion of 'removing the bias towards inclusion' (DfE, 2011: 4).

This is problematic, portraying a negative image of the concept of inclusion. It seems that special education may again embody a 'discourse of exclusion' (Barton, 2010). However, the overall approach to inclusion conceptualised within emerging government policy is confused, with tensions and contradictions. On the one hand, the notion of 'removing the bias towards inclusion' clearly positions the new government's understanding of inclusion as to refer to the position and placement of pupils with SEN and/or disability. Yet, at the same time, within the same documents, there is continued use of positive inclusive language and concepts around the notion of 'removing barriers to learning'.

It is essential that the government carefully defines its approach to inclusive education. Since the Salamanca Statement (UNESCO,1994), which drew together a range of countries to agree and sign commitment to principles of inclusion, including ensuring that all children are enrolled in 'regular schools' as a matter of course, much has been done to change attitudes towards how the needs of all children can be met most positively and effectively. For me, inclusion is not just about something that is 'done' to pupils with SEN and/or disabilities. Rather, it involves complex consideration and challenging questions about the appropriateness of educational experiences for ALL pupils. The flippant terminology used by the coalition government around 'removing the bias towards inclusion', for me undermines recent moves within the education system to more fully understand the complex notion of inclusion as an active process of removing barriers to learning and participation for all pupils (Booth and Ainscow, 2002; Ekins, 2010b).

While it is, of course, important to clearly understand the specific and particular needs of pupils with SEN, and to ensure that they are actively addressed through the implementation of support strategies to meet those needs, many have argued that this is most effectively achieved within school settings built on underlying principles of inclusive values (Corbett, 2001; Kugelmass, 2004; Ekins and Grimes, 2009). Unfortunately, the current suggestion of the need to 'remove the bias towards inclusion' represents a backwards step, where inclusion is once again considered only in terms of placement and where inclusion in mainstream is viewed in negative rather than positive ways.

So, what is, or should, inclusive education be about?

While the language and definition of inclusion, internationally, is also very confused with many different definitions, a useful typology of different approaches to inclusion within the English policy context is provided by Ainscow *et al.* (2006):

1   Inclusion as a concern with disabled students and others categorized as 'having special educational needs'.
2   Inclusion as a response to disciplinary exclusion.
3   Inclusion in relation to all groups seen as being vulnerable to exclusion.
4   Inclusion as developing the school for all.
5   Inclusion as 'Education for All'.
6   Inclusion as a principled approach to education and society.

Reflective activity 2.9

■   Where would you position recent Labour government policy on this typology?
■   Where would you position emerging coalition government policy?
■   What is the implication of this for the development of a fair and equitable education system for all?
■   Where would you position practice in your school?
■   Where would you position your own practice and understandings of inclusion?
■   Are there any tensions?
■   How may these be addressed?

In order to develop an education system that effectively meets the need of all pupils, there is a continued need to challenge and question underlying principles, in order to ensure that they really do meet the needs of all pupils and provide equitable educational opportunities for all. As Barton (2010) notes:

> the process will be challenging and disturbing, necessitating fundamental changes to the social and economic conditions and relations of a given society. This will include changes to the values informing the prioritization and distribution of resources, how society views difference, how schools are organized, how teachers view their work, the styles of their teaching and the nature of the curriculum.

For me, the development of inclusive practices will always be individualised, and will involve critical consideration and examination of the underlying values and principles impacting on the particular context. It is therefore difficult to provide a prescriptive blueprint for practice, and instead schools should be encouraged to critically examine their own practices in meaningful ways to consider the values and principles that are embedded.

As a starting point to support the understanding and development of inclusive practices, many schools that I have supported have found the following broad principles identified by Booth and Ainscow (2002), in the Index for Inclusion, to be helpful in enabling them to critically re-examine elements of their own practice:

■ reduce barriers to learning;
■ increase participation and access to learning;
■ support diversity.

These three principles can therefore provide a useful starting point to engage practitioners in discussions about the principles and values underpinning various practices within the school setting.

Research that I have undertaken (Ekins, 2010b) supports the development of a model within which these central principles can be understood in relation to a range of other variables, which can help to emphasise the unique character of individual school practice, development and appropriate agenda for change: this is shown below in Figure 2.1.

The model is not a simplistic checklist of actions and processes, nor a prescriptive model of development; instead it is a broad framework for rethinking existing tensions in

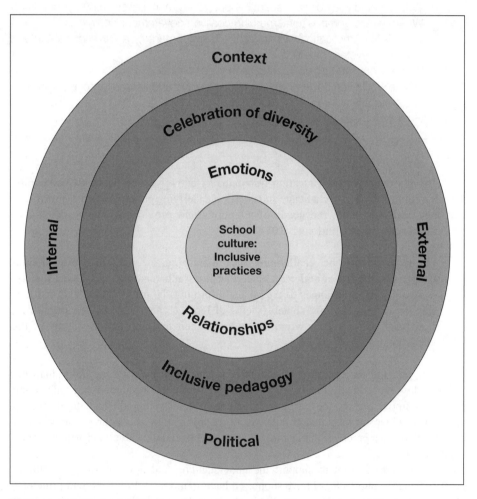

■ **Figure 2.1** Understanding the development of inclusive practices in schools
(Ekins, 2010b)

order for individual schools and settings to consider new ways forward. It is important to understand that change of this type is not simply about changing structures and processes. Rather, it is about deep cultural change (Howes *et al.*, 2009) and widespread 'reculturing' (Woods *et al.*, 1997), which can only occur when there is a shift in values and understanding in relation to the notion of inclusive education, and the position of inclusion within society.

The importance of the underlying culture within the school is emphasised, and placed at the heart of the model. This is seen to have the greatest impact on the potential development of inclusive practices, and cannot be simply prescribed or transplanted from other examples of practice, or from checklists of procedures. Recognition of the centrality of 'interpretation' of broad inclusive principles within different contexts producing different solutions and approaches is emphasised (West *et al.*, 2005; Ainscow *et al.*, 2006).

Culture is intricately linked with the emotions and relationships developed within the school, and these will be impacted on not only by changes within the school itself (staff mobility, changes in leadership, pupil changes) but also by changes in personal situations linked to individual staff members. In this it must be recognised that: 'the feelings and energy levels of headteachers and staff rise and fall, following the dictates of their personal lives as well as events at school' (Nias *et al.*, 1989: 124).

This aspect needs to be fully acknowledged as it demonstrates that change, development and the implementation of policy cannot be dictated in a mechanical way. It will always be filtered through the complex and unpredictable nature of staff emotion and relationships. As with culture, emotions and relationships cannot be easily prescribed through narrow checklists of how staff members should behave and interact with each other. Emotions and relationships are individual, complex and dependent on a range of variables and factors that cannot be structured and organised within the school context.

Around these complex factors that have emerged from the data, is a further layer of complexity, which is seen to be about staff members' celebration of diversity, and understanding of different learning styles in an inclusive rather than a stereotyped way. When diversity is seen to be a positive enabling feature within the school settings, rather than a barrier or limiting factor, this belief contributes to the development of the particular culture and ethos of the school. Inclusive pedagogy, including reflection and collaborative problem solving, is therefore also seen as key to the development of inclusive practices (Alexander, 2001; Kugelmass, 2004).

In the outer layer of the model is acknowledgement of the individual context of the school setting: that schools will all look very different and be at different stages of their particular development due to a range of complex and inter-linked contextual factors. Again, these contextual factors cannot always be planned and organised. They will include the impact of political and governmental agendas, internal and external factors. The model recognises that centralised policies cannot understand the complex dynamic of the individual school setting, and the impact that that policy may have on developing practices and cultures within the school setting. For some schools, a particular policy may reinforce and add support to principles and values already embedded within the school, and thus be a positive factor. For other schools, that same policy may be in tension and conflict with the underlying system of working and embedded principles and ethos within the school setting. It will only be those 'on the ground' who will be able to start to understand the complex relationship between centralised external policy and contextual factors, and the internal ethos and culture (Stables, 2009).

It is hoped that this model, taken with the broad principles of inclusive practice, will help to highlight the complexity of the issue of developing inclusive practices within the school setting, and will help to reinforce the individual nature of inclusive school development and the centrality of underlying culture and ethos that cannot be prescribed.

ACTION PLANNING

Identify three key points for individual reflection:

1 _____

2 _____

3 _____

Start to consider key issues to be followed up as points of action that have arisen from your reading of this chapter.

This may include:

▪ Working with staff to identify new policy drivers that may impact particularly on your school. Talk about ways that they may impact in positive or negative ways on existing systems and processes.

▪ Considering ways that innovative and individualised practices can be developed. What type of practices do staff in your school want to develop? In which ways will these be innovative? In which ways will they support improved outcomes for pupils with SEN?

▪ Considering ways to develop links with voluntary organisations. Which voluntary organisations operate in your area? How much do you currently know about the services, skills and expertise that they can offer? How can you develop effective links with a range of voluntary organisations to support the pupils and parents with whom you work?

▪ Examining personal and collective understandings and interpretations of inclusion: how are they similar and how do they differ? What may be the implication of any differences in interpretation on the development of inclusive practices across the whole school? How may the model in Figure 2.1 support the development of understanding about inclusive practice in your school setting?

▪ Others.

ACTION PLANNING TO ENABLE IMPACT

Use the format provided below to develop a clear action plan for future development of practices for either yourself, or for the school. Make sure that you do not identify too many different actions all at once, have a clear outcome for what you want to achieve in mind, and make sure that you clearly identify the different steps to take to achieve the outcome.

THE POLICY CONTEXT: ACTION PLANNING TO ENABLE IMPACT

Which key issues from the chapter do you want to focus on/ change/develop?	How will you effect this change or development (identify a number of small action steps to achieve your overall goal)?	Who else will need to be involved? How?	What will the outcome be (include timescales)?	Impact:

 # THE CHANGING SEN SYSTEM

THIS CHAPTER:

- critically considers flaws in the existing SEN system;
- reviews the language and terminology around SEN and/or disability;
- examines the gap between achievement for pupils with SEN and/or disability and other peers;
- considers ways that the existing SEN system is overly bureaucratic;
- reviews parental concerns with the existing SEN system, including problems with the existing statementing process.

REVIEW

Review of current SEN system

- What do you already know about how the SEN system works?
- What works well in your school context?
- Are there any problems with the existing SEN system for you and your practice in school?
- What are these?
- How do you overcome them?
- Which aspects of the SEN system do you think/know have been identified as failing pupils with SEN and/or disability?
- Would you agree with the findings from the OFSTED Review (2010) that the system is inequitable with those who are more able to make sense of it getting greater access to resources and support?
- What experiences have you had of this?

For some time, flaws in the existing SEN system have been identified, with calls for radical reform of the system (Warnock, 2005; House of Commons, 2006; Lamb, 2009; DCSF, 2010a; DfE, 2011). It has been recognised that the current SEN system is based on an outdated model, based on the 'social and legal context of 1981 . . . [which does not] always sit comfortably with more recent legislation and policy' (OFSTED, 2010: 59). The SEN system is therefore 'struggling to remain fit for purpose' (House of Commons, 2006: 12) to serve the needs of pupils with SEN and disabilities and their families in the twenty-first century. It is noted that the legislation around the area of SEN and disability is now far reaching, and there has been 'a tendency to add to rather than replace what is already there' (OFSTED, 2010: 59). While there have, therefore, been some 'well-intentioned reforms' (DfE, 2011: 15), these have simply added to an outdated and increasingly confusing SEN system, one often laden with tensions and inconsistencies.

What is even more worrying is the seeming inequalities that have evolved within the system, with OFSTED (2010) identifying that 'the review found a virtually unanimous feeling that the SEN system as it stands now is unfair: those who are able to make sense of it have quicker and greater access to resources and support' (OFSTED, 2010: 31).

Within the various reports that have recently been published to review the state of the current SEN system, a number of key failings in the system have been identified. These include, in no particular order:

■ problems with the definition and subsequent identification of SEN;
■ continued lack of achievement and gap between pupils with SEN and their peers;
■ overly bureaucratic;
■ adversarial for parents who find that they have to battle for the rights of their child with SEN;
■ problems with the current statementing system.

One of the most significant factors impacting on the SEN system, which draws on many, if not all, of the key issues above, is the underlying problem with widespread inconsistency in practice across the country. This variability impacts on many different aspects, as Lamb (2009) identifies:

> Throughout the Inquiry one of the most striking features of the SEN system has been the variation that we have seen. We have seen widely varying levels of parental confidence and there is variation at local authority level in a wide range of different indicators: from overall levels of SEN and the SEN–non-SEN attainment gap, to levels of exclusions, the number of statements issued and the time in which they are issued.
>
> (Lamb, 2009: 52)

The House of Commons (2006) also notes that the variability in practice includes poor practice in some areas.

REFLECTION

All of the reports mentioned above identified recommendations for changes to the existing SEN system. So, while government proposals for a 'new approach to SEN' (DfE, 2011) are heralded as a 'radical reform' (DfE, 2011: 15), we need to critically consider and reflect on how far it actually addresses these major flaws, and also the recommendations of previous reports.

The DfE (2011) sets out a commitment to develop a 'radically different system to support better life outcomes for young people; give parents confidence by giving them more control; and transfer power to professionals on the front line and to local communities' (DfE, 2011: 4).

As practitioners involved in working with pupils with SEN and/or disabilities and their parents, we need to consider how far the proposals actually propose a new approach to SEN and/or disability and how this new radical system actually address the previous concerns that have been raised. What were the problems underpinning the previous concerns with the system, and what is suggested in the new proposals and other research?

Reflective activity 3.1

Look at the table presented opposite, which provides summaries of recommendations from four key reports, which all identified the failings of the existing SEN system:

■ House of Commons Select Committee Report (2006);
■ Lamb Inquiry (2009);
■ OFSTED SEN and Disability Review (2010);
■ DfE Green Paper *Support and Aspiration: A new approach to SEN* (2011).

Please note that each of these reports identified a wide range of different recommendations for developing and overhauling the SEN systems. Thus, while it is not possible to present all of the various recommendations in full, those relating to specific key themes relevant to the themes discussed throughout the book are highlighted and presented for comparison.

Use the provided table as a tool to support reflection and discussion about what the key recommendations for changes and improvements to the SEN system are, and how far the proposals from the Green Paper (DfE, 2011) actually address the concerns and recommendations that are suggested.

Look first at the summaries of recommendations provided below, and use these as tools to support reflection and engagement in the remaining flaws in the current SEN system, and recommendations for how to address those, and then continue with the detailed discussions of the key areas of concern (identified above) and how these are proposed to be addressed through the Green Paper (DfE, 2011).

PROBLEMS WITH THE DEFINITION AND SUBSEQUENT IDENTIFICATION OF SEN

One of the underlying problems within the existing SEN system is the terminology itself. However, this is an area that still remains unaddressed within government proposals for the 'new approach to SEN'.

Currently, children are identified as having SEN 'if they have a greater difficulty in learning than the majority of children of their age which calls for additional or different educational provision to be made for them' (DfE, 2011: 18).

The term SEN originated with the Warnock Report (1978) that 'radically changed the conceptualisation of special educational needs. It introduced the idea of special educational needs (SEN), "statements" of SEN, and an "integrative" – which later became known as "inclusive" – approach, based on common educational goals for all children

Photocopiable resource: key recommendations

House of Commons	Lamb Inquiry	OFSTED	Green Paper
Identifying SEN:			
There is no single category of children with SEN. All children should be considered on an individual basis with a sliding scale of additional resource to meet their needs.	It is unhelpful to identify high numbers of pupils with SEN; need to address the underlying barriers to learning for pupils falling behind.	Schools should stop identifying pupils as having special educational needs when they simply need better teaching and pastoral support.	Focus on early identification and a new single early years setting and school-based category of SEN.
Inclusion:			
Supports the principle of educators pursuing an ethos that fully includes all children – including those with SEN and disabilities – in the setting or settings that best meets their needs and helps them achieve their potential, preferably a good school within their local community.	Need for an effective inclusion strategy within local schools.	The review found that no one model of educational support – such as special schools, full inclusion in mainstream provision, or specialist units co-located with mainstream settings – systematically worked better than any other.	Focus on 'Removing the bias towards inclusion'.
Training:			
Better guidance and staff training in dealing with disruptive behaviour by	SEN embedded in leadership training. *Achievement for All.*	Need to improve the quality of training for staff supporting pupils with SEN.	Focus on accredited training to ensure all staff have the specialist skills to work with pupils with a range of needs.

continued overleaf . . .

House of Commons	Lamb Inquiry	OFSTED	Green Paper
children with Autistic Spectrum Disorder, particularly Asperger's Syndrome, and social, emotional, and behavioural difficulties. More SEN training in Initial Teacher Education courses. Focus on SEN CPD for all staff.	Advanced training programmes in each of the five main areas of SEN. Preparation for working with pupils with SEN and parents included in Initial Teacher Education. Inspectors trained in SEN and disability.		New models of scholarship funding.
Statementing process:			
Break the link between assessment and funding of provision. Clear national guidance on the statementing process.	Need for national guidance on drawing up statements to accessible: reflecting the individual needs of the pupil without using too much jargon.	It is not enough for pupils to have a statement of special ensure they are clear and statement itself does not mean that current needs are being met.	A new single assessment process and 'Education, Health and Care Plan' by 2014. Greater independence in the assessment process using voluntary and community organisations.
Pupils:			
Increase the role of children and young people in reviewing, planning and designing services.	Ensure that pupils have a role in decision making, planning and review of provision. Children's outcomes need to be placed at the heart of the system.	Where children and young people are fully involved in decision-making and have a clear perception of their aims and aspirations, good outcomes are more likely to be secured.	

continued overleaf . . .

House of Commons	Lamb Inquiry	OFSTED	Green Paper
Collaboration:			
Between mainstream and special schools. Effective collaborative practices between schools and other services.	Need to develop a new role for special schools where they are fully resourced to share both their expertise and their facilities.	Need for effective collaboration across education, health and social care. Collaboration is more effective where protocols for sharing information across services are fully established.	Focus on innovative ways of working together, across agencies, within and between schools. Joint policy statements and approaches between Education, Health and Social Services.
SENCOs:			
Must be qualified teachers and in a senior management position. The role and position of a SENCO must reflect the central priority that SEN should hold within schools. Ongoing training against baseline standards.			Continued funding and commitment to National Award for SEN Coordination. SENCOs role identified as 'pivotal' to strategic leadership of the school.

continued overleaf . . .

House of Commons	Lamb Inquiry	OFSTED	Green Paper
Post 16:			
In terms of both availability and quality, post-16 provision is currently failing to meet the needs of young people with SEN and disabilities. Greater collaboration to support transition.		Evaluation of young people's progress within post-16 provision was limited, with limited consistent systems for tracking the outcomes for students.	A well-coordinated transition from child to adult services.
Parental involvement:			
Actively promote links with parents. Move away from an adversarial approach to appeals for parents.	Improve systems to engage parents.		Option of a personal budget for parents of pupils with an Education, Health and Care Plan by 2014. More control over the support that their child will receive. Real choice of school.

regardless of their abilities or disabilities: namely independence, enjoyment, and understanding' (House of Commons, 2006: 11).

The term 'special educational needs', however, is complex and raises questions and uncertainty within the education system:

■   What is a 'special educational need'?
■   Do all pupils that have a 'special educational need' have the same needs?/the same learning characteristics?/the same pattern of progress?

As Warnock has identified, the intention (with the Warnock Report, 1978) of introducing the term 'special educational needs' was to move away from categorisation of pupil needs under medical terms where pupils were considered 'uneducable' or 'educationally sub-normal' and to emphasise the possibility that pupils with SEN could be effectively educated within the mainstream. However, what has happened as a result of the introduction of the term, is that 'SEN has come to be the name of a single category' (Warnock, cited in House of Commons, 2006: 16).

Thus, there is an underlying grouping of all pupils with SEN into the same collective group, regardless of their actual needs and difficulties. This has been identified as the underlying flaw in a system that is embedded to the use of a meaningless and 'arbitrary distinction that leads to false classifications' (House of Commons, 2006: 16).

Reflecting on the impact of the Warnock Report (1978) nearly twenty years later, Warnock herself identifies that:

> one of the major disasters of the original report was that we introduced the concept of special educational needs to try and show that disabled children were not a race apart and many of them should be educated in the mainstream . . . But the unforeseen consequence is that SEN has come to be the name of a single category, and the government uses it as if it is the same problem to include a child in a wheelchair and a child with Asperger's, and that is conspicuously untrue.
>
> (House of Commons, 2006: 16)

This consequence has been significant, and has impacted on the conceptualisation and development of SEN practice ever since. Thus: 'the premise on which SEN provision is based – that there exists a single category of children with SEN – is fundamentally flawed' (House of Commons, 2006: 16).

In addition to this, a further difficulty with the differing uses and interpretations of terminology across different services is noted:

> the language of special educational needs has become highly contentious and confusing for both parents and professionals. Health services refer to 'disabled' children; social care services to 'children in need'; education to 'special educational needs', or, after the age of 16, to 'learning difficulties and/or disabilities'. The children and young people may find themselves belonging to more than one of these groups but the terms do not mean the same thing and they have different consequences in terms of the support that the young person will receive.
>
> (OFSTED, 2010: 8)

This is again an issue that remains largely unaddressed within developing proposals for the 'new approach to SEN' (DfE, 2011).

For me, the key issue to address is the complacent way in which practitioners, advisers, researchers and policy makers now use the terminology of SEN. SEN (as an acronym) has become commonplace within educational discourse, and as such, has lost its real meaning. It is acknowledged therefore, that 'the term "special educational needs" is used too widely' (OFSTED, 2010: 9) to refer to pupils who do not have a special educational need at all.

When we are talking about SEN, we are actually talking about a 'special educational need'. When phrased as such it highlights and emphasises the significant nature of the difficulties or needs that the child should be experiencing in order to be identified as SEN and placed on the SEN Register.

In addition, there needs to be more explicit understanding that the term 'SEN' refers to a large continuum of need: not to a single category. Any approaches to identification and assessment of need and provision of support therefore need to acknowledge this.

Currently, the term 'SEN' is over-used, and used largely to refer to 'relatively slow progress' (OFSTED, 2010: 9).

Indeed, the impact of the term 'SEN' also needs to be critically examined and challenged. There is widespread acknowledgement of the fact that, unfortunately, use of the term 'SEN' often leads to lowering of expectations for the pupil (Lamb, 2009; OFSTED, 2010; Florian, 2010; DfE, 2011).

There is the danger, as Florian (2010) notes that:

When students who encounter difficulties in learning are identified as having 'special educational needs', an intractable cycle is formed – students are assigned membership of the group because they are judged to possess the attributes of group membership, and they are believed to have the attributes of the group because they are members of it.

(Florian, 2010: 65)

Reflective activity 3.2

■ How is the notion of SEN conceptualised within your school context?
■ Does it lead to lowering of expectations for the pupil:

– By staff members?
– By the pupil themselves?
– By the parents of the pupil with SEN?
– By other pupils?

■ What is the implication of this for practice?

THE CHANGING PROFILE OF SEN

It is acknowledged that the profile of pupils with SEN and/or disability is changing (DfE, 2011). This includes:

Children who may not previously have survived birth are now entering school. These children include those with co-existing conditions such as autism and attention deficit and hyperactivity disorder, or profound and multiple learning difficulties and other who may be affected by other factors such as multi-sensory impairment or mental ill-health.

(DfE, 2011: 74)

There have been increases in the numbers of pupils identified with SEN in recent years, from 10 per cent of all pupils in 1995 to 18.2 per cent of all pupils (1.5 million pupils in total) in 2010 (DfE, 2011) and, as the discussions in Chapter 7 identify, there have also been changes in the prevalence and incidence of particular categories of need.

The DfE (2011) has identified that with the term SEN being unhelpfully associated with falling behind rather than a specific Special Educational Need, there is now a situation where particular groups within the school population are over-represented within the SEN population: 'Pupils with SEN are more than twice as likely to be eligible for free school meals than their peers. . . . Looked after children are three-and-a-half times more likely to have SEN compared with all children' (DfE, 2011: 22).

This over-representation also includes summer born pupils, with pupils born in August 60 per cent more likely to be identified as SEN than those born in September (DfE, 2011); over-representation of boys and also pupils who receive Free School Meals.

Reflective activity 3.3

Think about the implications of this for school practice, and also for the experience and self-esteem of summer born pupils.

It is significant that the DfE (2011) have identified that the correlation between summer born pupils and SEN is strongest at School Action – suggesting that this is related to pupils who are 'underachieving' in the context of national averages and expectations. Where pupils are identified with high level or more complex SEN, and need a statement of SEN, the correlation is not as strong- therefore providing clear evidence that the link between SEN and summer born pupils is not dependent on the 'summer born pupil' aspect.

What about boys and pupils receiving Free School Meals (i.e. those coming from areas of social disadvantage)?

Why are these groups of pupils over-represented within the SEN population?

Look at your own school data.

What does this show you about the progress and identification of summer-born birthdays?

What is the implication for teaching approaches and understanding of progress throughout the school?

In order to address problems with identifying pupils with SEN (although not addressing the underlying tension surrounding the actual terminology and definition of SEN), there are proposals to introduce a 'new approach to identifying SEN' (DfE, 2011: 4).

The existing graduated response through the three levels of SEN (School Action, School Action Plus and Statement) will therefore be replaced with a 'new single early years setting- and school-based category of SEN' (DfE, 2011: 4) (see Chapter 7 for full discussions about this change).

To support practitioners, professionals and parents to understand the changes, and the 'new approach to SEN', the government propose to review the SEN Code of Practice, to ensure that it will be 'much clearer in guidance for professionals about how to identify SEN accurately [and] shorter and clearer for professionals' (DfE, 2011: 67).

CONTINUED LACK OF ACHIEVEMENT AND GAP BETWEEN PUPILS WITH SEN AND THEIR PEERS

In the OFSTED SEN and Disability Review (2010) it was noted that 'the achievement of disabled children and young people and those who had SEN was good or outstanding in less than half the providers visited' (OFSTED, 2010: 7).

It is noted that 'children and young people with SEN don't achieve as they could' (DfE, 2011: 2) and that consequently the current SEN and education systems are failing large numbers of children.

Lamb (2009) notes that this is largely linked to the fact that 'the education system is living with a legacy of a time when children with SEN were seen as ineducable. Too often they are set the least demanding challenges. We found many examples where disabled children and children with SEN were sidelined rather than challenged to be the best that they could possibly be' (Lamb, 2009: 2).

Pupils with SEN and/or disabilities are still at risk of achieving lower outcomes than other pupils (DCSF, 2010a; DfE, 2011). The poorer achievement and levels of progress achieved by pupils with SEN and/or disability has been recognised (DCSF, 2010) and the DfE (2011) notes that pupils with SEN and/or disability are 'four times less likely to participate in higher education' (DfE, 2011: 22). The continuing impact of SEN on exclusion rates is also noted, with 'pupils at School Action Plus are 20 times more likely to receive a permanent exclusion and seven times more likely to receive a fixed-period exclusion than pupils with no identified SEN' (DfE, 2011: 22).

Despite intervention and identification, the gap between pupils with SEN and/or disability and those without SEN shows little sign of narrowing, and this is a concern within our education system today.

Reflective activity 3.4

It is not enough to accept such statistics.

■ Why is this happening?
■ What is creating the continued underachievement of pupils identified with SEN?
■ What is causing over-representation of disadvantaged groups?
■ Look at your own school-based data: is there over-representation of any disadvantaged groups on your SEN Register?
■ Why might this be?

---

continued overleaf . . .

> ■ How are pupils with SEN and/or disability performing?
> ■ Are they making good progress, or are they underachieving?
> ■ What are the implications of this for practice?
>
> Rather than accepting such inequitable situations for pupils with SEN, we need to continually question why this is.

OVERLY BUREAUCRATIC

The coalition government policy direction (as was discussed in Chapter 2) is generally to move away from an overly prescriptive approach and to reduce bureaucracy where possible, in order to emphasise a focus on the development of innovative approaches to improving teaching and learning. This goal is echoed within specific government guidance relating to the changing SEN system.

There is therefore acknowledgement that the existing system has been too prescriptive, with too many bureaucratic burdens being placed on practitioners (particularly SENCOs). A commitment is therefore expressed to 'transfer power to professionals on the front line and to local communities and strip away unnecessary bureaucracy so that professionals can innovate and use their judgement' (DfE, 2011: 4–6).

Guidance and advice to complete IEPs for pupils on the SEN Register will therefore be removed, with an acknowledgement of the range of other ways that schools are meeting this need in more effective ways, including through the use of provision mapping and developing more effective pupil and parent engagement in the target-setting process. It is therefore acknowledged that:

> In the period since 2001, when the Code was last reviewed and published, we know that many schools have developed new approaches to planning, reviewing and tracking the progress of all pupils that have enabled them to achieve what IEPs aimed to do without many of the associated bureaucratic burdens.
>
> (DfE, 2011: 98)

Statutory guidance relating to the completion of forms for the Annual Review process will also be removed, enabling schools to develop their own individualised and innovative ways to annually record, monitor and discuss progress and outcomes of pupils with SEN and/or disability with involved stakeholders.

A CHANGING SEN SYSTEM: NEW COMMITMENTS

The coalition government has also set out a commitment to address the fact that parents find the experience of engaging with the SEN system 'adversarial' and 'a battle'. They acknowledge that, currently, the SEN system is 'a system where parents feel they have to battle for the support they need, where they are passed from pillar to post, and where bureaucracy and frustration face them at every step' (DfE, 2011: 2).

Thus, emerging policy and guidance includes a clear focus on giving parents more control (DfE, 2011) and this reflects the findings of other reports, including Alexander (2010) and the Lamb Inquiry (2009) (see Chapter 9 for full discussions).

A key factor in parents' dissatisfaction with the SEN system has often been the complicated and bureaucratic statementing process. The coalition government has committed to address this through the introduction of a 'new single assessment process and Education, Health and Care Plan by 2014 to replace the statutory SEN assessment' (DfE, 2011: 4).

Proposals to improve this system, to be trialled over the forthcoming years, include addressing the problematic link between the assessment and resource/provision process, by 'introduc[ing] greater independence to the assessment of children's needs' (DfE, 2011: 6) through the possible involvement of voluntary or community groups to lead the assessment process.

Ways to improve and develop statutory responsibilities and duties for meeting needs across different agencies and services will also be explored in order to address the existing tension that, while many pupils with high levels of complex needs requiring statements of SEN have needs spanning education, health and social care, currently: 'although collaborative work across different services is encouraged, the ultimate accountability rests within education' (OFSTED, 2010: 59).

Ways to address this through joint policy statements across, in particular, health and education are therefore being considered (see also discussions about statementing in Chapter 7).

One of the key policy reforms identified within the White Paper (DfE, 2010a) was a strengthening of systems to manage behaviour, including giving greater powers to teachers and headteachers to search and discipline pupils, strengthening of headteachers' powers to maintain discipline and authority beyond the school gates and changes to the exclusions process. There is therefore a need to consider what the impact of these measures will be on pupils with behavioural, emotional and social difficulties.

Finally, in the context of the developing role and prevalence of settings and providers that are not directly accountable to the local authority, including the increase in numbers of Academies; the emergence of Special Academies and Free Schools; and also the move towards voluntary organisations becoming key providers of SEN provision and support, there remains a need to keep a focus on how the statutory entitlements of pupils with SEN are being protected. Without accountability to the local authority, and without the local authority being able to have a strategic overview of placement and provision to meet the needs of the pupils within their area, how will equitable entitlement and provision be ensured?

Reflective activity 3.5

■ What impact will these new commitments have on practice and provision for pupils with SEN and/or disability?

■ Are there any implications for the development of practice in your own school setting?

■ What will the advantages be?

■ Will there be any drawbacks or tensions?

ACTION PLANNING

Identify three key points for individual reflection:

1 _____

2 _____

3 _____

Start to consider key issues to be followed up as points of action that have arisen from your reading of this chapter.

This may include:

■ Working with others to consider the use of the term 'SEN' within your school context. How do staff, parents, pupils refer to pupils with SEN? What implications may this have on staff, pupil and parent perceptions and expectations?

■ Examining data to see if there are links between identification of SEN and other disadvantaged groups? Are pupils with SEN and/or disabilities underachieving? How can this be positively addressed?

■ Considering ways that bureaucracy relating to SEN can be reduced while retaining a focus on the impact and effectiveness for the pupil with SEN.

■ Considering the perceptions of parents, through the use of parental questionnaires or meetings, to find out whether existing systems are adversarial, and to discover if there are any new forms of support that would benefit parents of pupils with SEN.

■ Others.

ACTION PLANNING TO ENABLE IMPACT

Use the format provided below to develop a clear Action Plan for future development of practices for either yourself, or for the school. Make sure that you do not identify too many different actions all at once, have a clear outcome for what you want to achieve in mind, and make sure that you clearly identify the different steps to take to achieve the outcome.

THE CHANGING SEN SYSTEM: ACTION PLANNING TO ENABLE IMPACT:

Which key issues from the chapter do you want to focus on/ change/develop?	How will you effect this change or development (identify a number of small action steps to achieve your overall goal)?	Who else will need to be involved? How?	What will the outcome be (include timescales)?	Impact:

STATUTORY RESPONSIBILITIES FOR SEN

Whose job is it anyway?

THIS CHAPTER:

■ identifies existing statutory responsibilities for SEN and/or disability;
■ critically reflects on how these are managed within the school context;
■ examines ways that the *Achievement for All* approach enables a focus on whole school responsibilities for meeting the needs of pupils with SEN and/or disabilities;
■ considers the role of different staff members in relation to meeting statutory responsibilities for SEN;
■ explores the role of governors, the local authority and voluntary organisations in meeting statutory responsibilities for SEN.

REVIEW

It is essential that the needs of pupils with SEN and/or disability are being met as part of their legal entitlement in schools. Meeting the needs of pupils with SEN and/or disabilities fully and effectively can be more complex and challenging than meeting the needs of other pupils. As a result, the needs of pupils with SEN and/or disability are protected through statutory legislation.

Understanding what statutory responsibilities there are for meeting the needs of pupils with SEN and/or disability, and how these are managed within the school context, including the roles and responsibilities of different staff members, is therefore crucial for developing effective practice that fully meets the needs of pupils with SEN and/or disabilities.

There are, therefore, two key concerns and questions that we need to be asking of existing practices and understandings in school:

1   What are the statutory responsibilities, how are they being met within my school context, and how effective are those approaches?
2   Whose responsibility is it to ensure that statutory responsibilities for SEN and/or disabilities are being met within the school?

Review

▨   What are the statutory responsibilities for SEN and disability?

▨   Where can you go for information and guidance on these?

▨   Have these changed in recent years, and are they likely to change in the future?

▨   How will you find out about changes in statutory responsibilities or legislation?

▨   How are other staff in the school kept informed and up to date about SEN and disability legislation?

▨   Who is responsible in your school for meeting statutory responsibilities for SEN and disability?

▨   What particular approaches or systems have been developed to ensure that statutory responsibilities are met?

▨   Have these been embedded into whole school practices, or are they very separate and distinct practices?

▨   What impact do these have on practice and provision for meeting the needs of pupils with SEN and/or disability?

▨   Why is it important to have statutory responsibilities for SEN and/or disability?

Often, in response to questions about statutory responsibilities for SEN and disability, staff members in schools will automatically turn to the SENCO or headteacher, intimating that that is their responsibility. Clearly, the SENCO does have a very particular responsibility in relation to ensuring that statutory legislation is understood and adhered to. However, that responsibility should be one of leading the strategic direction of SEN practice, not one of doing it all themselves, and being solely responsible. Chapter 5 will therefore consider in more detail the complex, strategic role of the SENCO and the part that they play in meeting statutory responsibilities for SEN.

This chapter, however, looks at a different perspective. In this chapter, the importance of whole school embedded understanding and shared responsibility for meeting the statutory responsibilities for SEN and disability is highlighted.

REFLECTION

Before considering the shared responsibilities and duties of the whole school community in respect of meeting the needs of pupils with SEN, it is first important to identify and define exactly what those statutory responsibilities are. The table on p. 68 provides a summary of the statutory responsibilities for schools under SEN legislation:

Currently, expectations for how to meet the statutory entitlements of pupils with SEN are set out within the Code of Practice (DfES, 2001). All local authorities and maintained schools:

> must have regard to it. They must not ignore it. That means that whenever settings, schools and LEAs decide how to exercise their functions relating to children with special educational needs, and whenever the health and social services provide help to settings, schools and LEAs in this, those bodies must consider what this Code says. These bodies must fulfil their statutory duties towards children with special

Summary of schools' statutory responsibilities under special educational needs (SEN) legislation

Where a child has special educational needs (SEN) a school has statutory duties under the Education Act 1996, which include the following from sections 313, 317 and 317A:

■ The school should do its best to ensure that the necessary provision is made for any pupil who has SEN.

■ The school must ensure that where the headteacher or a nominated governor has been informed by a Local Authority that a pupil has SEN, those needs are made known to all who are likely to teach that pupil.

■ The school must ensure that teachers are aware of the importance of identifying and providing for pupils who have SEN.

■ The school must ensure a pupil with SEN joins in the activities of the school together with other pupils, so far as is reasonably practical and compatible with the child receiving the special educational provision their learning needs call for, the efficient education of the pupils with whom they are educated and the efficient use of resources.

■ The school must report to parents on the implementation of the school's policy for pupils with SEN.

■ The school must have regard to the **SEN Code of practice** when carrying out its duties toward all pupils with SEN.

■ The school must ensure that parents are notified of a decision by the school that SEN provision is being made for their child.

(Accessed from Teachernet: www.teachernet.gov.uk/
wholeschool/disability/summary/senleg/
accessed 28 March 2011)

educational needs but it is up to them to decide how to do so – in the light of the guidance in this Code of Practice.

(DfES, 2001: iii)

The Code of Practice is built on a number of fundamental principles, including that:

■ a child with special educational needs should have their needs met the special educational needs of children will normally be met in mainstream schools or settings

■ the views of the child should be sought and taken into account

■ parents have a vital role to play in supporting their child's education

■ children with special educational needs should be offered full access to a broad, balanced and relevant education, including an appropriate curriculum for the foundation stage and the National Curriculum.

(DfES, 2001: 7)

While currently the Code of Practice (DfES, 2001) and SEN legislation set out above continue to set the legislative context around statutory responsibilities for meeting SEN, the coalition government have noted that existing guidance is overly complex and confusing, and there is therefore a commitment to review, update and streamline SEN legislation to produce a more up to date and relevant SEN Code of Practice (DfE, 2011). This will be in line with the coalition government's emphasis on:

High expectations and good progress are entitlements for all learners. For learners with SEN these entitlements are supported by the actions that all schools are required to take to:

■ promote equality of opportunity and to anticipate and remove or minimise barriers for learners with disabilities;

■ use their best endeavours to ensure that the necessary provision is made for any learner who has SEN.

(DfE, 2010c: 6)

While the existing underpinning principles for statutory responsibilities for meeting SEN (DfES, 2001) are clearly based on inclusive principles, it will therefore be inter-esting to consider how, with the coalition government's plan to 'reduce the bias towards inclusion' (DfE, 2011: 4). The principles and values underpinning any new approach to SEN may therefore change and impact on statutory responsibilities.

In supporting teaching staff to understand their statutory responsibilities, it is still helpful to consider the principles of the National Curriculum Inclusion Statement (DES, 1999), reinforced within Removing Barriers to Achievement (DfES, 2004). This sets out the statutory principles that are essential for all teachers and schools to follow:

■ Setting suitable learning challenges.
■ Responding to pupils' diverse learning needs.
■ Overcoming potential barriers to learning and assessment for individuals and groups of pupils.

(DES, 1999)

Please see Reflective activity 4.1.

DISABILITY LEGISLATION

While it is not necessarily the responsibility of the SENCO to lead on statutory responsibilities in respect of disability legislation, there are clear points of overlap, with some pupils with SEN also having disabilities. It essential that all staff are aware of the duties set out in the Disability Discrimination Act (2005), and that the SENCO is also aware of implications that this may have for the development of practice and provision for any pupils on the SEN Register who may also have a disability.

From 1 October 2010 the Equality Act replaced most of the DDA. However, the Disability Equality Duty in the DDA continues to apply. The Disability Equality Duty states that ALL schools have a statutory duty to meet the requirements of the DDA, relating to all current and potential disabled:

■ employees
■ service users
■ pupils.

Reflective activity 4.1

- How aware were you of the statutory responsibilities and legislation governing SEN?
- How are the statutory responsibilities proactively implemented in practice within your own school?

To ensure that the statutory responsibilities are being fully and effectively met, it is essential to ensure that ALL staff have clear understanding of what they are: not just the SENCO or headteacher:

- Are all staff in your school context currently aware of the statutory responsibilities?
- How is this achieved/could this be achieved and further developed?
- How are all staff members within the school context supported to understand and individually meet the principles of the National Curriculum Inclusion?
- Does current practice in your school reflect these central principles?
- Are there aspects of practice or understanding that need to be developed further?
- Is this within individual staff members, or across all staff?
- What are the implications of this for how to address this? Would a whole staff approach work, or would individual support and training for identified members of staff be more effective?

There is a statutory duty to promote equal opportunities and be proactive, therefore consideration and strategic planning needs to not only respond to the needs of people with disabilities currently involved with the school, but needs to consider the potential needs of anyone wanting to engage with the school. Schools have to adhere to the General Duty, which relates to the statutory requirement to ensure that the general culture and ethos of the school reflects the principles and legislation of the DDA. They also have to adhere to the Specific Duty, which includes the requirement to put together a comprehensive Disability Equality Scheme, detailing how the views of all stakeholders with disabilities were consulted and gathered to inform the development of a proactive action plan to eliminate discrimination. As a result of the Equality Act (2010), this is now usually presented as part of a single Equality Scheme to meet the requirements of the three elements of equality legislation:

- race
- gender
- disability.

The definition of disability, as set out in the legislation, is complex and includes a wide range of impairments, including ASD, dyslexia, speech and language needs as well as physical disabilities. However, the impairment only amounts to a disability if the impact of it on the person's ability to carry out normal day-to-day activities is *substantial and long term.* Schools therefore need to consider the implications of this definition for the identification of pupils with disabilities within the school context.

Reflective activity 4.2

■ How are the statutory requirements of the Disability Discrimination Act (2005) and Equality Act (2010) applied within your school context?
■ How is whole school awareness, engagement and involvement in the development of the Scheme and Action Plan managed?
■ What are the overlaps between leading on disability equality, and leading on the development of appropriate SEN provision and practice?

There is also the need to consider that meeting the needs of pupils with SEN and/or disabilities is not just about statutory entitlements (although it is right that these should be protected by law). Rather, meeting the needs of all pupils, including those with SEN and/or disabilities should form part of the moral duty and purpose embedded within teaching. This building of a sense of moral duty and purpose helps to enhance positive actions and practices to meet statutory responsibilities: thereby turning SEN practice from something that is 'done because we have to' and is often achieved through an individual supporter role (e.g. the SENCO) into something that is embedded in a principled, inclusive, whole school approach to meeting the needs of all pupils. This is achieved in an embedded ethos and culture that supports inclusive understandings of the fundamental right of every child to an appropriate and meaningful educational experience.

SCHOOLS

From the outset, we need to emphasise that meeting statutory responsibilities for SEN is a whole school issue (Nasen, 2010: 2), it is not, and should not, be left to one person (the SENCO). This is acknowledged within the existing Code of Practice (DfES, 2001), although the reality of practice has meant that practices have often been sidelined to the SENCO: 'Provision for pupils with special educational needs is a matter for the school as a whole. . . . Teaching [pupils with SEN] is a whole school responsibility; requiring a whole school response' (DfES, 2001: 59).

Indeed, as Norwich (2010) and Hallett and Hallett (2010) identify, the statutory responsibilities linked to meeting the needs of pupils with SEN and/or disabilities are arguably too broad and wide ranging to be effectively contained within one role (the SENCO). Rather, there is a need to consider a whole school 'distributive' (Hallett and Hallett, 2010) approach to coordinating SEN provision and practice.

The issue, therefore, is whether there is need for a distinct specialist role for coordinating provision and practice for pupils with SEN and/or disabilities, or whether this is such an important part of whole school practice that it should fall within the responsibility of all; and also whether the coordination of provision really should only refer to pupils with SEN and/or disabilities, or whether it should be part of the development of practice for ALL pupils.

While, as Chapter 5 will discuss, there certainly is a need for a key role to strategically lead and develop practice and provision, there is therefore also a need to consider new ways to embed responsibilities and practices for SEN within a whole school approach.

Thus, although it is acknowledged that moves towards a completely 'distributive model of SEN coordination requires a radical rethink of practice' (Hallett and Hallett, 2010: 57), it is understood that 'Developing provision for a wider range of young people than the school has previously catered for is more likely to be successful if fully supported by the senior leadership team and embraced by the whole school community' (Sakellariadis, 2010: 25).

Part of the process of moving away from a distinct role solely responsible for SEN and disability, into a more distributed approach to collective responsibility for meeting SEN, will involve a shift in thinking and practice away from what 'has to be done because we have to' into a deeper understanding and acknowledgement of the rights of the child and ways that they can effectively be met.

This links to the earlier discussions about establishing a moral purpose behind practices in addition to responding on the surface to statutory responsibilities. Schools that have developed good practice are therefore continually reviewing and reflecting on, not only the statutory requirements, but also the underlying purpose, value and impact of practices to support improvements in outcomes for all pupils.

This approach supports a change of thinking and practice where it is acknowledged that 'The question, if one needs to be asked, should not be "can we?" but "how can we?"' (Sakellariadis, 2010: 25).

Reflective activity 4.3

■ What could be the benefits of a whole school embedded and distributed approach to meeting the statutory responsibilities of SEN legislation?

■ Which aspects of the system of SEN coordination could be effectively distributed to enable greater impact on practice?

■ Are there any benefits for retaining a focus on a SENCO role for some aspects of the role?

■ How far do you agree that 'SEN coordination with its multiple foci cannot all be located in a single role' (Norwich, 2010: 48)?

■ Could developing the SENCO role lead to 'deprofessionalisation' of other staff (Hallett and Hallett, 2010: 58)?

ACHIEVEMENT FOR ALL

The *Achievement for All* approach provides a model that highlights the need for a whole school approach. It emphasises the 'profound impact' (National College, 2010a: 1) that this can have on enabling a cultural shift in thinking, practice and understanding about how to best meet the needs of pupils with SEN and disabilities in a way that will lead to direct impact on outcomes for the pupils. This impact is not just about impact on attainment: rather, the focus is on improving:

    ▓   Access

    ▓   Aspirations

    ▓   Achievement.

(Blandford, 2011)

for all pupils, and particularly for those with SEN and Disabilities.

Thus, early findings from the University of Manchester evaluation, provides evidence of impact in terms of wider outcomes, including:

    ▓   improved relationships with hard to reach families. . . .

    ▓   Improved behaviour and fewer reported incidents. . . .

    ▓   Significant improvements in pupil attendance. . . .

    ▓   The overall number of pupils identified with SEND has reduced in the participating schools.

(National College, 2010a: 2)

To be able to do this, requires an approach that is embedded within the whole school ethos and culture. It cannot rest on the possible impact that one staff member may have on the pupil.

The focus is therefore on effective collaboration between all involved with the pupil: SENCO, senior leaders, teachers, parent, pupil and other professionals and schools. This collaborative approach is based on a well articulated and evidenced shared vision that emphasises the fundamental right of every child to access positive, effective and meaningful learning experiences. This vision is underpinned by shared understanding and recognition that all pupils can learn, commitment to removing barriers to enable pupils to learn more effectively, and a focus on ensuring that all involved have a clear understanding of what is expected, and how that can be achieved.

There has, therefore, already been evidence of the 'profound impact' (National College, 2010a: 1) that the *Achievement for All* approach has had on enabling cultural changes to occur. For one headteacher cited within the *Achievement for All* case studies, it has 'put SEND back into the classroom' (National College, 2010a: 2).

Reflective activity 4.4

▓   Where do SEN and disability practices currently reside within your school? Is the focus for SEN and disabilities in:

    –   All classes?

    –   Some classes?

    –   In the SEN office?

    –   In a separate SEN intervention area?

▓   What are the implications of this for your practice?

▓   How could you shift culture and practice in your school setting to ensure that the needs, understanding and practices to support all pupils, including those with SEND resides fully in ALL classrooms?

continued overleaf . . .

> ▩ What will this require in terms of:
>
> – Prioritisation and planning?
> – Resources?
> – Staff training and development?

TEACHERS

The importance and impact of high quality teaching on the progress and outcomes of pupils with SEN cannot be underestimated. It is therefore essential that time is prioritised to support teachers to understand their own statutory responsibilities in terms of supporting all pupils, including those with SEN. The evidence of the impact of teaching is convincing: US research (Sanders and River, 2006: cited by DfE, 2010b: 6) demonstrates that an 8 year old:

> consistently given a teacher in the top quintile of performance was found to perform 50 percentile points better three years later than a similarly performing 8 year old consistently given a teacher in the bottom quintile of performance. . . . This translates into a difference of between 6.7 and 7.9 National Curriculum points at Key stage 2 – which is more than two years progress.
>
> (DfE, 2010b: 6)

Despite this clear evidence, it is acknowledged that practices in schools often focus on placing the most vulnerable pupils, with the most complex needs, with unqualified support staff, while placing the best teachers with the highest ability pupils. As Lamb (2009) acknowledges, this demonstrates a 'hangover of a system, and a society, which does not place enough value on achieving good outcomes for disabled pupils and children with SEN. . . . We need the best teachers and better-targeted resources for those most in need' (Lamb, 2009: 2).

Meeting the needs of pupils with SEN therefore needs to be seen as a shared responsibility, involving all members of staff within the school community. Each teacher needs to carefully consider, respond to and meet the individual learning and special educational needs of pupils within their classroom. In this, it is important to ensure that teachers understand that they cannot rely solely on others (the SENCO, support staff or specialist teacher) to meet the needs of pupils with SEN, and in this 'All teachers are arguably considered to be 'special education teachers' (Garner, 2000), required to have the skills and confidence to support children with special educational needs in reaching their potential (DfES, 2004)' (Lawson and Nash, 2010: 160).

The *Achievement for All* approach emphasises this, highlighting that to improve outcomes and experiences, teachers need to change their embedded behaviours and expectations towards pupils with SEN and/or disability. There is a need to recognise the importance of supporting teachers to become 'inspirational' teachers (Blandford, 2011) to *all* pupils, rather than simply good teachers for some pupils.

By developing this approach, all staff may be supported to recognise that:

> Pupils with even the most severe and complex needs [are] able to make outstanding progress in all types of settings. High quality specialist teachers and a commitment by leaders to create opportunities to include all pupils [are] the keys to success.
>
> (Lamb, 2009: 31)

In supporting teachers to more effectively meet the needs of pupils with SEN and/or disability, it must be acknowledged that responding to pupils with challenging and complex SEN and/or disabilities can be very difficult for some practitioners. Research (MacBeath *et al.*, 2006; House of Commons, 2006; Ellis *et al.*, 2008) has noted the significant impact that trying to respond to the complex and challenging needs of some pupils (particularly those with challenging behaviour needs) can have on the self-esteem and professional identity of the teacher. The emotional impact of meeting diverse needs must therefore be acknowledged (Ekins, 2010b), and then supported through whole school approaches to training that will help to enhance the skills and, most importantly, the understandings and commitment to meeting the needs of all pupils, of all staff.

High quality provision for pupils with SEN and/or disability therefore depends on having teachers who are committed to supporting the diverse learning, social and emotional needs of all pupils; teachers who are trained to understand and positively address a range of needs and who have high expectations for the progress of all pupils.

SUPPORTING TEACHERS TO MEET THEIR STATUTORY RESPONSIBILITIES IN RESPECT OF SEN

In helping teachers to more fully understand and meet their statutory responsibilities for SEN, it may be helpful to provide clear guidance about how this can be achieved within their actual practice. It is therefore important to prioritise the development of teachers' skills and understandings as an approach to enabling all staff to more effectively and proactively meet their statutory responsibilities in relation to meeting the needs of all pupils, including those with SEN and/or disabilities.

Thus, rather than allowing teachers to become reliant on outside support (from the SENCO, support staff or specialist teacher), the most important factor in supporting pupils with SEN within the school context is the development of staff who understand their individual responsibility for meeting the needs of pupils within their class or teaching group, and providing support and practical guidance to enable teachers to develop increased understanding and a wide range of skills to better support those needs.

This can be achieved in a variety of ways, including through the development of Initial Teacher Education and Continuing Professional Development programmes for all staff, as well as by developing in-school approaches to developing and extending expertise.

For many years, commentators have therefore identified the need for clear, high quality training (both in initial teacher education and through Continuing Professional Development for those teachers already in post) (House of Commons Select Committee Report (2006); Lamb Inquiry, 2009; DfE, 2010a; DfE, 2011). This has been evidenced in recent years through the introduction of the Inclusion Development Programme (National Strategies, 2008). The Inclusion Development Programme provides an easy-to-use staff development tool to help extend understanding of some of the key high incidence SEN that teachers support every day within their teaching in mainstream schools. Recent training has also included the introduction of the National Award for SEN Coordination, a statutory postgraduate training course for SENCOs new to post.

Emerging government priorities also include commitments to ensuring that all staff are trained and confident to:

■ identify and overcome a range of barriers to learning;
■ manage challenging behaviour;
■ address bullying;
■ intervene early when problems emerge;
■ identify effectively what a child needs to help them to learn;
■ plan support to help every child progress well, reflecting the specific needs of children with SEN and those who may just be struggling with learning and need school-based catch-up support which is normally available.

(DfE, 2011: 9)

Reflective activity 4.5

■ How confident do you currently feel about being able to respond to all the areas identified above?
■ How well developed is practice across your school in relation to each of those areas?
■ Are there any areas to prioritise for further development?
■ How could this be achieved?
■ What is currently in place within your school context or your local authority to support teachers to respond to their statutory duties in respect of meeting the needs of pupils with SEN and disability?
■ How could this be further developed?

The DfE (2011) has set out a commitment to 'boost the availability of advanced-level continuous professional development' (DfE, 2011: 60), including proposals to 'fund scholarships for teachers to develop their practice in supporting disabled pupils and pupils with SEN, including in specific impairments' (DfE, 2011: 60).

This is an important and significant commitment. There is a need for increased numbers of classroom practitioners to have access to high quality training to better meet the needs of pupils of SEN and meet statutory responsibilities.

Indeed, at a time when specialist support services are increasingly being reduced within local authorities as a result of widespread restructuring to respond to the economic recession, there will increasingly be the need for schools to develop capacity, skills and expertise within their own staff groups. Ways to share this and work collaboratively in partnership with other schools will also be emphasised (see Chapter 5). Please now see Reflective activity 4.6.

The proposal of increased availability of advanced level professional development is therefore to be welcomed, and a strategic approach to this within individual schools and across clusters or partnerships of schools is to be encouraged. In this way, we can work towards ensuring that there are highly qualified staff, trained to understand and meet the needs of a wide range of different SEN working across schools, able to provide direct support and disseminate knowledge and understanding to others.

In addition to accessing a range of external CPD opportunities, it will be important for schools to consider and develop different ways to extend the skills and under-standings of staff members through approaches that are embedded within the whole school context. As the DfE (2011) acknowledge, working collaboratively and utilising

---

Reflective activity 4.6

▧ How can the need for quality CPD in relation to developing SEN expertise be positively embedded within the culture and ethos of your school setting?

▧ What systems are currently in place to audit and monitor the training, skills and expertise of all staff, including support staff?

▧ How is this information meaningfully matched to the actual needs of pupils within the school to ensure an effective match between need types and specialist understanding, resources and support?

▧ What more could be done?

---

opportunities to learn from each other, are powerful tools to support the development of skills across schools:

> Research shows that the most effective way for teachers to develop is by learning from each other. Teachers who have specialist knowledge and experience in working with young people with SEN are often well placed to develop the skills of their colleagues.
>
> (DfE, 2011: 60)

Reflective activity 4.7

▧ How does this happen in your school setting?

▧ What opportunities are currently available for teachers to work with and support each other?

▧ What impact does this have?

▧ Is there a clear focus on the impact of collaborative working?

▧ How is impact shared and disseminated more widely across the school to benefit the development of understanding throughout the school?

▧ Which staff members currently have skills, expertise and knowledge about different special educational needs?

▧ How is this information gathered and updated on a regular basis to ensure that it is used to benefit all staff and pupils within the school?

▧ How could collaborative working practices be developed further to enhance the skills and understanding of specific impairments and special educational needs in all staff?

As a starting point, it is important that schools engage proactively with the Inclusion Development Programme materials. These provide extensive, high quality resources to support the development of understanding of high incidence special educational needs. These can be used and adapted to suit needs within school settings, either used as a whole staff training and development tool, or used on an individual basis to support the development of individual expertise and understanding. The materials from the Inclusion Development Programme (IDP) can be used in different ways to support and meet the specific needs of staff within your own school setting. Do not be afraid, therefore, of adapting delivery and presentation of the materials to suit the particular training needs that you identify. The case studies below therefore provide two different examples of ways that the IDP has been used in schools to raise understanding and practice in relation to teachers' understanding of how to meet their statutory responsibilities for supporting pupils with SEN in their classes.

Case Studies **Use of the Inclusion Development Programme materials**

Case study 1

As a result of a strategic analysis of pupil needs data collated in the school, the SENCO and senior leadership team identified that there was an increasing rise in the prevalence of pupils with autistic spectrum difficulties across the school. This included four pupils with a medical diagnosis of Autism (all of whom had a statement of SEN); three pupils with Asperger's Syndrome (one of which was a very able and high functioning pupil) and a further eight pupils across different year groups who had social communication and interaction needs, although no formal diagnosis as yet.

It was noted that practice in terms of supporting these pupils was variable across the school, and that, during unstructured times in particular, the pupils were finding it difficult to cope with the school environment, resulting in recent rises in challenging behaviour.

The senior leadership team identified that one member of staff worked extremely effectively to proactively meet the needs of pupils with high level autistic needs. This member of staff had previously received training about autism, and was utilising the information and understandings that she had gained to develop whole class strategies that effectively enabled pupils with autism to access and participate in the teaching and learning experience fully.

It was identified that, as the profile of pupils with autism spectrum difficulties was growing in the school, it was important to raise the level of understanding of all staff. This would effectively reduce the problems currently experienced by pupils when they were in situations without their familiar class teacher.

The SENCO had recently accessed training about the IDP, through her local SENCO forum group, and it was agreed that time should be prioritised within staff meetings to provide whole staff training. This was placed on the School Development Plan as a key part of the strategic development of the school and staff for the forthcoming year.

When this was mentioned to teaching staff, it was also identified that to have real impact on the development of whole school understanding, it would also be important to include support staff, midday supervisors and administrator staff in this training. This would then effectively enable shared understandings of the issue, and the development of a consistent whole school approach.

The SENCO led the training, but ensured that opportunities were planned to enable other staff members to share their understandings and expertise. During the first training session, all staff completed the audit of understanding provided in the IDP materials.

This was shared and discussed by all staff, and enabled staff to collectively identify key aspects of the training that should be prioritised. In particular it identified the lack of understanding about the practical implications of ASD for the classroom teaching context.

Over a period of six months, regular training sessions were set up. As well as providing specific teaching and training about aspects of ASD, using the IDP materials, these sessions were also planned to ensure that all staff had the opportunity to feedback about how they were using and implementing the ideas in practice, with a focus on the *impact* of this.

A learning wall was set up in the staffroom, to support the development of understanding. Key questions and aspects that were being focused on were displayed clearly, with an expectation that over the six-month period, all members of staff would contribute something to the learning wall to support the development of practice in others. Over the six months, this became a vibrant and interactive display, supporting the development of collaborative practice across the school. Photocopies of articles about ASD were shared; key questions or challenges were posted – with other staff providing possible solutions and ideas for ways forward; and photographs or photocopies of work or planning were annotated and displayed to demonstrate changes in practice and the impact of those changes for pupils with autism. Resources, including picture symbols to support visual communication, were also shared to support the development of practice in others.

At the end of the six-month period, the IDP audit was again used to measure the impact of the training and the advancement of understanding. The improvements were significant, and this supported all staff to become more able to respond to their statutory duties for meeting the needs of pupils with this particular need type.

Case study 2

In this school, there is a pupil with complex literacy difficulties. He has made very slow and inconsistent progress for some time in mastering basic spelling and reading strategies and skills. His teacher is an outstanding practitioner, has understood his individual needs very well, and is supporting those needs through whole class teaching approaches. This approach, she has identified, not only helps the pupil to feel part of the class, and not singled out as different by needing different approaches and resources, but also supports wider needs within the class. The teacher has identified that although other pupils in her class do not have the specific difficulties that the individual pupil has, many would benefit from access to the same range of visual strategies to support weak auditory memories and difficulties with basic literacy skills.

It is agreed to have the needs of the pupil formally assessed, and, as was expected, a formal diagnosis of dyslexia was given.

Despite the excellent teaching and support provided by the teacher, once the diagnosis was formally given, the teacher expressed concerns to the SENCO that she was now not clear about how to meet her statutory responsibilities for that pupil, as she had no formal understanding about dyslexia as a specific special educational need.

The SENCO knew that what the teacher was already doing as part of her excellent classroom practice was effectively meeting statutory responsibilities in relation to that pupil, however, to reassure the teacher, the SENCO provided the teacher with a copy of the IDP materials for dyslexia to take away and look through. A meeting was booked for the following week to provide time for the SENCO and class teacher to discuss any issues to emerge. Having looked through the IDP materials individually, the class teacher was reassured that she was indeed already meeting the pupil's specific needs. In this case, use of the IDP helped to confirm for the teacher that, just because a pupil had now been given a specific 'label', the individual needs experienced by the pupil had not changed, and that, as an outstanding, experienced teacher she had been well placed to respond fully to his needs, thereby fulfilling her statutory responsibilities in relation to SEN.

It may also be helpful and useful to consider and share with all staff practical principles for effective class teaching: e.g. ideas of what teachers could/should be reflecting on and doing on a daily basis to ensure that they are meeting their statutory responsibilities in relation to meeting the needs of pupils with SEN and/or disability in their classroom context. In the OFSTED Review of SEN and Disability (2010), characteristics of best lessons were summarised:

Teachers had:

- thorough and detailed knowledge of the children and young people;
- thorough knowledge and understanding of teaching strategies and techniques, including assessment for learning;
- thorough knowledge about the subject or areas of learning being taught;
- understanding of how learning difficulties can affect children and young people's learning.

(OFSTED, 2010: 45)

Reflective activity 4.8

- Reflect on the characteristics of best lessons detailed above.
- Which characteristics do you feel secure with, and are confident are fully embedded within your daily teaching?
- Which areas are secure within whole school practice?
- How do you know?
- Are there any areas that could be identified to develop for the future?
- How can this be achieved?

OFSTED (2010) also identified a number of key factors that helped children and young people with SEN learn best. These have been presented as a checklist to support the review, reflection, action planning and impact cycle (see Appendix 2). This may be a useful tool to promote reflection about how teachers can best meet their statutory responsibilities in relation to supporting pupils with SEN in their everyday teaching.

Another useful resource to support teachers to better understand and engage in critical reflection about their use of effective teaching strategies is the Inclusive Teaching Checklist developed by the National Strategies. This is a simple to use checklist that provides a range of different teaching strategies that can be utilised to support pupil learning. It helps teachers to identify strategies that they are already using and are confident with, as well as helping them in a non-threatening way to identify strategies or approaches that they may not have previously considered. Teachers can then effectively match their use of teaching strategies to the needs of pupils within their class group to support them to evaluate how effectively they are matched, and the impact of this on meeting statutory responsibilities for pupils with SEN in all teaching (see Appendix 3 for a copy of the Inclusive Teaching Checklist).

A further strategy that has been useful to schools in developing and enhancing shared commitment, responsibility and understanding of ways to effectively meet the statutory entitlements of all pupils, is through the use of focused periods of collaborative staff development.

Once a key area for whole staff development has been identified, this can then be addressed, not just through a one-off staff training event (which often has limited impact beyond the immediate sharing of ideas) but instead through a strategic and collaborative approach to the development of reflective practice.

In this approach, the focus for development is collaboratively identified, to ensure whole staff commitment to the period of collaborative development. This is then discussed during an initial staff training session, to brainstorm the issues associated with it: why it is particularly relevant for the school context; areas of tension or misunderstanding that need to be understood; possible ways forward and strategies to trial. These discussions will then lead to the development of a shared and agreed Action Plan for development over the next term by all staff within the school.

During that period, five–ten minutes of each staff meeting is allocated for sharing of practice: to include questions to clarify the focus and ways forward; sharing of strategies or approaches that have worked; sharing of developing understanding and examples of impact on pupil experiences or outcomes. The collaborative staff development is also supported through the setting up of a staff Learning Wall within the staffroom, devoted to the particular area of focus. Thus, while Learning Walls have become established practice within classrooms, their usefulness has been neglected as a resource to support staff development. During the period of staff development, there is then an expectation that *all* members of staff contribute something to the Learning Wall to support the development of collective understanding and examples of practice relating to the area in need of change and development. The contributions could include any of the following (and the Learning Wall becomes most effective and useful in terms of developing practice when a diverse range of resources or contributions are shared):

■   photographs of activities that have supported the area of focus;
■   examples of planning – annotated to highlight the change or development in practice;

■   resources;
■   questions;
■   articles;
■   pupil evaluations;
■   staff evaluations.

This approach provides a powerful tool to support the meaningful development of thinking and practice across a whole staff group, and support the creation of more inclusive cultures and ethos that will support and enhance opportunities for all pupils to learn more effectively. It has more impact on the development of deep understanding and critical reflection than one-off staff meeting inputs achieve. This approach leads to increased engagement with the area to be changed or developed, leading to innovation and critical reflection about the issue. Discourse across the school can be transformed as discussions, both formal and informal, change as staff members reflect and share their collective experiences and the development of understanding and learning.

UNDERSTANDING THE STATUTORY RESPONSIBILITIES OF THE GOVERNING BODY AND THE SEN GOVERNOR

The governing body of a school, and identified SEN governor also have statutory responsibilities in relation to ensuring that practices within the school meet all pupils statutory entitlements as set out in SEN legislation. However, it is noted that this is often an 'untapped resource' (Pearson, 2010: 183).

Yet, there is a 'statutory requirement for the governing body of a school to be involved in issues relating to SEN provision' (Pearson, 2010: 188), with the DfE (2011) acknowledging that 'school governors are vitally important in improving outcomes for children with SEN' (DfE, 2011: 62).

The Code of Practice (DfES, 2001) currently sets out the specific responsibilities of the governing body:

The governing body of a community, voluntary or foundation school must:

■   do its best to ensure that the necessary provision is made for any pupil who has special educational needs;

■   ensure that, where the 'responsible person' – the head teacher or the appropriate governor – has been informed by the LEA that a pupil has special educational needs, those needs are made known to all who are likely to teach them;

■   ensure that teachers in the school are aware of the importance of identifying, and providing for, those pupils who have special educational needs;

■   consult the LEA and the governing bodies of other schools, when it seems to be necessary or desirable in the interests of coordinated special educational provision in the area as a whole;

---

continued overleaf . . .

■   ensure that a pupil with special educational needs joins in the activities of the school together with pupils who do not have special educational needs, so far as is reasonably practical and compatible with the child receiving the special educational provision their learning needs call for and the efficient education of the pupils with whom they are educated and the efficient use of resources;

■   report to parents on the implementation of the school's policy for pupils with special educational needs;

■   have regard to this Code of Practice when carrying out its duties toward all pupils with special educational needs;

■   ensure that parents are notified of a decision by the school that SEN provision is being made for their child.

(DfES, 2001: 11)

Reflective activity 4.9

■   How does the SEN governor and the governing body currently fulfil their statutory duties in relation to SEN?

■   How effective and meaningful are current practices for working with the governing body?

■   What is the role of the SEN governor?

■   How is this fulfilled?

■   What impact does the SEN governor visits have on supporting the effective development of SEN practices?

■   Are the visits and role of the SEN governor clearly defined and focused on developing practice and raising outcomes?

■   How could they be developed further?

The role of the SEN governor is vital in providing a direct link between practice in the school and the governing body. Ways to enhance the role of the SEN governor therefore need to be explored within the school, with consideration of the different ways that the role could be developed and defined. This may include the SEN governor becoming:

■   A champion
■   A critical friend
■   A source of support.

(Pearson, 2010: 183)

In order to be able to more fully utilise and develop this relatively 'untapped resource' (Pearson, 2010: 182), it may be helpful to consider the following questions that the DfE (2010a) have provided to support governors in their work. Building on from these questions, the SENCO can work directly with the SEN governor and, more widely with the governing body, to consider key questions that should be asked of practice to ensure that statutory responsibilities in relation to SEN are fully met throughout the school.

Ten key questions for governors to ask

1 What are the school's values? Are they reflected in our long-term develop-ment plans?

2 How are we going to raise standards for all children, including the most and least able, those with Special Educational Needs, boys and girls, and any who are currently underachieving?

3 Have we got the right staff and the right development and reward arrange-ments?

4 Do we have a sound financial strategy, get good value for money and have robust procurement and financial systems?

5 Do we keep our buildings and other assets in good condition and are they well used?

6 How well does the curriculum provide for and stretch all pupils?

7 How well do we keep parents informed and take account of their views?

8 Do we keep children safe and meet the statutory health and safety require-ments?

9 How is pupil behaviour? Do we tackle the root causes of poor behaviour?

10 Do we offer a wide range of extra-curricular activities which engage all pupils?

(DfE, 2010a: 72)

LOCAL AUTHORITIES

The role of local authorities is changing significantly. Over recent years, most local authorities have undergone periods of uncertainty and significant restructuring in order to respond to the current economic climate and the need to effect spending cuts. For practitioners in schools this has been evidenced in the cutting and restructuring of support services from whom to secure support and advice for individual pupils or staff within the school.

The role of the local authority has shifted from being in direct control of services and processes to support pupils, including those with SEN, to which schools are directly accountable. Now, the role, defined by the coalition government 'sets out the strong strategic role that local authorities will play in the new school system, acting as champions for parents and families, vulnerable children, and educational excellence' (DfE, 2011: 95).

Part of the new responsibilities of the local authority in respect of supporting the needs of pupils with SEN, is to 'communicate a clear local offer for families to clarify what support is available and from whom' (DfE, 2011: 8).

Local authorities are 'already required by the Special Educational Needs (Provision of Information by Local Authorities) (England) Regulations 2011 to publish the provision they expect schools to make for children with SEN but without statements and the provision made available for those children by the local authority. Ofsted tells us that this information is rarely provided clearly or effectively' (DfE, 2011: 45).

The DfE (2011) therefore set out that, in relation to school provision, this local offer would detail the additional to and different from provision provided by schools, covering the following key areas:

- Curriculum – how the teaching offers breadth and balance and is tailored to meet children's individual needs.
- Teaching – how teaching is adapted to meet children's SEN and how arrangements are made to secure specialist expertise.
- Assessment – how ongoing teacher assessment is used to identify barriers to learning for children with SEN.
- Pastoral support – how parents are involved in children's learning and how the school supports the education and wellbeing of disabled children and children with SEN.

(DfE, 2011: 46)

Reflective activity 4.10

- What is already in place within your local authority in terms of setting out the additional to and different from provision that is expected to be provided at school level and at local authority level?
- How could you use the information above to put together clear and accessible school-based information to all (including staff, wider professionals and parents) about the provision provided in your school to support the needs of pupils with disabilities and SEN?

This will be a useful activity to do as part of whole staff CPD to develop and enhance understanding of what is available, and also of what is expected as part of an inclusive school culture to remove barriers to learning and participation and support all pupils to make progress.

Thus, it is noted that 'as reforms of the school system and health services come into effect, the role of local authorities is likely to change. For children and young people with SEN or who are disabled and their families, there will be three core features of the local authority role:

- Strategic planning for services that meet the needs of local communities. . . .
- Securing a range of high quality provision for children with young people with SEN or who are disabled.
- Enabling families to make informed choices and exercise greater control over services.

(DfE, 2011: 95)

As voluntary bodies and community groups gradually start to take responsibility for some of the different aspects of SEN provision and practice, including assessment of need and provision of services, which have traditionally fallen within the remit of the local authority, there will be the need to carefully consider and monitor the implication and impact that this may have on statutory responsibilities for meeting SEN.

■ Will they become diluted, or dependent on interpretation by different voluntary bodies?
■ How will statutory duties be able to be monitored and regulated if they are undertaken by voluntary bodies?

ACTION PLANNING

Identify three key points for individual reflection:

1 _____

2 _____

3 _____

Start to consider key issues to be followed up as points of action that have arisen from your reading of this chapter.
This may include:

■ Completing audits of staff training needs to identify individual and whole staff training priorities. Using the Inclusive Teaching checklist, Inclusion Development Programme, and characteristics of good lessons as resources to support the development of staff expertise and understandings.
■ Implementing collaborative staff development focus areas, by collectively agreeing areas in need of development or change, setting up a staff learning wall, and initiating the model of brief reviews of the development of practice in staff meetings.
■ Finding out more about the *Achievement for All* approach and ways that this can support ways to embed a more whole school approach to meeting needs.
■ Considering ways that responsibilities for SEN can be distributed, and the implications of this for whole school practice.
■ Setting up links with the range of voluntary organisations in your area, to consider ways that you could work effectively together to more effectively support the needs of pupils with SEN and disabilities and their families.
■ Considering ways to develop the role of the SEN governor.
■ Others.

ACTION PLANNING TO ENABLE IMPACT

Use the format provided below to develop a clear Action Plan for future development of practices for either yourself, or for the school. Make sure that you do not identify too many different actions all at once, have a clear outcome for what you want to achieve in mind, and make sure that you clearly identify the different steps to take to achieve the outcome.

STATUTORY RESPONSIBILITIES FOR SEN: ACTION PLANNING TO ENABLE IMPACT:

Which key issues from the chapter do you want to focus on/ change/develop?	How will you effect this change or development (identify a number of small action steps to achieve your overall goal)?	Who else will need to be involved? How?	What will the outcome be (include timescales)?	Impact:

THE ROLE OF
THE SENCO

REVIEW

The role of the SENCO has undergone significant transformation and development in recent years, reflecting the repositioning of the SENCO away from the traditional 'coordinator' role of the SEN Code of Practice (2001) and into a strategic leader holding a 'pivotal position' within the school context (Education Act, DCSF, 2008; TDA, 2009; DfE, 2011). The role of the SENCO has become central within the school. Thus, it is acknowledged that:

> While headteachers and governors have the responsibility for ensuring that disabled pupils and pupils with SEN get the right support, it is frequently the SENCO who has the day to day lead. In many cases SENCOs work with teachers on mapping the provision for all pupils who need additional support, advising staff on appropriate and alternative interventions as a child moves through school, and modelling effective practice.
>
> (DfE, 2011: 63)

It is therefore important to take some time to critically review the current role of the SENCO, and then to reflect on the implications of recent changes to the positioning and legal status and responsibilities of the SENCO in order to evaluate how effectively existing practices in your school match what is now expected of the role, and what impact changes and developments to practice may have.

Understanding your own workload:

Take some time to make a list of all the tasks and responsibilities that fall into your role within your specific school setting:

■ Complete a 'work diary' over the period of one week, briefly detailing the different activities that you have completed.

■ Add in other activities that are central to your role but which occur at different times of the term/year.

■ Try and think about how much time you have to spend on each one.

■ Start to try and define which ones are:

- – administrative tasks;
- – strategic;
- – reactive;
- – enabling other colleagues;
- – direct work with pupils with SEN and/or disabilities;
- – other – specify.

■ What are the implications of this way of working for the effective development of SEN practices within your school setting?

■ If all/many of your current work tasks fall into the administrative or reactive categories, how will capacity be able to be built within your school context? How will practices improve and develop?

■ What does this brief review/analysis tell you about how to develop SEN practices and aspects of your own role and responsibilities for the future?

■ How will you achieve this?

■ Use just one adjective or noun to describe how you feel about your role.

■ Why have you described it in this way?

■ What feelings does this description evoke?

■ What implications does this have for practice

REFLECTION

A changing role

In recent years the role of the SENCO has changed, often leading to a certain degree of 'uncertainty' around the role (Hallett and Hallett, 2010: 6), with it being open to variation and interpretation (Norwich, 2010; Petersen, 2010).

While the Code of Practice sets out that the key managerial and administrative aspects of the role of the SENCO are:

■ ensuring liaison with parents and other professionals in respect of children with special educational needs;

■ advising and supporting other practitioners in the setting;

■ ensuring that appropriate Individual Education Plans are in place;

■ ensuring that relevant background information about individual children with special educational needs is collected, recorded and updated.

(DfES, 2001: 34)

Yet, the uncertainty around the role of the SENCO remains. Indeed, as Hallett and Hallett (2010) note, 'Reviews of practice conducted in the past five years have, somewhat unsurprisingly, reported that the reality of the role is clearly varied . . . and very much dependent on context and interpretation of sometimes contradictory legislation' (Hallett and Hallett, 2010: 51).

Part of the current variability in the role is therefore due to contextual differences. There is therefore a need to consider the unique and individual contexts within which SENCOs work. This will include the size and location of the school, and the number of pupils identified as having SEN and/or disabilities within the school context. A SENCO working in a large inner city school with high levels of pupils identified as having SEN and/or disabilities may therefore have a quite different role to a SENCO working in a small rural school with low numbers of pupils identified as having SEN and/or disabilities. The positioning and status of the role and overall approach to meeting the needs of pupils with SEN and/or disabilities will also impact on how the role is perceived and developed. This will include variation in whether the SENCO is seen as a senior leader, or not, and also whether there is shared responsibility for meeting the needs of all pupils, including those with SEN and/or disabilities or whether the responsibility rests solely with the SENCO.

For many SENCOs, the role has therefore become all encompassing, moving from a Special Educational Needs Coordinator to Inclusion Coordinators, with responsibility for monitoring the progress and provision for a widening number of 'vulnerable groups' within the school context.

Thus, in response to the question above about defining the role of the SENCO, common metaphors to emerge would include:

■ juggler
■ expected expert
■ counsellor
■ plate-spinner.

Through this chapter, and the book, the central message is to move the weight of responsibilities and statutory duties away from residing with just one person, into the development of a more effective and inclusive whole school approach. Within this approach the role of the SENCO remains central, but the metaphors and nouns change to those around being a:

■ facilitator
■ enabler
■ supporter

rather than someone who is charged with doing it all themselves (Ekins, 2010a: 111).

Since the review of SEN practices carried out by the House of Commons Select Committee (2006), concerns have been raised about the inconsistent role of the SENCO.

This review therefore identified the following recommendations for developing the role of the SENCO:

■ Special educational needs coordinators (SENCOs) should in all cases be qualified teachers and in a senior management position in the school as recommended in the SEN Code of Practice.

■ Firmer guidelines are required rather than the Government asking schools to 'have regard to' the SEN Code of practice.

■ The role and position of a SENCO must reflect the central priority that SEN should hold within schools.

■ SENCOs should be given ongoing training opportunities to enable them to keep their knowledge up to date as well as sufficient non-teaching time to reflect the number of children with SEN in their school.

■ These baseline standards for SENCOs to be given training both on and off the job should apply to all schools, including academies and trust schools.

■ Schools should set out in their SEN policy action to ensure that all SENCOs are adequately monitored and supported in their vital roles.

(House of Commons, 2006: 74)

Reflective activity 5.1

Which of the recommendations of the House of Commons Select Committee (2006) have now impacted on practice and are part of the role of the SENCO?
Are there any aspects that still need to be developed:

■ Nationally?
■ Locally?
■ In your own school?

The recent changes that have occurred through the Education (Special Educational Needs Coordinators) (England) Regulations 2008, set out the following requirements for the role of the SENCO:

■ SENCOs should in all cases be qualified teachers;
■ they should be in a senior management position in the school, as suggested by the SEN Code of Practice;
■ SENCOs should be properly trained.

(DCSF, 2008: 1)

You will notice that these statutory regulations do address some of the recommendations raised by the House of Commons Select Committee (2006) (see above). While these statutory regulations are to be welcomed, and have already helped to raise the status of the SENCO nationally, it is important to acknowledge that: 'This new emphasis, from a role bounded by a non-regulatory framework to one operating within statutory limits, requires a fundamental element of change in practice' (Hallett and Hallett, 2010: 4).

How these changes will fundamentally impact on practice therefore needs to be considered by schools.

In particular, the legal requirements have significantly impacted on raising the status of the SENCO, by specifying that the SENCO now must be a qualified teacher and that there is an expectation that they should also be in a senior management position. This has reversed the trend that has occurred through workforce restructuring in recent years, of teaching assistants often taking on the role of the SENCO, and has emphasised the range of leadership and management responsibilities held within the role. A key aspect of the role is also to be able to provide professional guidance, through modelling, mentoring, observation and coaching to other teaching staff to support colleagues to more fully meet the needs of pupils with SEN and/or disabilities. This is an aspect of the role that, arguably, could not be fully carried out by someone who is not qualified as a teacher.

While there has, therefore, in some schools, been the development of practice towards unqualified support staff or teaching assistants taking on the role, this needs to now be reconsidered in order to fulfil the recent statutory requirements for the role. As Petersen (2010) notes:

> twenty first century SENCOs need to have the time, status and support to enable them to be able to react and meet the demanding and challenging responsibilities that are now central to the role. No longer can we have a willing volunteer or a caring friend to carry out this extensive and diverse role. The professional SENCO has to be at the centre of change is a school wants to raise standards and improve its overall performance.
>
> (Petersen, 2010: 22)

It is this notion of the 'professional SENCO' that needs to be further considered and developed within schools.

Reflective activity 5.2

■   How far are you/your SENCO currently seen as a 'professional SENCO'?
■   What implications does this concept have for expectations of the role?
■   What resources (internally or externally) would be needed to enable you/your SENCO to develop as a professional SENCO?
■   What impact will this have on whole school practice?
■   What impact will it have on improving outcomes for pupils with SEN and/or disabilities?

In some schools unqualified members of staff have a wide range of expertise and skills in meeting some of the new requirements for the SENCO role. Schools must therefore carefully consider the wide range of responsibilities falling to the role of the SENCO, and could consider how to best utilise ALL existing skills and expertise – which may include having a SENCO who is a qualified teacher supported in identified aspects of the role by a highly experienced and knowledgeable unqualified member of staff. Indeed, as Norwich (2010) noted, the wide range of roles and responsibilities expected from the SENCO is not something that can easily be located within one person. Utilising expertise from a range of staff members within the school to move the role away from one that is just located within one individual to one that is shared to maximise expertise, but led by the SENCO may be something to develop.

THE NATIONAL AWARD FOR SEN COORDINATION

Central within the new statutory regulations for SENCOs is the introduction of specific requirements that those SENCOs new to the role must successfully achieve the National Award for SEN Coordination – the mandatory national SENCO training programme. This national training programme, delivered by approved training providers across the country, has embedded within it, through the required SENCO learning outcomes, clear expectations for the role and responsibilities of the twenty-first-century SENCO. Training providers must therefore: 'assure themselves that SENCOs meet all of the outcomes by the end of the programme in order to be awarded the National SENCO qualification (The National Award for Special Educational Needs Coordination)' (TDA, 2009: 16).

The introduction of mandatory training for SENCOs is significant, and will fulfil the recommendation that 'every school has a teacher to lead on teaching and learning for disabled pupils and pupils with SEN' (Lamb, 2009: 31).

However, the significance of the implementation of a mandatory national training framework to support the development of SENCOs goes beyond that. Mandatory training in order to be able to fulfil a particular position within a school is only statutory for two positions within the school context: the headteacher and the SENCO (Hallett and Hallett, 2010). This would therefore seem to highlight the importance of the SENCO role, raising its status within the school context as a key role for strategic whole school development. This therefore:

> seems to reflect a view that the SENCO is both an agent of change for individual pupils, and a change agent for schools; that is, it is both a process management role, and a strategic management role. This would seem to place the SENCO at the centre of the school development process, able to meet the needs of all pupils, while providing a specialist focus for those with additional needs.
>
> (Hallett and Hallett, 2010: 3)

The regulations for the national training programme are very specific. It is a Postgraduate Certificate course, so that on successful completion of the course, SENCOs will have achieved sixty Masters level credits (needing 180 Masters level credits to gain a full Masters degree). This course is therefore supporting moves within the education system to raise the status of the profession generally to a Masters-level profession. The course provides a careful balance between the development of the practical knowledge, understanding and skills that the SENCO needs to have to develop practice within the school and to be able to evidence the SENCO learning outcomes; as well as a focus on the development of Masters level skills such as:

■ reflection
■ criticality
■ enquiry.

Reflective activity 5.3

■　What do you think are the perceived benefits of a national training programme to support SENCOs new to post?

■　How will the national training programme help to develop the role of the SENCO nationally?

■　How do you think that the focus on Masters level skills will help to develop the role of the SENCO?

The development of this training programme has been seen as a welcome move – one that, with the other statutory requirements that came into force through the Education (Special Educational Needs Co-ordinators) (England) Regulations 2008, has helped to raise the status and skills of SENCOs. Indeed, as Petersen (2010) notes:

> As we enter the second decade of the twenty-first century we finally have high quality, professional development opportunities for our next generation of SENCOs. The National Award for SEN Coordination has been a long time coming but very welcome and the first step in the raised status that SENCOs deserve.
>
> (Petersen, 2010: 19)

WHAT ARE THE KEY RESPONSIBILITIES OF THE ROLE OF THE SENCO?

With the introduction of the mandatory National Award for SEN Coordination, we now have clear guidance about what is nationally expected from SENCOs as part of their role. This is provided in the fifty-five learning outcomes that all new SENCOs to post are required to evidence in order to gain the National Award for SEN Coordination.

While these 'should not to be interpreted as professional standards and do not replace the Professional Standards for Teachers, which apply to SENCOs in their schools in the same way as other teachers' (TDA, 2009: 16), they do provide a very clear overview of the expected knowledge, skills and understandings of the SENCO. These fifty-five learning outcomes (see Appendix 4) are divided into five key areas of responsibility, each with a number of key criteria:

Professional context

■　Statutory and regulatory frameworks and relevant developments at national and local level.

■　High incidence SEN and disabilities and how they can affect pupils' participation and learning.

■　Using evidence about learning, teaching and assessment in relation to pupils with SEN to inform practice.

continued overleaf . . .

Strategic development of SEN policy and procedures

- ■ Working strategically with senior colleagues and governors.
- ■ Strategic financial planning, budget management and use of resources in line with best value principles.
- ■ Strategies for improving outcomes for pupils with SEN and/or disabilities.

Coordinating provision

- ■ Developing, using, monitoring and evaluating systems.
- ■ Using tools for collecting, analysing and using data.
- ■ Deploying staff and managing resources.

Leading, developing and supporting colleagues

- ■ Providing professional direction to the work of others.
- ■ Leadership and development of staff.

Working in partnership with pupils, families and other professionals

- ■ Drawing on external sources of support and expertise.
- ■ Consulting, engaging and communicating with colleagues, parents and carers and pupils to enhance pupils' learning and achievement.

Reflective activity 5.4

- ■ Do you think that these five areas fully and adequately encompass the role of the SENCO?
- ■ Are there any key areas that you do not think are included?
- ■ Are there any areas, or aspects, that you do not think should sit within the role of the SENCO?
- ■ How do these compare with the broader definitions of the SENCO role provided within the Code of Practice (DfES, 2001)?

TENSIONS BETWEEN POLICY AND PRACTICE

While we do now have statutory regulations governing the role of the SENCO, we have to be aware of continuing inconsistencies between policy and practice.

Thus, while the notion of a 'professional SENCO' (Petersen, 2010: 22) is key to the future positioning and development of the role, there is much still to be done to continue to raise the status of the SENCO within all school settings. Fortunately, there is confirmed commitment to the role of the SENCO, as a strategic and 'pivotal' role within the school system (DfE, 2011). Yet, tensions do still remain, which need to be identified and addressed nationally, and also within individual schools.

While it is therefore widely accepted that, to be effective, the SENCO needs to be a strategic leader (DfES, 2004; House of Commons, 2006; Lamb, 2009; TDA, 2009; DfE, 2011), the reality in practice is that many SENCOs are still not senior leaders within their schools, and that in some schools there is a continuing situation where the Senior Leadership Team within the school actually undervalues and limits the SENCOs opportunities to effect real change and development within the school.

As the DfE (2011) note: 'The relationship between the SENCO and the senior management team within the school is critical to the effectiveness of [the SENCOs] pivotal role' (DfE, 2011: 63).

It is therefore essential that this is continually challenged and that efforts are made to move thinking and practice forward in all schools to ensure understanding and recognition of the 'major role [that SENCOs can play] in "building capacity for improvement"' (Nasen, 2010: 2).

A key way to ensure this, as identified in Chapter 4, when discussing whole school statutory responsibilities for SEN, is to ensure that there is whole school understanding of SEN, not as a separate issue, but as a key part in strategic whole school development. Thus, the SENCO 'should be viewed as integral to the "mainstream" rather than part of a separate SEN structure' (Nasen, 2010: 2).

Underpinning all of this is a fundamental lack of understanding and agreement about expectations for the role, which continue to be experienced by some SENCOs within some schools, despite the recent statutory regulations. Difficulties in the role of the SENCO are therefore 'exacerbated by inconsistencies in role expectation' (Hallett and Hallett, 2010: 2). Please now see Reflective activity 5.5.

Another tension that currently exists within our practice is in relation to the statutory requirement for SENCOs to undertake the mandatory SENCO training programme.

Currently, this is only statutory for those new to post, working in maintained, mainstream school settings. This therefore does not include the many experienced SENCOs (i.e. those who started working as a SENCO before 1 September 2008), or any SENCOs working in special schools and settings or independent schools. The regulations, while 'recommended' (DCSF, 2009) to Academies, who through the Academies Bill (2010) still have to adhere to SEN legislation, are again not statutory.

The omission of so many different settings within the statutory legislation is significant, and will impact on the consistency of SENCO support and the development of the role nationally.

Through this omission there is the danger that, while we are certainly developing a well skilled, professional body of SENCOs, there will be SENCOs who are 'left behind'. Although experienced SENCOs and those SENCOs working in special schools and settings or independent schools are certainly supported by training providers to access the National Award for SEN Coordination, there is no statutory requirement, or funding to support SENCOs to undertake the training.

In order to make significant and consistent national impact on the development of the 'professional SENCO' it is therefore essential that *all* SENCOs have access to high quality training to ensure that they are kept up to date with the changes in practice and regulation. It is also important that *all* SENCOs are supported to engage positively with

Reflective activity 5.5

Look again at the activity that you completed at the start of this chapter, relating to the identification of the roles and responsibilities relating to your own role in school:

- How have the expectations of your role been defined within your own school context?
- How are the roles and responsibilities defined within the Code of Practice (2001), as well as within the new required SENCO learning outcomes shared and agreed between all staff within the school?
- Are they all left to the SENCO, or do all members of staff take an active part in ensuring their effective implementation?
- What is the implication of this for the development of thinking, understanding and practice within the school context?
- Is your role defined as an Inclusion Manager/Coordinator, or as a Special Educational Needs Coordination?
- How does this impact on your role and responsibilities?
- How can practice in the school move from a separate SEN structure into the mainstream be effected?
- What impact will this have on practice?
- Is this an issue in your school, or have SEN practices already been embedded within whole school development?
- If SEN practice is already viewed as 'part of the mainstream', how has this been achieved?
- How can you share examples of the development of thinking and practice with other schools to support their individual development?
- If SENCO practice is not yet seen as 'part of the mainstream', how can you work towards this?
- Are SEN priorities and practices included as part of the School Development Plan, or are they on a separate Action Plan?
- What impact does this have on perceptions of the whole school community of the value and positioning of SEN practices within the school?

the SENCO learning outcomes to ensure that they review and develop their skills and role in line with national expectations. By doing this, we will have some impact on the current variability of practice across the country, and help to reduce the negative impact of the existing 'postcode lottery' of support, provision and practice affecting pupils with SEN and/or disabilities and their families.

IMPACT OF THE NATIONAL AWARD FOR SEN COORDINATION

Having worked with large numbers of SENCOs engaging with the National Award for SEN Coordination, since September 2009, I have been interested to reflect on the impact that the course is having, not only for individuals, but also for their schools, the pupils with SEN and/or disabilities, and their parents that they support, as well as for the development of the 'professional SENCO' identity nationally and in localised groups.

As course director, observing the engagement of the SENCOs in the course, and through the research that I have undertaken with the different cohorts (Ekins, 2011 forthcoming), I have noticed the following key points:

- Increased confidence and skills.
- Increased status in schools: many SENCOs are soon 'promoted' to become members of the Senior Leadership Team as a result of their engagement in the course.
- Dissemination of the course input to colleagues in schools, in creative and innovative ways (including the setting up of email bulletins, weekly newsletters, staff focus inputs, working parties, SEN representatives or 'ambassadors' to ensure consistency of practice across large schools) impacting on improvements in practice for pupils with SEN and/or disabilities across all staff.
- Increased engagement in legislation and theoretical frameworks, leading to greater understanding of the issues impacting on pupils with SEN and/or disability.
- Development of criticality and reflective thinking skills – leading to an increased ability to critically question and challenge existing practices.
- Development of professional networks: each cohort becomes a supportive resource, providing support and encouragement to others within the group – and this continues after the end of the teaching programme.
- Evidence of significant impact in schools: with many SENCOs providing evidence of appropriate actions that they have taken to significantly change and improve systems – particularly in relation to supporting colleagues to work in more effective ways to improve outcomes for pupils with SEN and/or disability; and also in monitoring and evaluating outcomes of support and provision in increasingly efficient ways.
- The development of a 'professional discourse' within the SENCOs.
- Opportunities to 'catch up' with new practices and information (particularly for experienced SENCOs and SENCOs from independent schools and special school settings).
- Greater understanding of the range of contexts, and an ability to reconsider practices in the light of greater understanding of the variety of different settings (benefiting from opportunities to share aspects of practice across primary and secondary schools; across maintained and independent settings; and across mainstream and special settings).

While there are, therefore, many positive aspects to engaging proactively with the statutory national SENCO training programme, there are also some tensions that continue to exist:

- For some SENCOs, while they personally benefit hugely from the course, they are limited in their ability to positively implement changes in practice by continued differences in perception of the role within their own school setting. Some SENCOs therefore become frustrated at not being able to change understandings of practice within the school context.
- The time requirements of the course are difficult – and again, SENCOs who are well supported by their school, which sees how much the course will benefit the

development of whole school practices, find this much easier to manage than those struggling to persuade senior leaders of the relevance of the course and teaching input.

■ For some SENCOs, having to complete assessed work at Masters level, as well as evidence of the development of practice in relation to each of the required SENCO learning outcomes is a difficult task.

■ Depending on the amount of time and status devoted to the SENCO role, it can be easier or more difficult to engage fully with the SENCO learning outcomes. For some very new SENCOs to role, they have required time to access the course and receive the taught inputs, followed by a period of time to start to implement changes in practice.

■ There does, therefore, have to be some understanding of the context within which the SENCO is working, in order to be empathetic to the type of changes that are possible for the SENCO to effect within what is actually a very small timescale. There also needs to be understanding of the complex nature of change. For some SENCOs and for some of the learning outcomes, change will take some time to occur, and therefore by the end of the course, only the beginning steps of a change that will occur over the next few years will be evidenced.

With the continued commitment by the government (DfE, 2011) to the role of the SENCO and the value of the National Award for SEN Coordination to support the development of the professional skills and identity of the SENCO, it will therefore be important to continue to evaluate and review the impact, making improvements to enable all SENCOs to positively engage with this statutory training programme.

BEING AN EFFECTIVE SENCO: TIME MANAGEMENT

One of the most difficult parts of the SENCO role, as evidenced in the research above, is finding the time to address the now very wide-ranging, strategic and whole-school responsibilities that fall within the role. The SENCO must therefore ensure that they develop effective time management skills, which may include appropriate and efficient delegation and prioritisation of tasks. This needs to be understood by the whole school, including the headteacher and senior leadership team.

Having a clear understanding of the role, is therefore a key starting point, and the required SENCO learning outcomes can support you in developing that understanding. Please now see Reflective activity 5.6.

Paperwork and bureaucracy always emerge as the key barriers taking up too much of the SENCO time. It must therefore be highlighted that, in the new national expectation of the role, there is not a separate learning outcome for 'completing paperwork'! This is NOT seen as a key aspect of the strategic role of the 'professional SENCO'.

It is therefore vital that the SENCO looks at ways to delegate out aspects of the role that are not needed to be completed by a strategic leader. Filing copies of targets or provision maps, for example, could be more efficiently completed by an SEN administrator; making initial contact with other schools to gather key information about new pupils transferring to the school (through the use of a shared and understood checklist of key questions) could also be completed by an SEN administrator. Getting pupil progress tracking data does not have to be separately completed by the SENCO: this should be a

Reflective activity 5.6

Use the Baseline Audit of existing skills and knowledge (Appendix 4), which is based on the statutory SENCO learning outcomes required for those SENCOs new to post completing the mandatory National Award for SEN Coordination.

Use this to complete a baseline audit of your own skills and knowledge, or the skills, knowledge, understanding and practices within the school as a whole:

■   What issues emerge as pertinent to the prioritisation of time for your role?
■   Are there any aspects of the role (e.g. leading, developing and supporting others; or strategic development) that perhaps you are not currently spending time on?
■   Are there any areas that you are spending too much time on?
■   What is the implication of this for practice?
■   Which areas have emerged as priority areas for development?
■   Which areas have you identified that you/your school already has well-developed expertise or practice?
■   How can you build on the existing strengths that you have identified?
■   How can you address the areas that you have identified where you have less existing knowledge or expertise?
■   What opportunities are there:

  –   Within your school?
  –   Locally, e.g. through local SENCO forum groups?
  –   Through accredited training programmes?
  –   For you to address any gaps in expertise and knowledge?

strategic whole school activity, and therefore any pupil tracking data and records should then be effectively shared to reduce time being wasted repeating tasks.

The SENCO also needs to consider simple techniques and strategies to enable key tasks such as monitoring provision and interventions, and undertaking classroom observations of practice to become more efficient.

Setting up simple systems (e.g. a traffic light system) to monitor pupil progress through interventions and provisions can enable the SENCO as strategic leader to monitor the impact that interventions are having and make any changes that are necessary to practise simply and efficiently (see case study below).

Opportunities to observe and support staff are important in enabling the review and development of practices within the school setting, but can be perceived as taking up too much time. Again, it is important for the SENCO to think proactively about how this can be best managed. By identifying a clear focus for the observation, a SENCO does not have to spend the whole lesson in one classroom. Instead, a 5–10 minute observation may be enough to get an understanding of the context, and any difficulties faced by the pupil and/or teacher. This would enable a SENCO to undertake a number of lesson observations within a morning or afternoon session, as well as attending to other issues such as meeting with parents and reviewing the progress of intervention groups.

Case Study **Effective time management**

The SENCO had worked with staff (teachers and support staff) to devise a simple to use monitoring form to be completed when pupils accessed intervention provisions. Clear outcomes had been identified at the start of the intervention, which were carefully matched against baseline skills, and against which progress through the intervention was rigorously evaluated.

During each intervention session the adult (teacher or support staff) would therefore judge whether the pupil was still a long way from achieving the set outcome (red); making progress but not yet secure (orange); or had achieved the set outcome (green).

By collecting the intervention records to review them every two weeks, the SENCO, as strategic leader, could then spend half an hour and quickly and efficiently be updated with progress that all pupils were making on the structured intervention programmes. Where a pupil, or group, were consistently not making progress towards the outcome (identified in red on the tracking sheets), the SENCO would intervene to talk to the staff involved (both teacher and support staff) about reasons for this, and ways to change the intervention to make it more effective for the pupil or group. Where a pupil or group were consistently meeting the end of intervention outcome (identified as green on the tracking sheet) and where there was still some time before the planned end of intervention, then again changes could be made. This may involve a decision to stop that pupil or group accessing the intervention, in order to enable another pupil/group to benefit from the input; or it may involve reconsidering the end outcomes, to further extend understanding and expected end outcome.

OFSTED (2011) provided clear guidance to OFSTED inspectors on aspects of practice that they expect to look for and judge during an OFSTED inspection. This also provides a useful resource to support SENCOs in helping to prioritise aspects of practice that need more time allocated to them. Appendix 5 provides a template where the key features that will be focused on during an inspection are identified to support with the review of existing practice and reflection and action planning about what needs to be further developed.

ACTION PLANNING

Identify three key points for individual reflection:

1 _____

2 _____

3 _____

Start to consider key issues to be followed up as points of action that have arisen from your reading of this chapter.

This may include:

- working with others to develop understanding of perceptions of the role of the SENCO within your school context;
- completing the audit of skills linked to the SENCO learning outcomes to understand implications for your own professional development;
- identifying ways to develop the role of the SENCO more fully within your own school context, including identifying appropriate training opportunities;
- using the adapted OFSTED (2011) template to identify priorities for whole school practice;
- others.

ACTION PLANNING TO ENABLE IMPACT

Use the format provided below to develop a clear Action Plan for future development of practices for either yourself, or for the school. Make sure that you do not identify too many different actions all at once, have a clear outcome for what you want to achieve in mind, and make sure that you clearly identify the different steps to take to achieve the outcome.

THE ROLE OF THE SENCO: ACTION PLANNING TO ENABLE IMPACT:

Which key issues from the chapter do you want to focus on/ change/develop?	How will you effect this change or development (identify a number of small action steps to achieve your overall goal)?	Who else will need to be involved? How?	What will the outcome be (include timescales)?	Impact:

NEW WAYS OF WORKING

REVIEW

No one person could ever effectively and fully meet the needs of a pupil with complex special educational needs and/or disabilities. Rather, what is required is the development of effective working practices to support collaboration between a range of different people, including the parent and pupil themselves and a range of professionals. This chapter focuses on the communication and collaboration that can and could happen between professionals from different services, including practitioners from different schools working together. The important issue of working effectively in collaboration with pupils and parents is then discussed in Chapter 9.

Currently, despite the previous Labour government's agenda for multi-agency working set out in *Every Child Matters* (2004) services and professionals do not consistently work effectively together to really place the child at the centre and provide a dynamic and interrelated service across different services to support that child. Despite individual examples of the development of some exceptional approaches to multi-agency working where the needs of the child or family really have been placed at the heart of the process, it is acknowledged that still 'parents tell us that it can feel like a struggle to get the right support for their family from education, health and social care services'. It can be slow and complicated, with different services working in isolation and each having its own approach (DfE, 2011: 6).

Collaboration between services is currently not working well enough to consistently and equitably support the needs of all pupils with SEN and/or disabilities. It is therefore essential that this is critically examined and explored in order to find ways to first identify the barriers to effective collaboration that currently exist between services, and then to find ways to remove those barriers.

Review

■ What examples of effective collaboration do you already have from your own practice supporting pupils with SEN and/or disabilities?

- – Who have you collaborated with?
- – How was the collaboration structured?
- – Who led the collaboration?
- – What was the impact/outcome of the collaboration:

  - – For the pupil with SEN and/or disabilities?
  - – For your own development of practice and understanding?
  - – For the school as a whole?

■ Can you think of any times when collaboration with others has broken down and not led to the effective development of practice for a pupil with SEN and/or disabilities?

- – How and why did the collaboration break down?
- – Are there any ways that the collaboration could have been saved?

REFLECTION

In an evolving and changing educational system, there is a need for new and innovative ways of working within and between schools, services and agencies to emerge. These practices need to be focused on putting the needs of the pupil with SEN and/or disabilities first, including finding practical and effective ways to meet the needs of that pupil. To be able to build new and innovative approaches to working together, principles of effective collaboration need to be understood and need to underpin our approaches to working with others. Unless we address the difficulties with effective working this will continue to be a significant barrier impacting on positive outcomes for pupils with SEN and disabilities: 'collaboration is a central element of inclusive practice because professional boundaries often become another barrier for young people to negotiate' (Parry et al., 2010: 3).

Whether we are considering collaboration between colleagues within the same school; collaboration between schools or collaboration between professionals from different agencies, a number of key principles will underpin whether the collaboration is effective and successful or not.

Reflective activity 6.1

■ What would you consider to be the most important principles of collaborative working?
■ Why have you identified those principles?
■ How do they relate to practice?
■ What is/can be the impact on practice when those principles are well developed?

Collaboration, to be meaningful and successful needs to be built on the following key principles:

■ a clear focus on the needs of the particular child as the reason for the collaboration;
■ a commitment from all to work towards meeting the needs of the particular child;
■ trust;
■ shared respect;
■ shared responsibility/accountability (OFSTED, 2010);
■ a team approach;
■ shared understanding of each other's perspectives: the individual knowledge, skills, expertise of each member of the collaborative group;
■ valuing and accepting the expertise of others;
■ clear protocols for sharing information have been established (OFSTED, 2010);
■ the development of a clear Action Plan that sets out the individual responsibilities of each member of the group, which is agreed by all, and which has a date for review;
■ time.

While it is important to acknowledge that over the last decade some very innovative and effective collaborative practices have evolved, and that these have served the needs of vulnerable children and families extremely well, it is clear that this is still not consistent everywhere, and that there are still large numbers of cases where parents and practitioners are experiencing difficulties securing the collaborative approach to meeting a child's needs that they require.

One of the key reasons that collaboration between agencies and services has been inconsistent, despite the introduction of *Every Child Matters* (DfES, 2004) and the increased expectation for services to collaborate to put the child and family at the centre of planning, is the fact that, to date, the accountability and responsibility for meeting pupil needs has been left to schools and education. While health and social services are also clearly working to support the needs of pupils with SEN and their families, the responsibilities and priorities for action are different, and they are not held accountable in terms of meeting outcomes for pupils with SEN. One way that this may be able to be developed more effectively for the future is to develop the concept of the school as a community resource to include health and social services within the location of the school, with professionals within each service working alongside each other to most effectively target and meet the needs of individuals and groups within the school community.

To have any significant long-term impact on the ability of different services to work effectively together will have to, however, also be addressed through shared policy and departmental statutory responsibilities. There is, currently, an indication that there will be a move towards joint policy statements (DfE, 2011) to support the development of shared accountability for outcomes for vulnerable pupils across all services. It is crucial that the impact of this is carefully monitored and evaluated though rigorous research that critically analyses the impact of this on individual experiences and the raising of positive outcomes for pupils with SEN and/or disabilities and their families, and also the consistency and sustainability of new approaches to ensure that all pupils with SEN and/or disabilities and their families receive a consistent, equitable experience wherever they may live.

The focus on competition between schools, with the use of league tables and push to raise standards, has also, arguably, impacted on ways that schools collaborate together. Over recent years there has, therefore, been an emphasis on raising standards within individual schools, rather than the development of a truly collaborative approach to meeting the needs of all pupils.

We now need to move away from an individualised approach to meeting pupil needs, where each school is competing against the other, and instead develop a more collaborative approach where the needs of the community are considered, and schools, services and agencies work collectively to meet these needs. Where there are areas of social deprivation, the responsibility for supporting the needs of children and their families to overcome the impact of social deprivation should become a shared responsibility within the community as a whole, rather than remain the 'problem' a single school has to address. Thus, as Lamb (2009) identifies:

> Schools, clusters of schools, local authorities, institutes of higher education and voluntary organisations need to work together to ensure that every child everywhere has access to teachers with the necessary skills and expertise to enable them to learn, progress and achieve good outcomes.
>
> (Lamb, 2009: 31)

Within such an approach, all individuals need to understand and respect the fact that expertise does not just lie with one service, agency or individual (OFSTED, 2010). Rather a collaborative approach that encourages the sharing of expertise from different perspectives will help to ensure that the best possible way to support the individual is identified.

Reflective activity 6.2

■ How realistic is the notion of shared accountability and more collaborative working practices across all services?

■ How could this be developed?

■ How realistic is the notion of schools working together to address the needs of a community, rather than individually and in competition with each other?

■ What impact would this have on current ways of working within and between schools in your local area?

■ How useful are the principles of effective collaboration for the development of a more effective approach to practice?

■ How could these be implemented in practice?

continued overleaf . . .

> ■ Are there any other key principles that you would add?
>
> ■ What other ideas could be developed to encourage better collaborative working and a collaborative approach to meeting the needs of a community between schools and services?

Building on these general principles for effective collaboration, the rest of this chapter focuses on different examples of collaboration, moving from within school to working with other schools and services/agencies, to support the practitioner to consider innovative ways to develop and enhance existing practices.

WITHIN SCHOOL

Practitioners should hopefully be used to working collaboratively, in different ways, with colleagues within their own school setting. However, this is not always the case, or has not always been developed to its full potential. Sometimes, there is little opportunity, or expectation, for colleagues to work together to discuss and develop innovative approaches to meeting needs. The importance of working together, and the impact that collaboration, either through team teaching, peer observation and discussion or just through sharing of ideas and strategies, can have on the development of practice needs to be acknowledged. This is one key way that inclusive and consistent approaches can be developed across the whole school (Ekins, 2010b), and this will support the development of shared responsibility for meeting the needs of all within the school community.

There therefore needs to be implicit understanding and commitment to shared responsibility for meeting the needs of all pupils embedded within the culture and ethos of the school. By doing this, we will move away from a practice where one member of staff is directly accountable for the progress of pupils with complex needs within their class group, to an approach that collectively acknowledges and takes shared responsibility for the challenging needs of particular individuals or class groups and works collaboratively to address them.

This approach will lead to the effective identification of whole staff training needs, which, rather than being dictated by the senior leadership team, or imposed by external bodies, will instead evolve through collaborative shared discussions about the emerging needs within the school. Staff development will therefore be understood and recognised as meaningful, as well as helping to build and develop whole staff inclusive principles, practices and collective responsibility for meeting the needs of all.

Indeed, the DfE (2010b) emphasise this notion of collaborative professional development, with an emphasis on providing opportunities for shared learning through the sharing of good practice and the use of observation. It is therefore noted that 'teachers learn best from other professionals and that an "open classroom" culture is vital: observing teaching and being observed, having the opportunity to plan, prepare, reflect and teach with other teachers.' (DfE, 2010a: 19).

It is thus helpful to consider ways to collectively identify aspects of practice to be focused on as part of a whole school development project, and to identify ways to enhance understanding of the issue through shared learning and observation of each others' practice. In this way, it is noted that 'collaborative CPD [continuing professional development] appears more likely to produce changes in teacher practice, attitudes or beliefs and in pupil outcomes' (DfE, 2010b: 11).

To support in the development of whole staff training, it is useful to consider and use the range of expertise and skills that individual members of the school community bring to the school, as a resource to support collaborative learning, and the development of whole school practice.

Reflective activity 6.3

■   Is practice within your school collaborative or competitive/individual? Do you work together to support each other, or just focus on your own class?

■   What is the impact of this approach on the overall culture and ethos of the school, and the outcomes that are achieved for all pupils?

■   How do colleagues currently collaborate together in your school setting?

■   Is use made of team teaching, or peer observations, of shared planning, or collaborative problem solving to share strategies to meet the needs of identified pupils with complex or challenging needs?

■   Is there a collaborative approach to removing barriers for all pupils, or is the focus on individual approaches to meeting needs?

■   How do you know and update information about the individual skills, expertise and experiences of individual members of staff?

■   How do you utilise those to support the development of practice across the whole school?

■   If a member of staff goes on training, how is the knowledge and information that they have gained shared with the whole school community?

Within the current changing school context, with reductions in external support common through the widespread restructuring of local authorities and specialist teaching services, there is an increasing need to build capacity within the individual school. This will involve identifying and understanding the training needs of members of staff, in relation to the profile of needs within the school context. That balance between staff training needs, carefully matched to the profile of needs within the school context is an important one to be aware of, and will result in increased effectiveness of approaches. Take a moment to consider and compare the two brief case studies provided below, which outline different approaches to planning training opportunities for staff:

Case Study 1

In this school, each member of staff was encouraged to identify and attend one key external training course to support their professional development each year. The Year 6 teacher identified and attended a literacy training course. The course focused on the use of a specific synthetic phonics approach. On her return to school, time was not prioritised for the teacher to share the information that she had received, and the teacher found that she was unable to utilise the training herself, as it would have been particularly useful for groups of children in Year 3. While the training had been interesting, it therefore had no direct impact on the teachers own practice, or on the development of practices within the school.

Case Study 2

This school had identified that the transition between Key Stage 1 and 2 was having an impact on pupil attainment and progress as they moved through Year 3 and 4. It was noted that more and more pupils coming into the school were struggling with the change in teaching structure, style and expectations between Key Stage 1 and Key Stage 2. A more collaborative approach to teaching and learning, which would make the transition between Key Stage 1 and Key Stage 2 smoother and easier for pupils, was agreed. To support this, the Year 2, 3 and 4 teachers all identified and attended the same training together, looking at aspects of literacy and mathematics teaching. Once back at school, time was given for the three teachers to work together to examine what they had learned and to identify key principles for practice. This was then disseminated to the whole staff through a staff meeting, which encouraged other members of staff to ask questions and input ideas and strategies. An action plan was developed that clearly set out positive changes to be made to the teaching structure, style and expectations through Year 2, 3 and 4, to enable a more graduated approach. This was trialled within school, and impact was evaluated with the whole staff. This led to the identification of key principles of effective teaching, which could be adapted and utilised by all teachers throughout the school, and the identification of future training courses that would build further understanding and expertise within the school context.

It is essential to ensure that staff training is appropriately matched to the profile of needs within the school context: general teaching and learning issues (as described above), as well as to specific areas of need. Therefore, if within the school or cohort it is identified that there are a significant amount of pupils with speech, language and communication needs, and if the staff working with those pupils have not already got a good grasp and understanding of those needs and ways that they will impact on learning, and implications of that for the development of appropriate teaching and learning strategies, then it is important to prioritise training in this area for the members of staff. In order to capitalise on the benefits of training, it is then important to ensure that training can be effectively shared and disseminated with all staff. Opportunities for other members of staff to observe the implementation of new strategies will also support effective collaboration, and the development of effective and consistent whole school practices.

In addition to accessing practical non-accredited training courses to support practitioner knowledge and understanding of the teaching and learning process for pupils with different needs, it will also be useful to take advantage of opportunities to build capacity within schools by enabling more staff to access accredited postgraduate training opportunities. This will particularly develop leadership capacity within the school, and, as teaching moves slowly towards a 'Masters-level profession' (with the recent introduction of the statutory National Award for SEN Coordination (NASC) for new SENCOs to post, and the Masters in Teaching and Learning (MTL) for staff in National Challenge schools) will promote the development and use of Masters level skills such as reflection, criticality and enquiry to enhance the teaching and learning process within the school.

The DfE (2011) have therefore emphasised commitment to ensuring that teachers are highly skilled, with access to a range of accredited training programmes to help them to most effectively meet the needs of all pupils:

We will boost the availability of advanced-level continuous professional development. . . . [and] also propose to fund scholarships for teachers to develop their practice in supporting disabled pupils and pupils with SEN, including in specific impairments.

(DfE, 2011: 60)

This commitment to funding and availability of advanced level courses, in a time of widespread budget cuts and removing of specification from government is significant and to be welcomed. It acknowledges the importance of developing a teaching profession highly trained and skilled at meeting the complex needs of all pupils: including increasing numbers of pupils with a range of specific impairments and needs.

Providing access to a range of training opportunities, and ensuring that they are carefully matched to the needs of both the staff and the pupils within the school, will therefore emerge as a key responsibility for the SENCO, as is emphasised within the required SENCO Learning Outcomes:

■ know the range of professional development opportunities available for staff (including support staff and beginner teachers) to improve their practice in working with pupils with SEN and/or disabilities;

■ advise on, contribute to, and where appropriate coordinate the professional development of staff so that they improve their practice in relation to pupils with SEN and/or disabilities.

(TDA, 2009)

Reflective activity 6.4

■ How do you currently support the professional development of others?

■ How do you ensure that all staff have 'sufficient access to continued professional development' (Sakellariadis, 2010: 32)?

■ How do you know what professional development opportunities are available?

■ Do you have up-to-date information about the range of accredited, post-graduate training courses that are available?

■ How can these be utilised to build capacity within the school?

■ How do you ensure that the professional development opportunities are meaningful and well focused on matching the needs of the staff member and the needs of the pupils?

A key feature of working effectively and collaboratively to understand and meet the needs of all pupils is therefore to 'empower staff to value and draw on resources available within the school' (Sakellariadis, 2010: 32). By doing this, you will effectively ensure that staff members within the school value their own expertise and their ability to problem solve collaboratively, rather than feeling that they continually have to seek the 'expert' knowledge of outside professionals, and that your colleagues do not feel 'disempowered from taking initiatives or implementing actions themselves' (Sakellariadis, 2010: 32).

BETWEEN SCHOOLS

There is now an increased focus on the need for schools to work together to support and meet the needs of all pupils (DfE, 2010a, 2010b; DfE, 2011). It is hoped that this collaboration will be 'driven by school leaders and teachers – not bureaucrats' (DfE, 2010a: 52). This focus emphasises a rights-based approach to meeting needs: with a move towards developing extended social responsibility within and across communities for ensuring that barriers are removed to learning, participation and access for all. This is a very welcome and positive move, although much will need to be done to counteract the recent years of competition between schools that have evolved in response to policy directives focused on standards and league tables. Indeed, as Davies and Hattersley (2010) note, 'Schools in competition will never be able to take responsibility for every child in their community without being worried about their position in the community and in the eyes of parents who are interested in "league tables"' (121).

We need to move away from situations common across the country where schools 'compete' for pupils coming from the most affluent backgrounds, with the embedded assumptions that those pupils will have the most positive impact on the perpetuation of high standards within the school. We also need to move away from some schools being cast as 'failing' simply because they are struggling to cope with the intensive demands of meeting the needs of disproportionately high numbers of pupils and families coming from areas of high deprivation or with high levels of need.

Ideally, we need to move towards a situation where needs are 'shared' between and across schools supporting a community. This may then provide all pupils with a much more equitable educational experience.

While this may currently seem more of an ideal than a reality, what can be achieved more easily is a more established and embedded approach to partnership working between schools, with strategic and collaborative shared problem solving about the needs of the cohort group across a community as a whole, as opposed to current discussions that are focused on comparisons between cohorts within individual schools. Such an approach will help to establish a more collaborative and proactive approach to the prioritisation and delegation of resources across a community. This may, for example, include:

- The sharing of a teacher or teaching assistant with specific skills in autism, so that that teacher or teaching assistant supports the school with the most amount of needs in that area, rather than remaining in the same school even if they do not have any pupils with autism at that time.
- The sharing of a specific resource (e.g. equipment) to support pupils with a particular need in different school settings.
- Shared prioritisation of funding within a particular school context to support the high levels of need identified within that school.

Existing expertise and resources need to be shared in order to support the development of more effective education for all pupils. In this way, there is a clear need for 'partnerships between schools to develop inclusion' (Davies and Hattersley, 2010: 121).

This notion is acknowledged by the DfE (2011), with a proposal to support the development of collaboration between schools: 'We intend to help local networks of schools develop teachers with specialist skills and knowledge that can be deployed across local clusters of schools' (DfE, 2011: 61).

This is an innovative and forward thinking strategy, which could be very usefully developed to move practices away from the traditional singular focus of individual schools thinking about their own practice in competition with other local schools, to an approach that may effectively put the child and their needs at the heart of localised decision making. For this to happen, however, requires committed practitioners who can think in innovative ways.

What is required is an approach that emphasises shared, collective responsibility for supporting and meeting the needs of vulnerable pupils with SEN and disabilities. This will move thinking and practice from individualised responses which, while benefiting an individual school in terms of raising their status in league tables, may not provide the most effective support for pupils and vulnerable families in the local area. Within a new approach it would be helpful to establish shared collective responsibility among a cluster of schools serving the same locality.

This principle is already supported by the DfE (2010a) through a commitment to try to address some aspects of competition impacting negatively on schools serving particularly deprived areas, through a collaborative approach to raising standards: 'We will incentivise schools to work together to raise standards, especially for disadvantaged pupils' (DfE, 2010a: 76).

There is therefore acknowledgement that 'Schools working together leads to better results. . . . And can support schools to improve more rapidly – by providing a common approach to professional development, sharing effective practice, and providing shared "back-office" support' (DfE, 2010a: 57).

This can happen formally through Academy chains, or federations of schools, or more informally through clusters of schools within a locality coming together to strategically prioritise needs across the range of schools.

While the focus of the £35 million 'collaboration incentive' is on improvements in attainment and narrowing the gap between deprived pupils and others, it is also hoped that such collaborations will bring with them benefits in terms of developing the full educational experience for all pupils, as well as providing opportunities to critically reflect on and develop appropriate and meaningful teaching and learning experiences for all. This should not be seen as simply another budget focused on providing intensive 'booster' support to enable pupils to 'get through the test'. Rather it should be seen as a wider opportunity to address embedded social inequalities, through the provision of extended opportunities, experiences and activities that will motivate and inspire pupils and subsequently help to raise their aspirations and levels of achievement. Such collaboration projects will also need to consider ways to use monies from the 'collaboration incentive' to develop community-based projects that will have impact on raising the motivations and aspirations within whole communities living within socially deprived areas. This will then have more meaningful, long-term impact on future education, attainment and aspirations of pupils coming from socially deprived backgrounds than will short-term intensive booster programmes just designed to raise standards within the school setting.

Reflective activity 6.5

■ How do you think that collaboration between schools could help to benefit all pupils living within the local community?

■ Would there be any drawbacks to such an approach?

■ How would these need to be addressed and how could this be achieved?

■ What particular strengths or expertise could different schools bring to a collaboration?

■ What existing barriers, relating to notions of competition between schools would need to be broken down and removed in order to enable this to happen effectively?

■ How could this happen?

■ What types of collaboration projects may benefit pupils living in your local community?

Another example of ways that schools are now being encouraged to collaborate to meet pupil needs rather than take an individual approach is through the new regulations for excluding pupils (DfE, 2010a). This is a particularly important issue for SENCOs and those interested in SEN and disability to be aware of, as data shows that increased numbers of pupils with SEN are excluded from schools than pupils with no SEN (being up to 'twenty times more likely to receive a fixed term exclusion than pupils with no identified SEN' (DfE, 2011: 22). With the publication of the Schools White Paper (DfE, 2010a) is the new notion that, while schools will still remain free to exclude pupils, they will however, remain 'responsible for finding and funding alternative provision themselves. . . . They could either collaborate with other schools to provide suitable places, or buy them from the local authority, the voluntary sector or local colleges' (DfE, 2010a: 39).

The school will therefore remain accountable for the pupil that they have excluded, and that pupil's assessment data would count in school performance tables.

It is hoped that these measures will help to reduce the amount of schools using exclusion as an easy way to simply pass the 'problem' to someone else. It will become the school's responsibility to find ways to support the pupil more effectively, either to remain within their own school, or by collaborating with other schools to identify more appropriate provision. This may help to reduce existing practices where some schools exclude pupils, before considering fully ways to make changes to the teaching and learning environment and approached used, in order to more fully meet the pupil's actual needs. Please now see Reflective activity 6.6.

Through a focus on collaboration between schools, we need to move to a system where the needs of children and families are placed centrally, above the needs of individual schools or staff members. We need an approach where expertise and individual excellence in terms of knowledge, skills and also resources can be shared for the benefit of the pupils, rather than remaining trapped and often underutilised within a particular school. Within such an approach, there can be an emphasis on the development of localised approaches that best match the needs of pupils and families in that area.

Reflective activity 6.6

■ What will be the impact of these new measures for schools in your local area, and for your school in particular?

■ Look back through recent exclusion data for your school over the last five years.

■ How many pupils have been excluded?

■ What were the reasons for their exclusion?

■ Could more have been done to make changes to the teaching and learning environment and approaches in order to remove the barriers to learning and participation that those pupils experienced?

■ Have you recently accepted pupils who have been previously excluded from other school settings?

■ How did you manage to address their complex or challenging needs?

■ What types of approach were needed?

■ How could collaboration between schools help to reduce exclusions from individual schools and raise the effective inclusion of pupils with complex or challenging needs?

■ How could a collaborative approach between schools help to identify and strategically plan and prioritise the resources (including alternative provision and developing staff expertise) that are needed to be developed to support needs within the local area?

■ How can you ensure that that developing expertise is shared to support the development of understanding and practice within all schools?

SPECIAL SCHOOLS

Linked to the notion of collaboration between schools to understand and address the needs of pupils within a community, is the need to recognise and utilise the expertise and specialist resources and experiences that are too often ignored within special schools. There is therefore a need to recognise, 'nurture, develop and disseminate' (Lamb, 2009: 31) the extensive expertise, resources and experiences that is currently located within special schools across the country. As the DfE (2011) note, special schools are uniquely positioned as 'hubs' for a wide range of other services, including therapies and support services to support pupils with complex and severe needs and their families. Finding out more about this resource may therefore help mainstream schools to reconsider new ways to approach the provision of support for pupils within their settings.

In the new model of collaborative working, it is therefore important that new and innovative ways are developed to enable special school staff to share their expertise, knowledge and resources in effective and creative ways in order to improve outcomes for pupils with SEN in all schools. The DfE (2011) acknowledges this, proposing that new approaches need to be developed to enable 'special schools to share their expertise and services to support the education, progress and development of pupils in other special and mainstream schools' (DfE, 2011: 9).

Thus, there can be the development of support to enable special schools to become 'centres of excellence offering support, guidance and specialist training to mainstream schools' (Petersen, 2010: 21).

Reflective activity 6.7

■ Are there any special schools or specialist provisions/units in your local area?
■ What particular area of SEN and/or disability do they support?
■ Have you/other colleagues from your school previously used the expertise or resources from the special school?
■ Have you/other colleagues from your school visited the special school to observe and reflect on different teaching and learning approaches, resources or strategies to support pupil learning?
■ What effective examples of collaboration between mainstream and special schools are you aware of?
■ What was the impact of the collaboration for the individual pupil, or for the growth of staff understanding and practice?
■ How could collaboration between mainstream and special schools be further developed?
■ What could be the benefit of this:

  – For staff from the mainstream school?
  – For staff from the special school?
  – For individual pupils with high levels of SEN and/or disability?
  – For parents of pupils with high levels of SEN and/or disability?
  – For all pupils within the mainstream school?
  – For all pupils within the special school?

Staff can therefore benefit from the development of links between special schools and mainstream school settings, as the sharing of practice may support all staff to develop effective understandings and practice to more effectively support pupils with complex needs attending mainstream settings, and so that 'they are able to meet a broader range of needs' (DfE, 2011: 73).

It is also possible to extend this notion further, to consider the benefit of increased opportunities for education practitioners, teachers and support staff to work across both special and mainstream school settings. This is an idea that is already being developed in Initial Teacher Education where there is an increasing focus on the need for students to have placements in both special schools and mainstream school settings. This can be developed to consider the potential impact of having teachers and support staff who at regular periods in their career have the opportunity of a secondment to work in a different setting. Thus, while the DfE (2011) acknowledge that 'working in special schools can provide a unique opportunity for teachers to develop their skills in teaching children with particular support needs' (DfE, 2011: 59), it can also work the other way. Developing simple systems to enable staff from both specialist and mainstream settings to work in each other's settings can help to ensure high expectations of all pupils across both settings, as well as enabling the effective sharing of expertise and understanding of support needs.

Special schools do not therefore just have to be thought about in terms of taking pupils who cannot access mainstream education. Rather, they can have an innovative and supportive role to play in supporting the development of inclusive practices that utilise the expertise and resources of special schools to effectively meet the needs of pupils with a range of needs within mainstream school settings. Within such an approach, it is again hoped that this will support a move towards an approach to education that prioritises the needs of the child, supporting the specific needs of the individual through creative, flexible and collaborative approaches across school settings, rather than discussions just focusing on placement and responsibility.

Recently, the development of innovative practices have often been hampered by the restricting bureaucratic processes involved. In a new era where there is policy commitment to reducing bureaucracy and encouraging innovation and flexible approaches, we therefore need to move towards an approach where meeting the needs of all pupils is a collective responsibility, thereby supporting special schools and mainstream schools to collectively and collaboratively support the needs of pupils, rather than appropriate support for the child being dependent on the naming of a specific school setting on a piece of paper.

WITH OTHER AGENCIES

There is an increased focus on the need for more effective collaboration between a range of services, agencies and professionals in order to meet the needs of pupils with SEN. Again, the issue needs to be about embedding collective responsibility for meeting the needs of pupils with SEN. While collaboration between professionals will require some leadership, and someone to take the lead role (the lead professional, as identified in *Every Child Matters*, DfES, 2004), this does not, and should not always be an education lead. Often, pupils with high levels of SEN have a range of complex needs, requiring significant input and attention from Health or Social Care. It may, even be that the educational needs are secondary to those. In such an example, it would therefore be most effective for the professional needing to provide the highest level of support to take the lead in collaborative discussions and decision making around that child.

This, however, requires shifts in prioritisation and accountability around meeting pupil needs throughout different services. Thus, while for some time there has been the underlying focus on different services working together to support the needs of the child through *Every Child Matters* (DfES, 2004), there has been little clear structural change to impact positively on the processes and systems to support vulnerable children and their families. It is therefore recognised that currently there is an unfair imbalance of duty and responsibility to meet the needs of pupils with SEN across different agencies and services:

> the responsibilities of local services for supporting children with a statement of SEN and their families differ. Local authorities have a duty to ensure that services specified in the education part of the statement are provided. Health legislation takes a different form; there is no corresponding requirement on health agencies, and there are different routes for redress. It is often unclear who is responsible for the delivery of services such as speech and language therapy, which may appear in the education part of the statement although they are funded and commissioned by local health services. This can lead to children with SEN not receiving the support that they need.
>
> (DfE, 2011: 35)

There is, therefore, a need to develop collaborative assessments of need (OFSTED, 2010). This will have the benefit of reducing the time taken to attend different assessments, and also increase understanding and a holistic view of the child and their needs across the range of services and agencies involved with the child. However, 'As long as accountability measures operate separately across different services, children's needs [will] not be met by a suitably holistic assessment and a common requirement to act on that assessment' (OFSTED, 2010: 60).

Issues impacting on the development of effective and more meaningful engagement and collaboration between services have also included a certain lack of professional trust across the different agencies. This lack of professional trust has meant that children have had to be reassessed before provision and support is provided by different services (OFSTED, 2010). Indeed, it is noted that, 'At times [different services] have worked competitively rather than cooperatively, blaming one another for perceived shortcomings. And perhaps most seriously of all, they have worked in ignorance of one another's values, priorities and achievements' (McConkey, 2010: 11).

As professionals supporting pupils with complex needs, often which span across education, health and social care, we must acknowledge that the pupil and their family may come into contact with many different professionals, sometimes with very different views about the prioritisation or presentation of needs. It is therefore essential that new and innovative practices that can break down existing lack of professional trust between different professionals are developed and established in order to improve outcomes for pupils with SEN and/or disabilities and their families. This will require opportunities for professionals to come together, either through 'joint professional training' (Farrell, 2010: 90) or through newly developed working practices, in order to build shared understanding of the issues impacting on each profession. Thus it is recognised that:

> When people are prepared to work together and learn from each other, the results are often innovative. In our view it is unlikely that any support addressing the complexities of equality issues will have any significant impact without creative thinking. Professionals must be prepared to look beyond their traditions, their training and their job descriptions and move towards changing the systems and settings that exclude and discriminate against young people.
>
> (Parry *et al.*, 2010: 3)

Where innovative projects and approaches have been developed to enable professionals from different services to work alongside each other, away from their traditional settings, improvements in practice, in terms of increased shared understandings and prioritisations of need have been noticed. Thus, OFSTED (2010) identified that, in Children's Centres, where 'professionals shared a site and worked as a team, informal interventions, as well as higher-level, more formalised intervention, were more readily forthcoming and more efficient' (OFSTED, 2010: 61).

In research undertaken, Workman and Pickard (2010) also identify that: 'the perceived threat to professional identity did not materialise; existing roles have been strengthened rather than undermined' (Workman and Pickard, 2010: 126).

In addition, it must be acknowledged that research (OFSTED, 2010) has also found that the difficulties between services are even further exacerbated where a pupil's support needs may span more than one local authority. There is therefore a need to ensure that the needs of the child are prioritised over differing localised interpretations of national guidance, in order to ensure a consistent and equitable approach to meeting the needs of all pupils.

Although the DfE (2011) acknowledges the importance of specialist roles, including speech and language therapists and educational psychologists, the reality, in many areas, has been that there has been a reduction in the numbers of these key frontline staff due to budget shortages, resulting in non-recruitment of staff to replace those who have left the service, while meeting increased demand from schools. In the context of a situation where direct contact with a range of services may be reduced, there is therefore a need to consider innovative and effective ways to utilise what availability there is. This may include:

■   shared problem solving sessions: where a cluster of schools come together with a range of professionals to jointly problem solve approaches to meeting needs;
■   access to specialist training to enable teachers to embed some of the basic principles of support, e.g. speech and language therapy.

It is therefore recognised that SENCOs will increasingly need to 'play a key role in coordinating work with a range of different agencies and parents in order to achieve as full a range of outcomes as possible' (Nasen, 2010: 1). Please now see Reflective activity 6.8.

It is as yet unclear how the issue of developing collaborative practices across services will be fully addressed, although there is an indication that the government want to build on joint working and joint policies between the traditionally separate government departments of Health and Education. It is therefore noted that 'the Department for

---

Reflective activity 6.8

■   Which services, agencies and professionals have you recently worked with to support the needs of pupils with SEN?
■   How effective has the collaborative working been?
■   Has there been a shared collective responsibility recognised and understood by all professionals in respect of ensuring that the specific needs of the individual are met?
■   What barriers to effective collaborative working across agencies, services and professionals have you experienced?
■   How could these be overcome?
■   How have the barriers impacted on the potential provision or progress of pupils with SEN?
■   Are there any other services, agencies or professionals that you think it would be beneficial to establish links with?
■   What has been the impact of local authority restructuring in your area in terms of accessibility and allocation of specialist support service staff?
■   How can new links be established to ensure that the needs of pupils are being met?

Education and the Department for Health will publish . . . a joint policy statement on the early years, setting out our vision for reform' (DfE, 2011: 31).

It is unlikely that until radical reform in terms of the nature in which the traditionally separate departments and services of education, health and social care work, real meaningful collaborative working will take place. Meaningful collaborative working across services and professions to really meet the needs of vulnerable children and families with SEN will only happen once there is shared commitment, prioritisation and resources across all services.

New government proposals, including the notion of setting up new local Health and Wellbeing Boards (DfE, 2011) that will 'bring together leading local councillors, the NHS, public health services, and local authority education and social care services. The new Boards will develop and maintain a joint analysis of the needs of their local community, which takes account of the needs of the views of children and adults who use local services' (DfE, 2011: 96) are therefore to be welcomed, but will need close scrutiny and analysis in order to ensure that they are effective in nationally meeting the needs of all pupils and their families in an equitable way.

COLLABORATION THROUGH THE NEW APPROACH TO STATEMENTING

One way that this may be evidenced, is through the new approach to the statementing process (see also Chapter 7 for further details about the new statementing process). The DfE (2011) therefore proposes that from 2014 statements will be replaced with a single assessment process and 'Education, Health and Care Plan'. This will detail the support required for that individual and will 'be clear about who is responsible for which services [including] a commitment from all parties across education, health and social care to provide their services' (DfE, 2011: 7). Please now see Reflective activity 6.9.

While the principles and vision behind the new 'Education, Health and Care Plan' are indeed to be supported, this new way of working will require more in-depth planning and understanding of the embedded differences in service delivery than is acknowledged within the Green Paper. It could be said that such a model has already been extensively

Reflective activity 6.9

■ How can you see this happening?
■ What will be the strengths of this approach?
■ What may be the barriers?
■ What have we already learned from the experience of *Every Child Matters*, the Common Assessment Framework, the notion of 'lead professionals' and 'team around the child' meetings that can support us to move towards this new model?
■ What aspects of good practice already exist in your area, and how could you utilise and build on those to ensure that the new model of providing support for pupils with high level needs is effective?

trialled in England, with the development of the Common Assessment Framework and systems to work collaboratively and across services to support the needs of the child forming the basis of the agenda for change within *Every Child Matters*. But yet, the evidence (House of Commons, 2006; Lamb, 2009; OFSTED, 2010; DfE, 2011) suggests that while some procedural systems have changed, there has not been the joining together of truly collaborative services that are centrally positioned around the needs of the individual child.

This is, however, not to say that there are not examples of good practice that has developed where services are working together in innovative and creative ways to put to one side differences in service delivery, to work more effectively to meet the needs of the child. These examples therefore need to be considered in more detail, to analyse the factors producing success and to consider ways that this can be adapted to individual contexts to support the development of a more collaborative and multi-professional approach to supporting needs.

NEW WAYS OF WORKING WITH VOLUNTARY ORGANISATIONS

As discussed in Chapter 2, in the new policy context there is a new emphasis on community and voluntary bodies taking responsibility for providing a range of services and support for meeting the needs of pupils with SEN and/or families. There are indications, for example, in the proposal that voluntary organisations take over responsibility for leading the assessment of need for pupils requiring statements or the new 'Education, Health and Care Plans' (DfE, 2011), and the requirement for parents to have keyworkers to support them in understanding and managing personal budgets (DfE, 2011), that some of those processes will be formalised. However, there is also the need for innovative thinking about ways that schools can utilise much more effectively the support that is already available, in terms of expertise, training and resources, from voluntary organisations.

In a time of decreased access to specialist support and professionals from restructured local authorities, the role and scope of voluntary organisations therefore needs to be considered.

Reflective activity 6.10

▨ Do you currently work with any voluntary organisations?
▨ Which voluntary or community organisations currently operate in your area?
▨ What different types of support could they offer:

- To the school?
- To the pupil with SEN and/or disabilities?
- To the parents and families of the pupil with SEN and/or disability?

▨ How could you work effectively with voluntary organisations to plan a more 'strategic alliance' that places the needs of the pupils with SEN and/or disabilities at the heart of the planning process?

ACTION PLANNING

Identify three key points for individual reflection:

1   _____

2   _____

3   _____

Start to consider key issues to be followed up as points of action that have arisen from your reading of this chapter.

This may include:

- Using the principles of collaborative working to consider ways to develop existing collaboration and embed new ones.
- Auditing current staff training needs (teachers and support staff) and matching those against the profile of need within the school context to strategically identify future training needs and ways that those could be addressed.
- Identifying a range of training opportunities that are locally available: including short courses and accredited advanced-level courses in order to build capacity within the school.
- Considering ways and developing practices to ensure that all new training is fully disseminated and utilised.
- Working with other schools to consider new and innovative ways to work together to identify and address needs across a community.
- Making more effective links with local special schools: exploring what support and resources they have to offer staff and pupils in your school setting, and also what experiences or support you can offer to the special school.
- Considering the range of support available through voluntary organisations, and new ways to access that.
- Others.

ACTION PLANNING TO ENABLE IMPACT

Use the format provided below to develop a clear Action Plan for future development of practices for either yourself, or for the school. Make sure that you do not identify too many different actions all at once, have a clear outcome for what you want to achieve in mind, and make sure that you clearly identify the different steps to take to achieve the outcome.

NEW WAYS OF WORKING: ACTION PLANNING TO ENABLE IMPACT:

Which key issues from the chapter do you want to focus on/ change/develop?	How will you effect this change or development (identify a number of small action steps to achieve your overall goal)?	Who else will need to be involved? How?	What will the outcome be (include timescales)?	Impact:

IDENTIFICATION OF SEN

THIS CHAPTER:

■ examines how special educational needs are currently identified;
■ examines the relationship between SEN and/or disability and underachievement;
■ considers perverse incentives impacting on the identification of SEN and/or disability;
■ critically considers the impact of inconsistencies in assessment of need;
■ considers categories of need;
■ examines the importance of early identification;
■ considers new ways forward;
■ critically reviews proposed changes to the statementing process.

REVIEW

> Identifying children's support needs early is vital if they are to thrive, and enables parents and professionals to put the right approach in place quickly.
>
> (DfE, 2011: 6)

This is not surprising. However, for many years the system for accurately and consistently identifying pupils with SEN and/or disability has been confusing, problematic and inconsistent – exposing large variations between regions, local authorities and even within local authorities. Please now see the Review box on p. 106.

Currently, children are identified as having SEN 'if they have a greater difficulty in learning than the majority of children of their age which calls for additional or different educational provision to be made for them' (DfE, 2011: 18).

OFSTED (2010) identifies that the term 'SEN' is used for those pupils that have a 'learning difficulty' that requires special or additional provision to be made for them. A 'learning difficulty' is defined as meaning that the pupil:

■ has a significantly greater difficulty in learning than the majority of children of the same age;

Review

■ What systems do you currently have in place to identify pupils with special educational needs within your school setting?

■ Who is responsible for identifying special educational needs?

■ Do class teachers have ownership in this process?

■ If they do, how confident are they in this?

■ What are the implications of this for practice?

■ Are there systems in place within your school to identify underachievement as separate to SEN?

■ Is there understanding across your school setting that underachievement does not necessarily mean that a pupil may have a SEN?

■ How is this discussed/tackled?

■ Do you have systems for moderating judgements about placement of pupils within your school and across the local authority?

■ has a disability that prevents or hinders them from making use of the educational facilities of a kind generally provided for children of the same age in schools within the area of the local education authority.

(OFSTED, 2010: 15)

For pupils over the age of 16, in post-16 education or training, the term 'learning difficulties and/or disabilities' is used, and applied if the same criteria as above is met (OFSTED, 2010: 15).

The current system for identifying SEN within schools, set out within the Code of Practice, is based on three different levels, and the notion of a 'graduated response' to support pupils to ideally move down and off the SEN Register (DfES, 2001):

■ School Action: at this level, the school identifies the need to provide something that is 'additional to or different from' the differentiated approach that is usually provided within the school for all pupils for a particular pupil.

■ School Action Plus: at this level the school consults and involves external specialists and services.

■ Statement of SEN: at this level, it is acknowledged that the pupil requires support beyond what the school can provide alone. The local authority becomes involved in carefully assessing the pupil's need, and identifying support needs. This may include specialist provision, but not always.

In January 2010 the number of children identified as having SEN was reported to be 21 per cent of the national school age population. Of this 21 per cent, 11.4 per cent of the school population were identified at School Action (approximately 916,000 pupils), with 6.2 per cent of the school population at School Action Plus (approximately 496,000 pupils) and 2.7 per cent of the school population having a statement of SEN (approximately 221,000 pupils) (DfE, 2011: 18).

As well as being identified at different levels on the SEN Register, pupils are identified by different categories of need. The Code of Practice (2001) introduced four key categories of need:

■ cognition and learning
■ communication and interaction
■ behaviour, emotional and social difficulties
■ physical and sensory needs.

REFLECTION

Identification of SEN at School Action and School Action Plus

OFSTED (2010) considered whether inconsistent identification of SEN at any of the three levels of the existing system actually mattered, and concluded that:

It does matter if:

■ the standard offer of education or care is insufficiently adapted for frequently found needs;
■ such identification is the only way parents and schools can gain access to expertise or support from a range of 'in-house' or external services;
■ special educational needs or disability are used as a reason for lower expectations and an excuse for poor outcomes.

(OFSTED, 2010: 24)

But that it does not matter if:

■ the total package of services and support is appropriately customised to each pupil's individual needs;
■ the provision that follows identification is, in any case, of poor quality and is not effective.

(OFSTED, 2010: 24)

Reflective activity 7.1

■ How do you feel about this?
■ Does it matter if we inconsistently identify special educational needs?
■ What are the implications of inconsistent identification:

– Nationally?
– For school practice?
– For the pupil?
– For the parent?

Identifying SEN consistently and accurately is a key issue within the world of SEN. A range of reports have recently identified the problems inherent within current systems for identifying and allocating support for SEN (House of Commons, 2006; OFSTED, 2010; DfE, 2011). While the difficulties around the actual terminology of SEN have already been discussed (see Chapter 3), this chapter focuses on issues impacting on the identification and placement of pupils at different levels on school SEN Registers.

Thus, the notion embedded within the Code of Practice (DfES, 2001) that pupils should be identified as having SEN when they require interventions that are 'additional to or different from' those provided for other pupils, as part of differentiated practice, has created a situation where some schools are able to argue that they need to provide 'additional to or different from' strategies, which, in another school setting, would be part of the inclusive Quality Teaching strategies and approaches used to support and meet the needs of all pupils (OFSTED, 2010).

The terminology within the Code of Practice (DfES, 2001), rather than providing clear guidance, has therefore led to a situation where there has been no really clear national framework for the consistent identification of pupils with SEN. The terminology is open to interpretation. Thus, while the main indicators for identifying SEN are: the need for provision that is 'additional to and different from' that required for other pupils; and the existence of a greater difficulty in learning, the DfE (2010c) identify the tensions and levels of variance impacting on effective identification of SEN:

> A child or young person should not be assumed to have special educational needs just because they have fallen behind in their learning. Equally, it should not be assumed that a learner working at age-related expectations does not have a SEN or learning difficulty.
>
> (DfE, 2010c: 3)

It is also noted that:

> In the case of children and young people who need complex and specialist support from health and other services to enable them to thrive and develop, the term 'educational needs' does not always accurately reflect their situation.
>
> (OFSTED, 2010: 9)

While the notion of SEN is complex, and it is difficult to fit pupils with wide-ranging needs into neat categories or levels of need (see discussions later in relation to categories of need), there is a need for some form of national benchmark criteria for the level, or range of need associated with identification of SEN. This may help to address the current inconsistent practices that we have in relation to the identification of SEN, and the inappropriate identification of pupils who are underachieving rather than have a specific SEN.This is not easy to do, and is fraught with tensions relating to the way that we perceive and construct understanding around individual difference and need.

Currently, identification of need is achieved through the 'graduated response' of the Code of Practice (DfES, 2001). However, the lack of a clear national framework or criteria for identification and placement on SEN Registers has lead to the prevalence of widely different levels of SEN being recorded across different local authorities, where the 'total proportion of pupils with SEN by local authority in January 2010 ranged from 11.9% to 33.5%' (DfE, 2011: 19).

It is as a result of such varying practices that some of the criticisms of the 'postcode lottery' affecting pupils with SEN has arisen. Identification and placement on the SEN Register for an individual pupil can, therefore, literally be affected by their geographical location, and moving to a neighbouring school that may happen to be situated within a different local authority can then impact directly on whether the pupil is identified with SEN, and even whether a statement of SEN will be issued. Pupils with SEN are therefore not experiencing equitable and fair access to support and identification to meet their needs (OFSTED, 2010).

SEN OR UNDERACHIEVEMENT: OVER-INFLATED LEVELS OF SEN?

Recently, significant concerns about the number of pupils who are inaccurately identified with SEN have been highlighted (OFSTED, 2010; DfE, 2011). It has been noted that pupils that do not have special educational needs, but instead are falling behind and underachieving within the school context are being incorrectly identified as having SEN (OFSTED, 2010), leading to a 'considerable increase in recent years in the number of pupils without statements, from 10% of all pupils in 1995 to 18.2% or 1.5 million pupils in 2010' (DfE, 2011: 20).

There is therefore a real need to clarify and make a clear distinction between those pupils who have a genuine special educational need, and those pupils who have a shorter term need, or are simply in need of some focused support in order to help them to keep up and make effective progress in relation to their starting points. Indeed, as Lamb (2009) notes, 'The conflation of 'falling behind' and SEN is unhelpful and may have contributed to the growing numbers of pupils identified at School Action and School Action Plus' (24).

OFSTED (2010) therefore identifies that 'as many as half of all pupils identified at School Action' (OFSTED, 2010: 9) are incorrectly identified, and that this could be addressed through a closer focus on improving teaching and learning for all.

The over-identification of pupils on the SEN Register needs to be reconsidered and critically examined as it is said to:

> harm pupils who do not have SEN but who are identified as having SEN [as] too often the label excuses inaction: slow progress by some children is deemed satisfactory because of a non-existent special need. This problem of over-identification sustains a culture of low expectations for these children and can mean that they do not get the right help.
>
> (DfE, 2011: 67)

It has therefore perhaps become 'too easy' to explain away pupils who have fallen behind in their learning, under the justification that they have SEN and 'well, what more can be done?' (Lamb, 2009).

This notion of the 'culture of excuses' is important, and it is essential that practitioners in schools work hard to identify and address this whenever and wherever it is experienced. It is not acceptable that an attitude of 'what more can we expect' can pervade the educational settings of pupils with SEN. It is essential that we build and develop cultures of high expectations and aspirations in all within the school community; to include teachers, parents and pupils.

While recent messages have therefore been blunt and consistent: that schools should reconsider the effectiveness of their overall teaching and learning approach, as well as approaches to pastoral support and care, BEFORE resorting to labelling pupils as having SEN (OFSTED, 2010; DfE, 2011), it should be understood that part of the problem may lie in the overarching policy context within which SEN practices sit. Policies emphasising the raising of standards and competition between schools in the form of league tables may therefore exacerbate difficulties with the over-identification of SEN. It is therefore essential that, as critical and reflective practitioners, we challenge policy frameworks that may lead to such practices.

Reflective activity 7.2

Understanding the difference between underachievement and a specific special educational need is important within the school context, and supports a reconsideration of wider whole school practices to support the progress of all pupils:

- How many pupils within the school context do actually have a special educational need?
- How many are underachieving, not because of a special educational need, but as a result of other factors impacting on the pupils?
- Is there a 'culture of excuses' within your school setting?
- Is the 'SEN label' used as an excuse to explain the slow or limited progress that pupils are making?
- How is this evidenced?
- How can this be addressed?
- What other factors could be impacting on the progress of pupils who do not have a special educational need, and, instead, are underachieving?
- How could they be positively addressed in order to enable all pupils (those who are underachieving, as well as those with correctly identified special educational needs)?

To further support you in your reconsideration and examination of practice, consider the case studies below:

Case Study 1

This school is situated in an affluent urban setting. End of Key Stage 2 data is extremely good, with 94 per cent of all pupils achieving Level 4 or above at the end of Year 6. Many of those pupils achieve high Level 4's and Level 5's.

This school, however, had identified 33 per cent of the school population as needing to be placed on the SEN Register.

When challenged about this high proportion in relation to such high results, it was noted that staff were consistently and regularly identifying pupils in all year

---

groups who were working below the accepted level for that school group. Therefore, for example, pupils working at Level 2C in Year 2, or Level 4C in Year 6, where the expected average for their peers would be Level 3C in Year 2 or Level 4A in Year 6, were therefore being identified and placed on the SEN Register.

For this school, they considered that they were having to provide something 'additional to or different from' their expected curriculum delivery to meet the needs of those pupils.

However, can it be considered that these pupils (who were operating within broadly average ability levels) actually did have Special Educational Needs?

Case Study 2

This school is situated within a deprived inner-city area. Ninety-four different languages are spoken within the school community, with most children having English as an additional language.

This school had identified that 64 per cent of the school population has SEN.

When challenged about this very high level of SEN within the school, the SENCO identified that all pupils with English as an additional language are placed on the SEN Register. All pupils who received any intervention support, even if only in the form of 'booster' catch-up intervention, were identified as having SEN and placed on the SEN Register. Staff argued that this was done to provide a record of the support that was provided within the school.

Here there are real issues about the understanding of Special Educational Needs, with staff needing to recognise that just because pupils may have English as an additional language, this does not constitute in itself a Special Educational Need. Staff also need to recognise their duty to provide a range of differentiated support and provision, including booster, catch-up intervention support for pupils without needing to label the child as having a Special Educational Need.

Reflective activity 7.3

■ What does the term SEN mean within your school context?

■ Is there shared and consistent understanding of what SEN is, and ways to identify pupils who may have special educational needs within your school context?

■ Review your SEN Register. What criteria has been used to make consistent judgements about which pupils should be placed on the SEN Register?

■ Is the criteria rigorous enough? Does it emphasise that the pupil has a special educational need, rather than just requiring additional support for a shorter period of time? Is the criteria used consistently throughout the school? Is it also used consistently throughout the local authority?

It is essential that schools understand that, in the identification of SEN, there should be a focus, not only on the additional support required for the pupil, but also the criteria that the pupil will have a 'significantly greater difficulty in learning than the majority of their peers' (OFSTED, 2010: 23), in order to ensure that identification and placement of pupils at the current School Action level really do have a special educational need, rather than just underachieving.

There are similar tensions and inconsistencies in practice relating to the identification and placement of pupils at School Action Plus across the country. While the Code of Practice (DfES, 2001), states that at School Action Plus, the school involves and consults with external professionals, the guidance is open to interpretation leading to inappropriate identification and levelling of need. Examples of practice have therefore been identified where any pupil receiving external support (including pupils attending asthma clinics, or having social services support) are identified and placed at School Action Plus, regardless of whether they actually have any special *educational* need.

At the other end of the spectrum, at a time of cutting back of external agency support across local authorities, many schools are finding it increasingly difficult to get the individual support from external professionals that they may once have had. Some schools are therefore finding it difficult (based on the Code of Practice (DfES, 2001) guidance about the need to involve external professionals) to actually identify any pupils at that level, due to the shortages of professionals in their area.

This is leading to vastly differing practices emerging across different areas of the country, which is not in response to differing levels of pupil need, but instead is in response to varying resources in terms of money and external agency staff.

The same differences in practice are even evident in regional variations in statementing, with it being acknowledged that pupils with very similar needs, in one local authority would receive a statement of SEN, while in another would not.

In schools developing good practice, however, there is a move away from a resource and provision focused model, towards a model of practice based on inherent understanding of the need to continually review the impact and effectiveness of teaching and learning approaches on positive outcomes for all pupils. Thus, where high numbers of pupils are identified as requiring additional support, such schools do not simply add more and more pupils to the SEN Register. Rather, they engage in critical and reflective examination of the underlying factors impacting on positive achievement for all. This involves a critical examination of existing teaching and learning strategies, the embedded expectations and assumptions of staff (to ensure that there is a consistent focus on high expectations from all pupils) and an appropriate and meaningful match between support, including pastoral support and care, and the needs of the pupils within the school.

Indeed, it is noted (OFSTED, 2010) that in schools where the practice and skills of teachers were judged very good and outstanding, there was evidence that additional support and provision was not required to meet the needs of individual pupils: their individual needs instead were fully met through inclusive and outstanding whole class teaching.

Such an approach is embodied within the *Achievement for All* approach, which, rather than promoting a focus on strategies specifically for pupils with SEN, rather, encourages schools to critically review practice, and make improvements to teaching and learning practices, ensuring the setting of consistent high expectations for all pupils by all staff members.

Thus, it has been identified that, in *Achievement for All* schools, there is a move towards 'declassifying children previously identified at School Action, because with a culture of high expectations and provision of personalised school-based support the label itself is no longer necessary' (DfE, 2011: 65).

Reflective activity 7.4

■ Are there any ways that you think this could happen in your school context?
■ What would be the implications?
■ What would be the benefits?
■ What would be the drawbacks?

PERVERSE INCENTIVES IMPACTING ON SEN IDENTIFICATION

It is now recognised and acknowledged (OFSTED, 2010; DfE, 2011) that the recent focus on league tables and audits of numbers of pupils with SEN within the school, linked to Contextual Value Added data, created 'perverse incentives to over-identify children as having SEN. There is compelling evidence that these labels of SEN have perpetuated a culture of low expectations and have not led to the right support being put in place' (DfE, 2011: 9). Thus, some schools continued to believe that 'identifying more pupils with special educational needs resulted in a positive influence on the school's contextual value-added score' (OFSTED, 2010: 22).

Misconceptions about the impact of SEN levels on the school, are also evidenced in some schools in relation to confusions about the relationship between funding and the number of pupils identified as having SEN, with OFSTED (2010) again identifying that where the 'formula for funding schools took into account the proportions of children identified as having special educational needs, this gave an obvious motivation to identify more such children' (OFSTED, 2010: 23).

Reflective activity 7.5

■ What is your experience of this?
■ In discussions with colleagues, either in your own school or others, what reasons have been given for placement of pupils on the SEN Register, or for not actively reducing numbers on the SEN Register?

In many schools, the reason for this may have been linked to embedded misconceptions and confusions about the links between levels of SEN and levels of funding for the school; or the impact of reduced numbers of SEN on the Contextual Value Added data for the school.

---

continued overleaf . . .

However, in many local authorities, the direct link and correlation between funding and numbers on the SEN Register was identified some years ago, and measures have been taken to cut the link, through different funding formula. While this may have happened, new messages have not always effectively filtered through, and systems and practices that perpetuate the continuation of high levels of pupils with SEN on the SEN Register may remain due to that inaccurate misconception:

- ▨ What are the perceived incentives for keeping pupils on the SEN Register in your own school setting?
- ▨ What would happen if you suddenly removed all of the School Action children from your Register, and reduced the numbers at School Action Plus?
- ▨ Is this a real threat, or a perceived threat based on perpetuation of a misconception about the link between SEN and funding/data?

INCONSISTENCIES IN ASSESSMENT OF NEED

Another factor impacting on the successful and accurate identification of pupils with SEN, is the fact that assessments of need differ widely, both within and between local authorities, and across different services. Thus, it was identified by OFSTED (2010) that 'children with similar needs were being assessed as requiring different levels of additional support' (OFSTED, 2010: 10).

Across different services, it was also noted that the thresholds and expectations or requirements of levels of need varied before support and intervention was provided. Thus, if a pupil was assessed by health professionals, the response, assessment and identification of need may be very different to, for example, educational psychologists coming from, and working within an educational context.

As a result, it is acknowledged that there has often been the need for multiple assessments of need, repeated across the different agencies and services, often leading to inconsistent plans being drawn up (OFSTED, 2010; DfE, 2011). The delays, repetition of assessment and inconsistencies in intervention or support plans have caused frustration for parents of pupils with SEN and/or disabilities.

As previously noted (see discussions in Chapter 3) there are also significant differences in interpretation of need across different services, with different assessment thresholds, terminology and responses.

Where there is this level of inconsistency and variance in practice, this clearly provides evidence of a confused and flawed approach to the national identification of pupils with SEN.

CATEGORIES OF NEED

Another issue causing tensions and confusion relates to the labelling of pupils under different categories of need. Both the actual labels themselves, and the underpinning philosophy and approach to labelling, with the inherent impact on perceptions and expectations, need to be questioned and challenged.

The Code of Practice (DfES, 2001) introduced the notion of four categories of need:

- Cognition and Learning.
- Behaviour, Emotional and Social Difficulties.
- Communication and Interaction.
- Sensory and/or Physical Needs.

So, how helpful is labelling in helping practitioners to understand and meet the needs of pupils with SEN and/or disability?

On one level, an understanding of the type and range of needs, for an individual, a specific cohort, or indeed across a whole school can help to strategically identify trends and patterns of need. This can be helpful in terms of planning strategic responses to training or resourcing within and across a school. Identifying the key area of need impacting on a pupil can also help to focus support and strategies that may be appropriate to meet that particular area of need (although it is to be noted that the notion of SEN specific teaching and learning strategies is problematic). Yet, understanding that the pupil's primary area of need is, for example, communication and interaction, leads to a much more effective understanding of the needs and difficulties that the child may experience, and ways to effectively remove barriers to learning for that pupil, than if the pupil was simply identified as having 'SEN'.

However, pupils are complex. It is therefore not always easy to assign a specific label to their individual learning needs. Some pupils may have complex needs, which span across many, if not all, of the different categories of need. New conditions are also emerging, and becoming increasingly prevalent within education as a result of changes in society (including medical advancements, and improved assessments). It is for this reason that the DfE (2011) now recognise many more areas of need than the four traditionally identified in the Code of Practice (DfES, 2001):

the term SEN encompasses a wide range of types of need. The established categories of SEN are: specific learning difficulty, moderate learning difficulty, severe learning difficulty, profound and multiple learning difficulty, behavioural, emotional and social difficulties, speech, language and communication needs, hearing impairment, visual impairment, multi-sensory impairment, physical disability and autistic spectrum disorder.

(DfE, 2011: 19)

It is also acknowledged that identification by category or area of need is subject to interpretation, and therefore inconsistent approaches are used nationally, within and across local authorities and different schools. As OFSTED (2010) identify: 'evidence during the review showed that interpretations of need differed considerably within the categories established by the Department for Education' (OFSTED, 2010: 20).

It is also increasingly acknowledged that the use and application of a label to a pupil may inaccurately define their actual needs, and may, in fact, mask the actual primary difficulty and may lead to lowering of expectations by others to the abilities and potential of the pupil. Thus, as the DfE (2011) note, in the case of pupils with behavioural, emotional and social difficulties:

the term puts too great an emphasis on the presenting behaviour. We want to ensure that assessments of SEN and any assessments of children displaying challenging behaviour, by any professional, identify the root causes of the behaviour rather than focus on the symptoms.

(DfE, 2011: 70)

Reflective activity 7.6

The DfE (2011) pose the question: 'Is the BESD label overused in terms of describing behaviour problems rather than leading to an assessment of underlying behaviour?' (DfE, 2011: 70).

- ▪ What do you think?
- ▪ How is the term BESD used in your school?
- ▪ Does it help to understand the underlying factors causing the difficulties, or does it mask those underlying difficulties?
- ▪ What about other SEN categories or labels?

Thus, while it is important to analyse trends and patterns in prevalence of different 'need types' within our schools, there is the danger that such a focus may ignore the important individual characteristics of pupils with SEN. We need to critically challenge and re-examine our continuing use of labels to refer to pupils with SEN. What impact does this have on our practice, and on the outcomes, aspirations and self-esteem or identity of pupils?

In any discussion about categorising and labelling needs, it is therefore essential to consider the impact on the pupil's perception of their personal identity. As practitioners,

Reflective activity 7.7

As a staff group, consider the impact of labelling on the child, their perception of their own identity and also attitudes of others to that child:

- ▪ How does the child with SEN define themselves?

    - by their label?
    - in comparison to their peers?
    - in relation to their needs?
    - in relation to their strengths?

- ▪ How do others identify them?
- ▪ What is the implication of this for practice?
- ▪ Is the label used always the 'right' one, or does it sometimes mask other difficulties and issues?

we need to be aware of how we talk about pupils identified as having SEN and/or disabilities, both with colleagues and in front of the pupils themselves. It has become all too common to find colleagues discussing the 'SEN pupils' or the 'language group', which tends to neglect and ignore consideration of the pupil as an individual, and instead simply assign them to a group (the SEN pupils). Please now see Reflective activity 7.7.

As reflective practitioners we need to beware of ignoring the child and just focusing on the label. The child is the important issue, and they should be considered as an individual: not as a 'condition'. Care is therefore needed that 'classification of a disorder or disability does not come to be seen as a classification of the child' (Farrell, 2010: 55).

There is therefore the acknowledgement that 'we should not only move away from the current system of categorization of needs but also start to think critically about the way terms are used' (OFSTED, 2010: 9).

Currently, our education and SEN systems have become embedded to the use of categories and labels, and any move would require a radical shift in thinking and practice to reconsider the individualised learning needs, and learning strengths, of pupils: perhaps along a continuum of learning support and provision (House of Commons, 2006). Rix (2010) offers another alternative way forward:

> An alternative to traditional deficit labels are labels of opportunity which 'clearly position the barriers faced by individuals within the school structures around them, not within the individuals themselves'.
>
> (Rix, 2007: 28)

> For example, Down's syndrome is not a useful term in the majority of contexts in which a person with that label finds themselves.
>
> (Rix and Sheehy, 2010: 315)

Rix (2007) therefore suggests that it would be more helpful for practitioners to describe the needs of the individual rather than their disability: a 'person supported by signing and visual communication' rather than a person with Down's syndrome. What does the label actually tell us about the individual, and ways that they can access and participate in the world?

Reflective activity 7.8

■ How could this help to develop or change practice and cultures of expectations within your own school?

■ Would this be a helpful model?

■ How?

■ What impact may this have on perceptions and assumptions from the teacher?

– The pupil?

– The parent?

– Peers?

PREVALENCE OF SEN AND HIGH INCIDENCE SEN

Having identified tensions and difficulties with the underlying concept of labels and categories of need, it is important to acknowledge that this is the system within which we currently operate. Data is therefore nationally gathered relating to the growing incidence and prevalence of different categories or types of need. This data shows us patterns and trends in increasing or emerging areas of need, and it is therefore useful to consider the implications of the data gathered for reconsidering practices across the country and within individual schools.

In addition to increases in numbers of pupils identified as having SEN, it is also noted that there have been increases in the prevalence of particular categories of need. Recent data therefore identifies the following issues:

■ In the five years between 2005 and 2010:

   – numbers of pupils with behavioural, emotional and social difficulties has increased by 23%;
   – numbers of pupils with speech, language and communication needs have increased by 58%; and
   – numbers of pupils with autism have increased by 61% (DfE, 2011: 20).

■ In 2010, for pupils with statements, the largest numbers of pupils were identified as having:

   – autistic spectrum disorder (18.8%);
   – moderate learning difficulty (18.2%); and
   – behavioural, emotional and social difficulties (14.2%) (OFSTED, 2010: 20).

■ In 2010, for pupils at School Action Plus, the largest numbers of pupils were identified as having:

   – Moderate learning difficulty (26.8%);
   – behavioural, emotional and social difficulties (26.3%); and
   – speech, language and communications needs (17.6%) (OFSTED, 2010: 20).

Reflective activity 7.9

■ What does the information presented above tell us about high incidence needs?

■ What could be the causes for those increases in identification within certain categories of need?

■ What are the implications of this for developing practice: nationally and within your own school context?

■ Has there been any change or development in the pattern of need type within your own school setting?

■ What is the most prevalent need type?

■ How is this positively and strategically addressed within your school setting?

continued overleaf . . .

> – E.g. has training been planned and implemented to ensure that all staff are confident in meeting the needs of pupils with that particular need type?
> – Have trends and patterns in need type been shared with all staff to raise their awareness of those needs, and the range of day-to-day teaching strategies that they can implement to support those needs?

MOVING FORWARD

Early identification

The importance of early identification of SEN and early intervention is generally recognised and acknowledged (House of Commons, 2006; Lamb, 2009; DfE, 2011), with a recognition that:

> too many children are still falling through the net and starting school without the necessary skills or behaviours for formal learning (particularly in speech, language and communication) because of a failure to spot or address a developmental problem. This can also mean that support is put in place needlessly late.
>
> (DfE, 2011: 29)

In order to address this, there is now a move towards acknowledging that 'all professionals who come into contact with families have a part to play in identifying those children whose needs are not being adequately met' (DfE, 2011: 29).

In particular, there is an explicit notion of moving towards health visitors having a greater role to play in the early identification of special educational needs (DfE, 2011).

Thus, there are proposals to introduce developmental assessments at the age of two-and-a-half, in order to identify SEN at the earliest possible opportunity.

Reflective activity 7.10

■ How can SEN be most effectively identified at the earliest possible stage?
■ How early (in terms of age or development) do you think that it is possible to identify SEN?
■ What are the possible implications of health visitors becoming increasingly involved in the identification of SEN, possibly at the age of two-and-a-half, through the developmental assessment?

> – What will be the benefits of this approach: nationally, and for your school?
> – What may be the drawbacks or limitations?

continued overleaf . . .

> ■ Will this approach to a developmental assessment force a return to a medical model of SEN, where there is too sharp and wide a distinction between those who are identified and labelled early as having 'SEN' with the assumption that this will probably be based to a large part on a medical diagnosis of need, impairment or disability; and who then are expected to require one type of response); and others who do not have SEN?
> ■ What are the implications of this for the development of an inclusive education system and society?

While currently there are no clear indications relating to what the developmental assessment will look like, and how this will link to the notion of early identification of SEN completed by health visitors, a number of issues and tensions do need to be identified and considered throughout the development of these proposals:

■ While the principles of early identification are sound, we need to critically consider and question how early it is possible to identify SEN. There are some children who from birth, or early in their development, it is possible to identify their specific and complex SEN, but for others, is two-and-a-half years of age really an appropriate time to start labelling them as having a special educational need?

■ How can we know that it is a special educational need, and not a developmental one?

■ Will the development of a practice that seeks to identify SEN as early as possible, simply exacerbate the existing system where children coming from socially deprived backgrounds are overly represented in numbers of SEN pupils?

■ What can be done to address that?

■ While the move to increase the health visitor workforce is to be welcomed, how can health professionals be supported to make assessments about future 'educational' needs?

■ How will clearer understanding and agreement about SEN be achieved?

■ What implications does this have for the development of closer working practices?

A SINGLE EARLY YEARS AND SCHOOL-BASED CATEGORY OF SEN

> With accurate identification and early action there should be no need to move up through the stages of the Code of Practice.
>
> (Lamb, 2009: 26)

We therefore need to critically challenge the notion of the graduated response, with the in-built expectation that, as pupils fall increasingly behind their peers (often as a result of the lowered expectations for progress linked to them) then they will need to progress through the stages of the Code of Practice. Instead, once a pupil's needs have been identified (whether they are SEN or not) there should be an automatic commitment to addressing and meeting that pupil's needs, whatever that requires.

The system that we currently have is built on a focus on provision rather than a focus on outcomes. Thus, identification of need is usually linked directly to what type of provision or support is provided as a result. When pupils are identified at School Action, there is therefore often the provision of group support; at School Action Plus, there will be the provision of varying levels of specialist support. However, often there is little – if any – review or analysis of outcomes or progress from the provision given. As OFSTED (2010) identified: 'The additional provision was often not of good quality and did not lead to significantly better outcomes for the child or young person' (OFSTED, 2010: 7).

This needs to be addressed. In order to improve the identification of need and address the needs identified through the assessment and identification process, therefore needs to be a much clearer focus on outcomes for the pupil.

To be able to move forward, there needs to be greater acceptance and understanding of difference and diversity as a strength, rather than a barrier or problem to be overcome (Ekins, 2010b). As Florian (2010) notes:

> Difference is not the problem; rather, understanding that learners differ and how the different aspects of human development interact with experience to produce individual differences become the theoretical starting point for inclusive pedagogy.
>
> (Florian, 2010: 66)

This is fundamental to an approach that will inclusively meet the needs of all pupils within a true personalisation agenda.

The move to re-examine and change the existing system of a graduated response through three SEN levels (School Action; School Action Plus and Statement of SEN) is therefore to be welcomed. As has been identified earlier, there have long been inconsistencies and problems with that system in terms of the meaningful identification and placement of pupils at different levels. Proposals now suggest that this will be replaced with a single early years or school-based category of SEN:

> We intend to tackle the practice of over-identification by replacing the current SEN identification levels of School Action and School Action Plus with a new single school-based SEN category for children whose needs exceed what is normally available in schools.
>
> (DfE, 2011: 10)

While the details of how this is to be set up, and the criteria for identification of need within that single category of SEN are still to be developed, the hope is that this will in some way address the issues previously discussed relating to the over-identification of pupils who really do not have SEN and instead simply require appropriately differentiated support and provision within the school context.

Reflective activity 7.11

■ What will be the implication of this change for your school practice?
■ Do you think that the change is a welcome one?
■ Are there any tensions or difficulties in the proposed new single category of SEN?
■ How will you support colleagues to understand the changes as they come into force?

There are concerns that the move away from the three levels in the Code of Practice (DfES, 2001) will impact on the graduated response provided to meet the needs of pupils with SEN. However, this notion of the 'graduated response' does need to be challenged and examined.

The 'graduated response' outlined in the Code of Practice (DfES, 2001), in reality, actually encouraged an approach where pupils were identified with SEN, and, in some situations, were then seen as someone else's responsibility (e.g. the SENCO, or support staff providing the intervention). In reality, the graduated approach perhaps, in some cases, encouraged a move up through the levels. The 'graduated response' in this approach, really only started once the pupil had been identified as having SEN.

While we are still waiting for the system to be fully developed, understood and implemented, I am hopeful that the new approach to a single category of need may actually encourage a more effective, and inclusive, graduated response to meeting educational needs for all pupils. With the shift away from identifying pupils at School Action (many of whom do not have specific special educational needs, but instead are falling behind or underachieving), I hope that this will encourage and develop a greater graduated response in terms of the provision and support that will be developed *before* a pupil is identified with SEN.

This would produce a more inclusive approach to meeting need, although we still need to guard against an exclusive situation emerging where the differences between those with SEN and those without SEN are sharply exaggerated. As practitioners, we will therefore need to ensure that the move towards a single school-based category of SEN will not result in an approach to meeting need, where pupils are increasingly segregated: with those with 'SEN' receiving one type of education, and having one level of expectations in terms of progress and engagement; and pupils with 'no SEN' having another.

CHANGES TO THE STATEMENTING PROCESS

The current statementing process has been widely criticised (House of Commons, 2006; Lamb, 2009; OFSTED, 2010; DfE, 2011) as:

■ overly complex;
■ bureaucratic;
■ inconsistent;
■ resource/money led rather than need and outcome driven;
■ inequitable;
■ ineffective in effectively meeting the needs of pupils with SEN and/or disability and their parents;
■ adversarial, or a 'battle' for parents.

There is evidence of the 'postcode lottery' that exists as a result of localised variations in the assessment of need, the interpretation and prioritisation of need, and the problematic linking of the assessment process being carried out by the body responsible for funding any support or provision required (e.g. the local authority).

Currently, it is acknowledged that points of transition, e.g. between primary and secondary are significant drivers for requests for statutory assessment, with a significant rise in the number of requests for pupils in Year 5 (OFSTED, 2010). There is also a lack of understanding relating to what a Statement of SEN will actually do, or provide for the pupil with SEN. In many local authorities, the Statement of SEN no longer brings an allocation of money or an amount of support staff hours. Inconsistent understandings between different professionals and parents relating to the value and purpose of the statement therefore need to be addressed.

Reflective activity 7.12

▨   In your own area, what difference will the Statement of SEN make to the pupil with SEN?

▨   Is there consistent understanding about the value and purpose of a statement across all professionals, and parents?

▨   How could this be further developed and addressed?

▨   What is the implication of the rise in statements between Year 5 and Year 6, as a result of transition between primary and secondary schools?

▨   What does this tell us about educational experiences and provision between primary and secondary?

▨   What else could happen to ensure that pupils are supported to access secondary education effectively?

▨   Is this trend a result of tradition, or is there deeper underlying reason for the need for pupils to access specialist provision and services once they reach secondary age?

As a result of the deeply embedded problems within the existing statementing system, changes are proposed to the statementing process, with the introduction of a 'new single assessment process and "Education, Health and care Plan" to identify their support needs' (DfE, 2011: 36)

Initial proposals suggest that this would include more information and planning around longer term life outcomes in addition to the information about support and provision that the statement of SEN currently contains.

It is also suggested that changes will be made to both the assessment process and the accountability and duties of different services to meet the needs of pupils requiring an Education, Health and Care Plan.

As was discussed in the previous chapter, while this is a worthy goal, it must be noted that the principles underpinning this seem to be the same, or very similar, to those underpinning the previous Labour Government's *Every Child Matters* (DfES, 2004). While, with *Every Child Matters*, there were examples of exceptional multi-agency working and understanding developing, this was still far from being consistent across all areas of the country, and even across all areas within the same local authority.

In order to achieve this goal, there is therefore the need for very careful planning around how this is to be achieved, which will include the need for joint policy commitment and statutory responsibility to the process across all services.

Linked to these proposals, is also the suggestion that voluntary or community organisations will take over part of the assessment process, in order to break the links between assessment of need and funding/provision of resources currently both held by the local authority.

It is noted that these changes will take some time to implement, with the suggestion that this may develop by 2014. In the meantime, there are proposals to speed up the current statementing process, reducing it from 26 weeks to 20 (DfE, 2011).

ACTION PLANNING

Identify three key points for individual reflection:

1 _____

2 _____

3 _____

Start to consider key issues to be followed up as points of action that have arisen from your reading of this chapter.

This may include:

■ Reviewing the existing SEN register to consider whether all children have a specific special educational need, or whether some are placed on the SEN register because they are simply underachieving.

■ Providing training for all staff to ensure consistent whole school understanding of the differences between SEN and underachievement.

■ Working with staff to develop understanding of the terminology and notion of 'removing barriers to learning': and the responsibility of staff to proactively work with all pupils to remove barriers to learning.

■ Reconsidering the use and impact of labels on staff and pupil perceptions and expectations: ensuring high expectations for all pupils, including those with SEN and/or disabilities.

■ Working with staff and parents to understand and embed new information about the single school-based category of SEN, and also the new Education, Health and Care Plan.

■ Others.

ACTION PLANNING TO ENABLE IMPACT

Use the format provided below to develop a clear Action Plan for future development of practices for either yourself, or for the school. Make sure that you do not identify too many different actions all at once, have a clear outcome for what you want to achieve in mind, and that you clearly identify the different steps to take to achieve the outcome.

IDENTIFICATION OF SEN: ACTION PLANNING TO ENABLE IMPACT:

Which key issues from the chapter do you want to focus on/ change/develop?	How will you effect this change or development (identify a number of small action steps to achieve your overall goal)?	Who else will need to be involved? How?	What will the outcome be (include timescales)?	Impact:

8 COORDINATING, IMPLEMENTING AND EVALUATING PROVISION

THIS CHAPTER:

- identifies the range of systems involved in the effective coordination, implementation and evaluation of provision, and ways that these systems have changed as a result of changing policy;
- emphasises the need for a strategic and inclusive whole school approach to the coordination and evaluation of provision to achieve the best outcomes for pupils;
- critically examines the need for an approach focused on impact and outcomes rather than just based on provision;
- critically considers the role of support staff in coordinating, implementing and evaluating provision;
- considers practical measures to enhance the overall effectiveness of systems to coordinate, implement and evaluate provision.

REVIEW

The issue of planning and implementing effective provision to meet the needs of pupils with SEN and/or disabilities in our schools is not new. It has evolved and developed over recent years to include a wide range of different practices. Please now see the Review box on following page.

The number of systems and processes that have been introduced and are recommended as good practice (OFSTED, 2004, 2011; DCSF, 2007, 2008; OFSTED, 2011; DfE, 2011) over recent years have included:

- pupil tracking;
- identification of pupils who are underachieving, or who are experiencing barriers to learning;
- intervention planning/provision mapping;
- intervention monitoring, evaluation and review;
- target setting;
- self-evaluation.

Review

■ What systems and processes are in place to support the coordination, implementation and evaluation of provision in your school?

■ How are decisions made about the most effective and appropriate provision to implement for a pupil?

■ Who is involved directly in the coordination, implementation and evaluation of provision?

■ Do the systems that you use directly link to changes and improvements in practice and outcomes for each pupil? Or: are they paper-based activities with little direct link to what actually happens on a day-to-day basis within the classroom?

■ What works well?

■ Why and how is this effective?

■ Are there any aspects of your current system or process that do not work so well?

■ Why?

■ How could this be addressed?

Recently, with the development of the new required learning outcomes for those SENCOs new to post completing the National Award for SEN Coordination, the importance of effective practices to support the coordination of provision has been emphasised, with one of the five key sections specifically about Coordinating Provision.

This section therefore sets out the requirement for new SENCOs to focus on:

Developing, using, monitoring and evaluating systems – training should enable SENCOs to develop, monitor, evaluate and review systems for:

■ identifying pupils who may have SEN and/or disabilities (using classroom observation, data, assessment and other forms of monitoring);

■ informing all staff about the learning needs, behaviour and achievement of pupils with SEN and/or disabilities;

■ helping colleagues to have realistic expectations of behaviour for pupils with SEN and/or disabilities and set appropriately challenging targets for them;

■ planning approaches and interventions to meet the needs of pupils with SEN and/or disabilities, geared to removing or minimising barriers to participation and learning;

■ recording and reviewing the progress of pupil with SEN and/or disabilities towards learning targets;

■ assessing the effectiveness of provision for pupils with SEN and/or disabilities;

continued overleaf . . .

■ ensuring appropriate arrangements are put in place (in classroom practice and for the examinations/tests themselves) for pupils sitting national tests and examinations; and

■ liaising with other schools to promote continuity of support and progression in learning when pupils with SEN and/or disabilities transfer.

Using tools for collecting, analysing and using data – training should enable SENCOs to:

■ know how school, local authority and national data systems work, including RAISEonline; and

■ analyse and interpret relevant, local, national and school data to inform policy and practices, expectations, targets for improving the learning of pupils with SEN and/or disabilities.

Deploying staff and managing resources – training should enable SENCOs to:

■ delegate tasks appropriately, deploy and manage staff effectively to ensure the most efficient use of teaching and other expertise to support pupils with SEN and/or disabilities;

■ make flexible and innovative use of the available workforce, recognising and utilising particular strengths and expertise.

(TDA, 2009)

In addition to the specified learning outcomes within the coordinating provision section, others within the Strategic Development section identify the need to:

■ work with senior colleagues and the governing body to establish appropriate resources to support the teaching of pupils with SEN and/or disabilities, and the means of monitoring their use in terms of value for money, efficiency and effectiveness; and

■ develop and provide regular information to the head teacher and governing body on the effectiveness of provision for pupils with SEN and/or disabilities to inform decision making and policy review.

■ how to manage and make best use of available financial, human and physical resources, including how to use tools such as provision mapping to plan, evaluate and improve provision for pupils with SEN and/or disabilities, including identifying ineffective or missing provision.

The issue of coordinating, implementing and evaluating provision is therefore central to ensuring that all pupils, particularly those with SEN and/or disabilities, receive support and provision that is effective at meeting their specific needs and that enables them to make effective progress.

REFLECTION

The impact of new policy and guidance

Currently, the systems and processes identified above remain fundamental to the effective coordination of provision and support for pupils with SEN. There has been commitment to the continuation of the National Award for SEN Coordination, which centrally positions these important processes. However, it is important that practitioners are aware that the emphasis on some systems and processes is changing as a result of the new political context and priority areas (DfE, 2010c; DfE, 2011).

There has therefore been a change to the requirements for all maintained schools to fill in and update a standardised Self Evaluation Form (the SEF). While the requirement to complete the standardised form has been removed (DfE, 2010a), the principles of rigorous self-evaluation to support the development of good practice in schools is emphasised. Thus, it is noted that:

> We strongly support the view that good schools evaluate themselves rigorously. But we do not believe that imposing a very long form in a standard format, which requires consideration of many issues which may be of limited importance to a particular school, helps schools to evaluate themselves in a focused way against their priorities.'
>
> (DfE, 2010a: 29)

Schools will therefore have greater freedoms to develop innovative ways to evaluate their own practice and to present these in meaningful ways.

There has also been removal of advice and guidance that emphasise IEPs as the way to plan for pupils with SEN (OFSTED, 2011; DfE, 2011). It is therefore noted that 'in order to remove bureaucratic burdens on schools we will remove advice and guidance on using IEPs and encourage schools to explore the ways in which other new approaches can be used to enable pupils with SEN to develop, progress and fulfil their potential' (DfE, 2011: 99).

Guidance provided to OFSTED Inspectors (2011) also highlights that there is 'no statutory requirement to have individual education plans; reviewing and reporting progress against the objectives within a statement is all that is required' (OFSTED, 2011: 6).

These changes in government emphasis and direction therefore open up the potential for schools to develop processes and systems that best respond to the context of their own school and also to the needs of the pupils that they serve.

There have also been shifts in terminology around what has been the model of Waves of Intervention, set out over recent years by the National Strategies (2002, 2003). The Waves of Intervention model was a powerful model for whole school inclusive development, which emphasised the importance of focusing considerable attention on ensuring that the day-to-day teaching approaches and strategies of the teacher are appropriate and effective in ensuring progress for all pupils, before implementing additional support and provision.

With the recent change in government, the principles of the model have been retained, although rather than the National Strategies terminology of Waves of Intervention; the DfE focus is increasingly on Quality Teaching and then intervention. This can, however, still be transplanted onto the original model first introduced by the National Strategies shown in Figure 8.1.

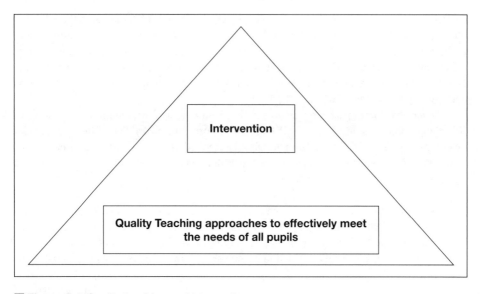

▨ **Figure 8.1** Quality teaching and intervention

The importance and significance of the way in which the triangular model is presented, demonstrates and draws attention to the fact that the most important foundation and basis for effective teaching and learning to take place, is through an emphasis on and understanding of quality teaching approaches: not through an emphasis on withdrawn or specialised intervention.

While there is less emphasis on the Waves of Intervention within DfE guidance documents, there is still a noticeable confusion in the seeming linking of Waves of Intervention with the graduated response to meeting SEN. Thus, DfE guidance (2010c) provides the following as a key prompt for School Improvement Partners: 'How closely is the "Waves" model of intervention aligned with the SEN Code of Practice's "graduated response?"' (DfE, 2010c: 44).

This is a concern, as it is continuing to embed confused approaches about the Waves of Intervention, linking them solely with SEN, rather than as a whole school strategic tool for responding to and meeting the needs of all pupils, through a graduated approach to quality teaching approaches to meet the needs of all; 'catch-up', or 'keep-up' intervention to provide short time-limited support for those pupils at risk of falling behind; and more intensive and specialised support for those with longer term needs (Ekins and Grimes, 2009).

Reflective activity 8.1

■ What are the implications of the changes outlined above to:

- the self-evaluation process;
- IEPs;
- Waves of Intervention.

to the development of practice within your school context?
■ Are there any inconsistencies or confusions that may need to be addressed?
■ How will this be addressed?
■ What are the implications of the changes referred to above for the ability to effectively meet the needs of all pupils with SEN and/or disability?

THE NEED FOR A STRATEGIC AND INCLUSIVE WHOLE SCHOOL APPROACH TO THE COORDINATION AND EVALUATION OF PROVISION

For systems and processes to be effective in meeting the needs of pupils with SEN and/or disabilities, there is the need for a shift in thinking and practice away from all of the systems being the responsibility of one person (usually the SENCO); or a model of practice where aspects of the different processes are the sole responsibility of different members of staff, with no communication or collaboration between the different staff members (e.g. the assessment coordinator takes responsibility for data; while the SENCO takes responsibility for target setting, with no link between) to a model where there is embedded whole staff ownership, commitment to and responsibility for the range of processes (Ekins and Grimes, 2009).

Ultimately, coordinating provision needs to be seen as a whole school responsibility, with all staff members actively involved, and this builds on the central principle of shared collective responsibility and ownership running throughout the discussions in this book. Such an approach can help to move thinking and practice away from seeing the various processes (target setting, provision mapping, etc.) as a paper-based exercise completed just for pupils with SEN and/or disabilities; to embedded, shared understanding of the importance of effective approaches to coordinating provision, and the impact that they have on the day-to-day teaching and learning experiences of all pupils.

This shift in thinking and practice is demonstrated in the Inclusion in Action model (Ekins and Grimes, 2009) shown in Figure 8.2 on the following page. This model helps practitioners to consider how the range of systems to coordinating provision can be used more strategically. It sets out a more strategic approach, where, instead of each system being seen as separate and distinct, the processes are seen as part of the whole model, each dynamically impacting on another to enable a more proactive and effective approach to planning and implementing provision within the school to occur.

Elsewhere (Ekins and Grimes, 2009) we have set out case studies of schools at different stages of development, demonstrating how, as schools move towards Stage 3:

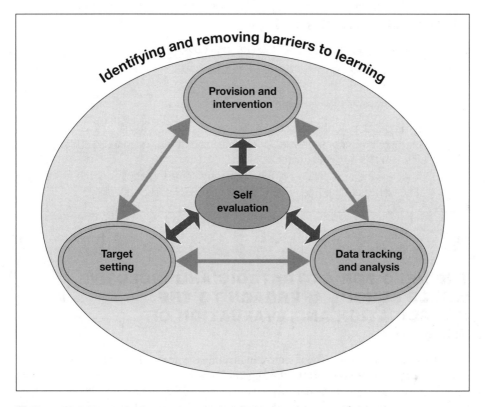

▪ **Figure 8.2** The Inclusion in Action model (Ekins and Grimes, 2009)

Inclusion in Action, the processes become shared, collaborative and meaningful, with the teacher (the professional with the most important direct link to the pupil with SEN and/or disabilities at the very heart of the processes) fully involved, and benefiting from increased levels of understanding and engagement in the processes. The processes move from being seen as something that has to be done three times a year, and then filed; to processes that support the day-to-day planning and support of all pupils.

As can be seen by the model presented above, all of the processes are linked to each other, with self-evaluation playing a central part, supporting teachers to evaluate current practices, by drawing on the different information available, and using it to inform judgements, rather than leaving the information gathered in separate folders, only used by identified individuals. This also fits with the principles of the 'Impact-focused approach to the development of practice' model introduced in Chapter 1, and underpinning the discussions throughout the book.

A FOCUS ON IMPACT AND OUTCOMES RATHER THAN JUST BASED ON PROVISION

Any approach to coordinating provision has to be based on setting high expectations of progress for all pupils: including those pupils with SEN and/or disabilities. For too long, the progress of pupils with SEN and/or disabilities has been impacted on by low expectations, and a focus on placement and provision rather than on the setting of realistic and high expectations of outcomes and progress.

The chapter places an emphasis on the evaluation of the impact of provision on pupil learning. The issue is therefore about being able to evaluate 'the *effectiveness* of interventions – not just [describe] what is provided' (OFSTED, 2011: 6).

There is also the need to focus on the relevance of planned support. The focus should be on the impact that any support or provision has on meeting and addressing the pupil's underlying needs, rather than just focusing on providing something. As OFSTED (2010) noted: 'The support [pupils] were allocated was not always appropriate to their needs. For example, some were allocated support for behaviour when, in fact, they had specific communication needs.'

An approach to critically reviewing all provision therefore needs to be developed in schools in order to ensure that it all remains relevant and closely matched to actual pupil need. This critical review needs to include a focus and evaluation of the provision on a number of different levels:

1 The appropriateness of the provision:

- How closely does it match actual need?
- Or is existing provision based on traditional intervention programmes which no longer match the profile of needs within the cohort or school?

2 The outcomes of the provision:

- Is there clear understanding of baseline skill levels and what is hoped to be achieved through the intervention by all involved?
- Is the expected outcome of the intervention clearly identified at the start, and shared with all staff, pupils and parents involved?
- How is progress through the intervention monitored?
- Are flexible systems set up to enable the expected end outcomes to be extended or reduced to respond positively to pupil learning through the intervention?
- Are ways to transfer and apply learning and skills into the classroom context fully explored to ensure meaningful impact on learning?
- Are final outcomes assessed to check progress against baseline data?
- Is sustained impact on skills after the end of the intervention monitored and recorded?

3 Whether the intervention is value for money:

- Work out the cost of running an intervention against the outcome in terms of pupil progress, e.g. calculate the number of hours a week × the number of weeks the intervention runs for × staff member hourly rate and divide by the number of pupils in the intervention group to calculate the cost of running the intervention per pupil.
- Is the intervention providing good value for money?
- Could it be delivered in a more cost-effective way?
- What would be the impact on outcomes?

In a time of changing financial contexts, schools will need to consider notions of getting 'better for less': it is therefore essential that time is taken to consider 'value for money' in terms of evaluating outcomes and impact. Schools will need to consider ways to maintain effective provision within reducing school and local authority budgets. With some flexible and creative thinking and planning, schools need to start to consider ways to use resources more effectively, thereby providing better provision for less money.

It will therefore become 'more important than ever that SENCOs have a full understanding of the delegated school budget and the specific amounts available to support children and young people with SEN' (Petersen, 2010: 21).

While this is important, the traditional notion of separate 'SEN budgets' does need to be challenged. In a time where more funding is being devolved straight to schools, without the previous ring-fencing of budgets held either centrally or by local authorities to support the needs of pupils with SEN, it is important to move thinking and practice away from conceptualising a finite amount or 'budget' to meet the needs of pupils with SEN, and into an approach that understands that the school receives a budget to meet the needs of all of its pupils. It is therefore the responsibility of leaders within the school to ensure that that total school budget is used effectively to provide all pupils with the support that they require to enable them to make progress. For some schools, with high levels of pupil mobility, or working in areas of high social deprivation, this may require very flexible approaches to managing budgets to ensure that at any time money and resources (including human resources) can be reallocated to support the specific and complex needs of different individuals.

THE ROLE AND DEPLOYMENT OF SUPPORT STAFF

A key consideration when looking at coordinating provision effectively is the need to consider the role and deployment of support staff. Support staff will, in most cases, constitute the most expensive resource within the school setting, and it is therefore essential that they are deployed in the most effective way to maximise pupil outcomes, rather than being deployed according to traditional structures: often, in the primary school context, relating to a teaching assistant being placed in each class, regardless of consideration of levels of need within and between class groups.

The evidence on the impact of teaching assistant support on improvements in pupil outcomes and learning is very mixed, and it is essential that practitioners take time to critically review, question and challenge embedded models of practice to ensure that an expensive collective resource, such as support staff, is really deployed in a way so as to maximise impact on pupil outcomes.

Indeed, OFSTED (2010) therefore note that support staff can become a 'barrier to learning' when not deployed in the appropriate way. It is therefore acknowledged that: 'Within schools, support staff can make a real difference to the achievement of pupils with SEN, but they need to be deployed and used effectively in order to do so' (DfE, 2011: 63).

Without careful consideration relating to the effective deployment of teaching assistants and support staff, research has noted the:

> negative impact on children's progress from using support staff as substitutes for teachers. There is a clear relationship between support from teaching assistants (TAs)

and lower attainment and slower rates of progress for pupils with SEN. Further, there is a relationship between the amount of support received from TAs and pupil attainment: the more support, the lower the attainment.

(Lamb, 2009: 29)

At a time where the use and deployment of teaching assistants and support staff, often to work with individuals with complex special educational needs, or with groups requiring additional intervention support, is commonplace within schools, this finding is significant. It requires schools to reconsider the use and deployment of staff.

Reflective activity 8.2

■ Reconsider Lamb's (2009) statement above.

■ Why do you think that there is this negative impact and correlation between support from teaching assistants and progress of pupils with SEN and/or disabilities?

■ What happens in your school setting?

■ Is there a positive or a negative correlation between support from teaching assistants or support staff and pupil progress?

■ How do you know?

■ How is it measured?

■ Is it regularly reviewed in order to make changes to ensure a clear focus on achieving improved pupil outcomes?

The reasons for this 'barrier to learning' and 'negative impact' on the progress of pupils with SEN and/or disabilities may include:

■ reduction in opportunities for the pupil with SEN and/or disabilities to engage in independent learning;

■ the focus for the TA may be on task completion (sometimes to the extent of doing parts of the task themselves) rather than on development of learning;

■ the pupil with SEN and/or disabilities does not develop a range of independent learning strategies, including understanding when and how to ask for help, or problem-solving;

■ lack of understanding of support staff of different ways to question pupils to extend thinking and learning;

■ missed opportunities to discuss and collaborate with the teacher, so that the support staff is not fully aware of the wider context within which the learning takes place;

■ lack of training for the teaching assistant in the particular intervention, or in more general understanding of child development, including ways to learn and barriers to learning.

It is therefore acknowledged that 'to ensure that children benefit from the support of teaching assistants there has to be a ruthless focus on the impact of how they are deployed and on the skills they need to support children's learning. Underpinning this is a core principle that the teacher takes responsibility for the outcomes of every child, through planning and the monitoring of progress' (Lamb, 2009: 28).

As previously discussed (Chapter 4), a focus on the direct involvement of teachers in improving outcomes for pupils with SEN and/or disabilities is essential. It must therefore be emphasised and understood within the school context that the teacher is the qualified professional and that it is critical that pupils with complex needs receive the professional, high quality support from the teacher trained to understand learning needs and child development, that they require.

Thus 'teaching assistant time should never be a substitute for teaching from a qualified teacher. Too often, the most vulnerable pupils are supported almost exclusively by teaching assistants. . . . This practice is not acceptable. Children with SEN need more, not less, time with the school's most skilled and qualified teachers' (DfE, 2011: 63).

Support staff can and do have a significant impact on positive pupil outcomes, both in terms of attainment and on wider outcomes including improvements to pupil self-esteem, in some situations. However, for this to occur, there needs to be a strategic approach to the 'training, support, deployment and management' (DfE, 2011: 64) of teaching assistants as part of a whole school approach to improving teaching and learning for all.

Reflective activity 8.3

▪ How is that managed within your own school setting?
▪ What changes need to be made?
▪ How can these be addressed?
▪ Are there any remaining barriers?

- Staff expectations and perceptions about teaching assistant deployment and support?
- Lack of training and skills?
- Mismatch between levels of need and levels of trained support to meet those needs?

▪ How can these barriers be positively overcome?

PRACTICAL MEASURES TO ENHANCE THE OVERALL EFFECTIVENESS OF SYSTEMS TO COORDINATE, IMPLEMENT AND EVALUATE PROVISION

In order to effectively coordinate, implement and evaluate provision that will have a positive impact on pupil outcomes, there is a need to engage meaningfully in a cyclical and dynamically linked process of assessing pupil progress, identifying needs, planning and implementing interventions and support, target setting and monitoring and review of interventions and targets.

As understood within the Inclusion in Action model (Ekins and Grimes, 2009) these processes are not linear or hierarchical. Rather they should be flexible, each impacting on the understanding and application of the next part of the process.

This section supports the reader to develop increased understanding of the different aspects of the cycle and overall process of coordinating provision, in order to highlight key issues and tensions that may exist within changing policy contexts.

ASSESSING PUPIL PROGRESS

Meaningful use of data is an important aspect of coordinating provision.

Most schools are already familiar with this issue, and systems are in place to regularly assess pupil progress. The new government have therefore continued to emphasise the need to use data, including data using the P Levels for pupils with SEN effectively to 'help [teachers] track pupils' progress, identify strengths and areas for development, and improve teaching and learning' (DfE, 2011: 77).

While the DfE (2010) have declared their support of 'the view that skilled and precise assessment of pupils' work – both of the level at which children are working and of what they should be learning next – is an essential part of good teaching' (DfE, 2010a: 30), the new policy context recognises that this can happen in different and more effective ways. There is recognition therefore that 'we do not need to impose national requirements as to how this should be done. So we will not be prescriptive about the use of the "Assessing Pupil Progress" materials and the new National Curriculum will not specify the methods teachers use' (DfE, 2010a: 30).

In terms of the national use of data, there will be a greater emphasis placed on progress data rather than on performance measures such as CVA (Contextual Value Added), which is said to 'entrench low aspirations for children because of their background' (DfE, 2010a: 68).

There is therefore a commitment to 'measure schools on how much value they add for all pupils, not rank them on the make-up of their intake' (DfE, 2010a: 68).

However, the most important issue to note is not the type of assessment undertaken (whether informal, or national testing) but rather what the data tells us about what needs to be done to secure positive outcomes for individuals and whole cohorts. The assessment process itself is therefore only the start of the process, and staff need to be supported to look beyond the simple assessment data produced, and instead engage in a much deeper strategic process of reviewing and evaluating the 'so what?'; 'why?' and 'how?' questions that the data may raise. Thus, as the DfE (2010c) note:

> One of the most important purposes of assessment is to inform teaching and learning. Assessment enables schools to track pupil progress accurately, to design future learning, to adjust, commission new or decommission existing provision and to review expectations and learning trajectories.
>
> (DfE, 2010c: 8)

To ensure that a meaningful and strategic system is established, some key critical questions therefore need to be considered, including:

■ What does the data show is working well?
■ What is not working so well? For individuals, groups and whole cohorts?

■   What does this tell us about aspects of provision and practice that need to be developed or prioritised within the school context?
■   What does this tell us about staff training needs: either for individual members of staff, or for whole staff groups?
■   How can this be addressed?
■   What action will be taken immediately to address issues identified through the analysis of data?
■   Who needs to be involved?
■   How?

The key issue is therefore about the action that will happen as a result of the analysis of data: an approach to clear action planning that will develop and improve practice needs to be embedded to enable and inform strategic planning for improved outcomes for all pupils, including those with SEN and/or disabilities.

IDENTIFYING NEEDS

Central to, and running alongside, the process of strategically analysing data and deciding on appropriate interventions, support and strategies to be put in place, is the issue of identifying and understanding needs. This includes appropriate and accurate identification of pupils with SEN and/or disabilities, including awareness of what their primary area of need may be (see Chapter 7), but will also include the identification of other groups 'vulnerable to underachievement' (OFSTED, 2000). This process helps all staff to further understand and be aware of the range of barriers to learning that the pupil may face.

The process of putting together Profiles of Need (Ekins and Grimes, 2009) can therefore be a very helpful activity to support strategic planning both at an individual class level and at a whole school level. At its most simple level, this process simply involves a full class list, against which any 'needs' that the pupil may have are indicated. The process allows for the fact that pupils are complex, and therefore may have both a range of needs, as well as possibly contradictory needs (i.e. identified both as having SEN and being gifted and talented).

For most schools, identifying the following key areas of need is helpful, and this is then added to by the school to identify any other 'vulnerable groups' particular to the school context:

■   SEN: by level of need and area of need;
■   gifted and talented;
■   looked after child;
■   social services involvement;
■   English as an additional language;
■   Gypsy, Roma or Traveller.

By identifying the needs of individuals by cohort and across the whole school staff will have a much clearer understanding of the range of needs impacting on progress and outcomes across the school: including any new or rising trends or patterns of need. Against this, the pupil tracking data can be analysed: to make links between the needs of different identified groups of pupils, and the progress that they make. This should lead into strategic consideration of whether the needs of particular groups are being effectively met by the existing interventions and strategies on offer, or whether new and different systems need to be developed, which leads into the next part of the dynamic process – planning interventions.

PLANNING INTERVENTIONS

Against the background of clearly understanding and identifying needs, is then the development of an effective approach to planning interventions: interventions that are closely focused on and matched to pupil needs, to ensure positive outcomes. Again, a number of key principles are fundamental to an approach that is effective. In particular this includes:

- The need to recognise the importance of high quality inclusive teaching approaches and strategies that are utilised by the class teacher, and that actually match the needs of the pupils with whom the teacher is working.
- Where pupil progress outcomes (identified through effective analysis of pupil tracking data – see p. 137) identify that individuals, groups or whole cohorts are not making the progress required, or expected, then attention needs to be paid to addressing whole class teaching issues: rather than immediately focusing on the need to implement additional interventions.
- Interventions should then build on this foundation of effectively matched support provided through inclusive teaching strategies (Ekins, 2010a).
- Where additional intervention is required, there is a need to ensure that this is achieved in a sensitive and inclusive way, which does not inadvertently emphasise, draw attention to or exacerbate the differences that it seeks to address (Florian, 2010).
- Understanding that it is difficult to provide interventions that are based simply on 'categories of need'. Therefore, not all pupils with Autistic Spectrum Disorders will require or benefit from the same approach: what is needed are individualised approaches that reflect the actual needs and difficulties that the pupil is experiencing.
- Interventions need to be time-limited and closely focused on outcomes: 'what consistently worked best was a close analysis of [pupil needs], often as they changed and developed, matched to a clear view of the impact of intervention on outcomes for them' (OFSTED, 2010: 11).
- Progress towards the outcomes needs to be monitored and reviewed regularly through the intervention to ensure that the intervention is effective for the identified pupils. Where progress is not being made, immediate changes and adjustments to the delivery or planning of the intervention can be made (Ekins and Grimes, 2009; OFSTED, 2010).
- In deciding on which interventions to use, evidence bases need to be used to support effective decision making (see also Chapter 10 for discussions about the need for evidence-based practice). This can include evidence that will be available from the government about 'interventions which are effective in supporting the achievement of disadvantaged children including, for example, intensive support in reading, writing and mathematics' (DfE, 2010a: 81). But, may, and should, also include localised evidence-based practice in the form of internal evaluation (including Action Research) about the impact that interventions have had on pupil progress, and discussions with other schools about what has been implemented and how effective it has been.

- Ensure that interventions take into account wider contextual factors. OFSTED (2010) have therefore identified that: 'Interventions that were carried out in isolation from the range of contextual factors influencing the development of a child or young person, for example their home or community, did not make enough of a difference to progress or well-being, particularly in the long term' (OFSTED, 2010: 32).
- Consider the most effective implementation of provision and intervention: 1:1 is not always the most effective in terms of pupil outcomes, or value for money. Therefore, OFSTED (2010) identified that provision (e.g. speech and language therapy) was more effective when provided to groups of pupils, rather than in the traditional 1:1 clinical model. Communication skills even for those with severe needs were improved at a faster rate in such a setting.
- Ensure that interventions include planned opportunities for group and collaborative work.

Reflective activity 8.4

- Which of these key principles are already effectively embedded in your school approach to planning intervention?
- Are there any that are not, and which need to be?
- How will this be addressed in your school context?
- Who will you need to involve?

PUPIL PROGRESS REVIEW MEETINGS

Recently, schools have developed the use of Pupil Progress Review Meetings (DCSF, 2007; Ekins and Grimes, 2009). Where used well, this has been a positive development, and can be seen as a key tool in enabling the Inclusion in Action model to work in practice. The meetings therefore draw together many of the specific elements of an effective approach to coordinating provision, including:

- strategic and analytical discussion of pupil tracking data;
- identification of needs: including underachievement by individuals, groups of pupils, or indeed whole cohorts;
- planning discussions about what type of provision or support would be most appropriate;
- discussions about targets/outcomes that are needed to support pupil(s) to make effective progress;
- these discussions can then effectively be recorded onto a Provision Map, which provides a clear and accessible document to enable strategic evaluation of provision across different cohorts within the school context.

Pupil Progress Review Meetings have become popular within schools, and are recognised as a useful and effective way to draw information together to inform judgements and planning for future resource and support needs.

This model of practice links in extremely well with the principles underlying the Inclusion in Action model. As with the Inclusion in Action model, the Pupil Progress Review meeting enables the different systems to come together, and be discussed together to support dynamic and strategic planning. The teacher should be at the centre of these discussions, which should be self-reflective and evaluative, and should be supported by a range of other key staff concerned with monitoring the needs, progress and provision of pupils, as relevant to the individual school.

The discussions should be positive and proactive, and in the most effective meetings, the class teacher is given ownership of the process, by taking the lead and using the range of information available to them to evaluate pupil progress and identify areas in need of development, not only at an individual level, but also at a small group level and a whole class level. As part of the process effective provision maps can be drawn up. Provision maps should be developed to include more than a simple list of what is available within the school context, such as some strategic and evaluative information about how and in which ways pupils are accessing the range of available interventions, and the impact that they are having. The best provision maps therefore 'showed which interventions were particularly effective' (OFSTED, 2010: 63).

With the proposal to remove advice and guidance about the specific use of Individual Education Plans (IEPs) (DfE, 2011), Pupil Progress Review meetings, and provision maps that are meaningful and clearly linked to strategic planning for improved outcomes for pupils with SEN will become increasingly important.

Reflective activity 8.5

■ Do you currently hold Pupil Progress Review meetings in your school?
■ How could these be developed to become an effective tool to support the meaningful development of strategic planning to meet the needs of all pupils, including those with SEN and/or disability?
■ How are targets/outcomes currently set for pupils with SEN and/or disabilities in your school?
■ What are the benefits of using IEPs?
■ How could other systems, such as provision mapping, make the system of target setting more meaningful and effective?

ACTION PLANNING

Identify three key points for individual reflection:

1 _____

2 _____

3 _____

Start to consider key issues to be followed up as points of action that have arisen from your reading of this chapter.

This may include:

▓ Critically reviewing the effectiveness of existing systems used in school to implement, monitor, review and evaluate the coordination of provision.

▓ Considering ways to embed a whole school strategic approach to coordinating provision, which is intricately liked to the whole school development cycle, rather than seen as separate to it.

▓ Working with staff to identify how existing systems are used to have a direct impact on day-to-day practice and improving pupil outcomes.

▓ Critically reconsidering the impact of deployment of support staff on pupil outcomes.

▓ Using the Inclusion in Action (Ekins and Grimes, 2009) to support the review of existing processes.

▓ Reconsidering the current use of IEPs: are they needed, or could more innovative ways be found to provide the information that is currently recorded on an IEP? Is the information used and referred to? How?

▓ Others.

ACTION PLANNING TO ENABLE IMPACT

Use the format provided below to develop a clear Action Plan for future development of practices for either yourself, or for the school. Make sure that you do not identify too many different actions all at once, have a clear outcome for what you want to achieve in mind, and make sure that you clearly identify the different steps to take to achieve the outcome.

EFFECTIVE COORDINATION OF PROVISION: ACTION PLANNING TO ENABLE IMPACT:

Which key issues from the chapter do you want to focus on/ change/develop?	How will you effect this change or development (identify a number of small action steps to achieve your overall goal)?	Who else will need to be involved? How?	What will the outcome be (include timescales)?	Impact:

9 WORKING WITH PUPILS WITH SEN AND/OR DISABILITIES AND THEIR PARENTS

THIS CHAPTER:

- reviews the experiences of parents of pupils with SEN and/or disabilities;
- highlights issues around working meaningfully with pupils with SEN and/or disabilities to review provision and support needs;
- considers key principles of effective communication systems for working with parents;
- considers the need for a focus on outcomes when working with parents;
- discusses the structured conversation;
- considers the impact of engaging parents as partners for the school, for parents and for the child with SEN and/or disabilities;
- examines the range of information that parents should have access to, and more effective ways that this can be provided;
- considers the new proposals for personal budgets for parents of pupils with an 'Education and Health Care Plan' and implications of this for support and partnership working between school staff and parents.

REVIEW

> Engagement with parents is critical to children's progress.
>
> (Lamb, 2009: 32)

The issue of working with parents has emerged as a significant theme within new government policy (DfE, 2010a; DfE, 2011), reflecting the findings and discussions of other recent government and independent research reports (House of Commons, 2006; Lamb, 2009; Alexander, 2010). These reviews and reports on practice identified the variety of experiences that parents had of the educational system and how it supported them and the needs of their children with SEN and/or disabilities:

In talking with parents of disabled children and children with special educational needs (SEN), we met some of the happiest parents in the country and some of the angriest. Many had children who are well-supported and making good progress. But we also met parents for whom the education system represents a battle to get the needs of their child identified and for these to be met. The crucial issue is that both experiences happen within the same system. While the aims of the SEN framework remain relevant, implementation has too often failed to live up to them.

(Lamb, 2009:2)

This statement gives us much food for thought, and we need to critically review the implications of this for the development of practice that is effective in actually understanding and meeting the needs of pupils and the families of pupils with SEN and/or disabilities.

Review

■ What systems do you currently have in place in your school to support and involve parents of pupils with SEN and/or disabilities?
■ How helpful/effective are they?
■ What would be helpful/effective?
■ How could this be achieved?
■ What are the existing barriers?

A range of systems for working with, or communicating information to parents currently exist as common practice within schools. These may include:

■ formal teacher/parent consultations;
■ formal parent/SENCO meetings: including Annual Review meetings for pupils with a statement of SEN;
■ CAF (Common Assessment Framework) and TAC (Team Around the Child) meetings;
■ parent groups;
■ letters sent home to inform parents of targets or provision.

While these may be common, and may be one way of engaging with parents, we need to critically consider how effective these measures actually are, and how they can be enhanced to enable parents to have a stronger, more respected voice within the decision making and planning process.

REFLECTION

Involving pupils

The importance of pupil voice and involving pupils in meaningful discussions about their learning and provision has recently been highlighted (Lamb, 2009; OFSTED, 2010).

However, while in recent government policy (DfE, 2010a; DfE, 2011) there has been an increased focus on the need to engage effectively and meaningfully with parents, there seems to be a noticeable omission relating to ways to work more meaningfully with pupils with SEN and/or disabilities themselves. Government guidance and proposals (DfE, 2011), while providing a range of commitments and proposals for developing systems to work more effectively with parents, therefore contain very little about the important issue of working meaningfully with pupils with SEN and/or disabilities themselves.

Although there has been a focus over recent years (Lamb, 2009; Alexander, 2010) on involving pupils more meaningfully, with acknowledgement that 'the voice of children needs to be strengthened within the system' (Lamb, 2009: 5), it is noted that: 'there remains frustration among young people with SEN and disabilities, which is that teachers do not listen to or understand their needs' (Bradbury et al., 2010: 207).

Despite this acknowledgement, this is an issue that is not fully addressed or raised within recent government policy and guidance.

Reflective activity 9.1

■ What systems do you have in place to involve, listen to and respond to the views of pupils with SEN and/or disability?

■ How meaningful are those systems?

Parry et al. (2010) note that: 'Using children's views should be seen as integral to all levels of providing support: planning; delivery; decision making; and evaluation' (Parry et al., 2010: 4).

■ How are pupils views heard and listened to to inform those individual elements of:

– planning
– delivery
– decision making
– evaluation

in your own school context?

Over recent years, many schools have developed a range of systems and processes for involving pupils. At a basic level, this usually involves imparting information, for example, about targets that have been set, to the pupil; or the setting up of a School Council.

Schools need, however, to critically review and evaluate the actual impact and effectiveness of existing systems to engage with and involve pupils with SEN and/or disabilities in a range of meaningful decision-making processes. The ESRC (2001) notion of a 'ladder of participation' explored in Durrant and Holden (2006) is interesting to utilise when reconsidering practices. The 'ladder of participation' has as its first stage the use of pupil questionnaires, which is seen to only enable pupils to be a 'respondent to an imposed agenda' (Durrant and Holden, 2006: 93), while, moving through the stages of participation, opportunities for pupils to participate with teachers in decision making are provided, leading to pupils having an 'active role in enquiry and decision making themselves . . . setting agendas, planning interventions and evaluating impact' (Durrant and Holden, 2006: 92).

In order to move practices forward, there needs to be embedded understanding, by all staff, pupils and parents of the benefits of engaging pupils in decision-making processes. Research therefore identifies that:

- Pupils have a unique understanding of issues impacting on their learning, and are therefore able to offer unique insights into what will work.
- 'Pupil solutions are often practical and simple and the impact of them would appear to enable pupils to have greater access to learning' (Bradbury *et al.*, 2010: 207).
- Pupil progress and learning was improved when pupils were given the opportunity to engage in the decision-making process (OFSTED, 2010).
- Often, pupils prefer low key support which does not make them feel different to their peers (OFSTED, 2010).
- The ways to engage pupils also need to be meaningful, and to respond appropriately to the actual needs of the pupils involved.

Reflective activity 9.2

- How can this be achieved?
- How can decision-making processes be developed to enable pupils to take an active part?
- What are the barriers?
- What are the opportunities?
- What impact will this have on pupil engagement, participation and outcomes?

Bradbury *et al.* (2010) identify a number of key considerations that staff need to be aware of when reviewing ways to encourage pupils to take an active part in decision-making processes:

- need to establish communication systems that will be meaningful and appropriate for the pupil;
- it needs to be acknowledged that 'difficult to express ideas cannot be rushed and sensitive advocacy may be needed to help difficult to raise issues to be raised';
- adults need to devote time to putting aside their 'personal agendas', to ensure that the voice of the pupil is allowed and enabled to be heard.

However, it is also noted that:

- if the child is able to offer their view, there needs to be a careful consideration of the weight this view should be given. Children's views may not be stable over time and their priorities may not always be in their best interests.

(Bradbury *et al.*, 2010: 209)

Reflective activity 9.3

■ How can the tensions be addressed and understood within the school context?

■ What balance can be struck between giving pupils enough opportunity to engage actively in decision-making processes, while ensuring that this engagement does not impact negatively on what would be the most appropriate outcomes for the pupil?

PARENTAL EXPERIENCES OF THE CURRENT SEN SYSTEM

Currently, parents note that: 'the system is bureaucratic, bewildering and adversarial and that it does not sufficiently reflect the needs of their child and family life' (DfE, 2011: 4). This negative image of parental experience is also highlighted within the OFSTED Review:

> Many parents and carers felt that an adversarial approach was often established from the beginning of the assessment of special educational needs. Parents and carers felt the need to argue to have their child's needs formally recognised in order to gain the resources or support required.
>
> (OFSTED, 2010: 68)

There is clearly much work to be done on reconsidering and developing systems that meet the needs of parents supporting children with SEN and/or disabilities:

Reflective activity 9.4

Think about recent experiences that you have had working with parents of pupils with SEN and/or disabilities. This may be in supporting parents to understand the support available within the school setting, or it may be supporting the parents during larger multi-agency meetings, supporting parents to navigate the existing statementing process.

Perhaps you are the parent of a pupil with SEN and/or disabilities, or have friends or family who are parents of a pupil with SEN and/or disabilities. Consider your/their experiences of the existing systems:

■ In what ways may parents feel that the SEN system is bureaucratic?
■ Would you agree with this?
■ In what ways may parents feel that the SEN system is bewildering?
■ Would you agree with this?
■ In what ways may parents feel that the SEN system is adversarial?
■ Would you agree with this?
■ Having considered the existing systems in place and identified practices that may seem bureaucratic, bewildering or adversarial for the parent, how could you change the practices or overcome the barriers?

Improving parental confidence is readily achievable through good communication, shared information and a change of approach. It is not overly demanding of expertise or resources and the mutual respect that develops can transform relationships between authorities and parents.

(Lamb, 2009: 3)

However, a number of key areas in the system which do not work effectively for the child and the family have been identified:

■ children's support needs [are] identified late;
■ families are made to put up with a culture of low expectations about what their child can achieve at school;
■ parents don't have good information about what they can expect and have limited choices about the best schools and care for their child;
■ families are forced to negotiate each bit of their support separately.

(DfE, 2011: 4)

Please now see Reflective activity 9.5.

Emerging government policy has a clear focus on the centrality of parents and families within the SEN system. It suggests that changes to the existing SEN system need

---

Reflective activity 9.5

Consider the systems and practices that you currently have in place in relation to each of the identified criticisms of the existing system:

■ What do you do already to address the concerns that have been raised?
■ What more could you do?
■ How? Who would need to be involved?
■ In your experience, either of supporting parents, or as a parent of a pupil with SEN yourself, are there any other areas of concern that should be addressed?
■ How could you work towards achieving the principles identified by Lamb (2009)?
■ What systems would support a change or development in practice?

Use the table on p. 150 as a planning grid to start to identify the answers to these questions. Use the blank rows to work with colleagues to identify any other areas of concern that need to be addressed in relation to working with parents in your particular school setting.

One of the SENCO learning outcomes from the National Award for SEN Coordination is to 'help staff to achieve constructive working relationships with pupils with SEN and their parents/carers' (TDA, 2009).

■ How is this achieved?

Area of concern for parents:	Current practices to overcome this:	What more needs to be done?	How can this be achieved?	Who will be involved?
Child's support needs are identified late				
Culture of low expectations about what their child can achieve at school				
Lack of clear information about what to expect and limited choices about best schools and care for their child				
Forced to negotiate each bit of support for their child separately				

to be made to more fully position processes and systems around the needs of the family. It identifies that 'the system to support children and young people who are disabled or who have SEN often works against the wishes of families' (DfE, 2011: 4), and emphasises the need to reposition 'parents at the heart of any discussions and decisions about their child' (DfE, 2011: 42).

This may be a challenge for some practitioners and may perhaps undermine the professional identity that some practitioners have constructed around their role as the 'expert' working in schools. What is required therefore is an approach that emphasises the coming together and shared nature of learning and expertise. Both the teacher and the parent will have expert, individual knowledge of the pupil/child, and when effective discussions are developed to utilise and share this, more meaningful understanding of the range of needs or difficulties that the child may experience is achieved. In particular, collaborative and empathetic approaches will be improved if the practitioner takes time to consider the experience of having a child with SEN and/or disability from the perspective of the parent. Thus, the impact on parents of pupils with SEN and/or disability, who may feel anger, denial, frustration, resentment, as well as parental love for their child needs to be acknowledged: 'When children are identified as being disabled [or of having SEN]. . . . Parents can feel overwhelmed. They may be coming to terms with a future very different from the one they had imagined, and can encounter an unfamiliar and seemingly complicated system' (DfE, 2011: 42).

Practitioners therefore need to understand and respect this in their interactions and relationships with parents of pupils with SEN.

Reflective activity 9.6

■ How is this developed in your own school context?
■ How are all staff supported to understand the individual perspectives and experiences, including the emotional experience of having children with SEN and/or disabilities?
■ Could the sharing of understanding and experiences be further developed within the school context?

KEY PRINCIPLES OF EFFECTIVE COMMUNICATION

We have heard a clear message: parents need to be listened to more and the system needs to be more ambitious for their children.

(Lamb, 2009: 1)

Please now see Reflective activity 9.7.

Drawing on research into the experience of parents engaging with the SEN system (House of Commons, 2006; Lamb, 2009; OFSTED, 2010; DfE, 2011), the following key principles for developing effective communication systems with parents need to be highlighted and considered within the context of the individual school:

Reflective activity 9.7

■ What would you identify as the key principles for effective communication?
■ How are these embedded within approaches that are developed within your own school setting?
■ What aspects still need to be developed?
■ What would be the impact of those changes?
■ How could they be achieved?

■ open communication channels;
■ honesty;
■ listening to the parents: not just talking to/at them;
■ taking time to learn about and understand the issues from the parent's perspective: which may be different to the perspective and understandings gained within the school context;
■ collaboration and willingness to share the decision-making process;
■ commitment to simplifying systems by reducing the amount of inaccessible jargon used during communications;
■ providing support and approaches that reflect the parent or families individual circumstances;
■ valuing the expertise that the parent can bring, acknowledging that 'parents know their children best' (DfE, 2011);
■ developing systems that empower parents to be able to become more involved and active within decision-making processes;
■ trust between practitioner and parent.

Communication is not a one-way system: it is not just about practitioners and professionals talking to/at parents. Effective communication involves practitioners and professionals investing in time to create opportunities for parents to be listened to. It is therefore essential to develop a 'culture that values listening to parents [with recognition that] everyone working with parents of disabled children and children with SEN needs to be prepared to be part of that culture' (Lamb, 2009: 32).

Effective communication systems also need to be individually created and developed to ensure that they actually do meet the needs of the parents involved. This is an important issue to consider: the same communication system may not work for all parents. Some may prefer an informal approach, whereas others may prefer a more formalised arrangement where they have definite dates and times for formal reviews and discussions about their child's progress.

WAYS TO IMPROVE SYSTEMS FOR INVOLVING PARENTS

Before describing some practical strategies that may be utilised to support the development of more effective partnership working and communication between parents, it is important to highlight two central principles that underpin the approach to be taken:

1   There is a need to move discussions with parents away from being centred on provision and placement, into more meaningful discussions about outcomes, including shared expectations for realistic outcomes for the pupil. Therefore, we need to move away from a culture of practice where there remains:

> little focus on outcomes for children. Rather the focus was on the type and amount of provision and often on agreeing a number of hours of support from a learning support assistant. What was apparent was that few of the parents the Inquiry met seemed to have been encouraged to have a discussion about the outcomes they expected, or aspired to, for their child or how best these outcomes might be achieved.
>
> (Lamb, 2009: 20)

2   There is a need for a clear shared understanding across all staff and parents of the benefits of partnership working, with practices built on an embedded culture of respect and valuing the expertise and specific individual knowledge that the parent may bring of their child's individual needs.

Reflective activity 9.8

■   How are these principles currently embedded in the culture of understanding and practice within your school?

■   What type of outcomes do parents want?

■   How do you know?

■   How relevant are those outcomes?

■   How can school and parents work together to achieve these outcomes for the child?

■   How will a shift in focus away from provision and placement, and onto outcomes improve practices for the pupil?

■   How can a shared understanding of the need for effective partnership working be embedded across the school?

Mitchell (2008) draws on DoE (1988) five levels of parental involvement:

Level 1   Being informed. At this most basic level, the school informs parents about its programmes and in turn, is asked for information.

Level 2   Taking part in activities. At this level, parents are involved in activities, but to a limited extent.

Level 3   Dialogue and exchange of views. Here, parents are invited to examine school or classroom goals and needs.

Level 4   Taking part in decision making. At this level, parents are asked about their views when decisions affecting their child are being made.

Level 5   Having responsibility to act. This is the highest level, with parents making decisions in partnership with the school and being involved in both planning and evaluating parts of the school programme.

(Mitchell, 2008: 70)

This is a helpful model to use to reflect on the practical suggestions for improving communication and partnership working with parents set out below.

To aid and support effective communication between parents and school practitioners, we need to consider ways that information is presented for parents, to ensure that it is the most useful and helpful in supporting parents to make informed choices and decisions.

The DfE (2011) note that findings from the Council for Disabled Children have identified four key areas of information that parents would find helpful for schools to focus on:

■ The school's statutory responsibilities.
■ The school's approach to SEN.
■ How this approach was consulted on.
■ The provision normally available in the school for children with SEN.

(DfE, 2011: 46)

Reflective activity 9.9

■ What information do you currently have available for parents?
■ Does it cover the four key areas identified above?
■ Is there any further information that is needed to add?
■ How could you do this?
■ Are there ways that you could involve parents of pupils with SEN in decision making about the range and format of information that would be useful for parents?
■ How do you know about what information parents would find useful?
■ Have you/can you find out from parents what information would be useful to them, and ways that it could be usefully presented?
■ How can you differentiate the presentation of information so that it is fully available and accessible to all: consider presenting information in different languages, in accessible language (avoiding jargon and complex terminology), through emails or texts rather than just through written letters?

Parents need to have more information about what is available, and the potential impact of different options for their child. As the DfE (2011) report, currently:

> Some parents report that they have little choice in reality because they are not clear about their options, because their local mainstream schools are not able to offer appropriate provision for their child, or because there is a shortage of special school places locally.

(DfE, 2011: 51)

More and better information presented to parents in accessible and meaningful ways will therefore improve choice for parents. This is particularly significant within the current context, with a focus on empowering parents, and providing them with real choice about key issues, including the type of school and provision that their child receives. Within the context of Free Schools, Academies and Special Academies, parents therefore need to have access to meaningful information about the choices that are available to them, how to access different provisions, and the impact and implications of their choice for improved outcomes for their child.

Once the parent has chosen the school that is appropriate for their child, a further range of information needs to be accessibly presented and available to further empower parents to understand the provision and support that is available for their child. In this, there is an acknowledgement, particularly from Lamb (2009) that schools should ensure that information about SEN and/or disabilities is readily accessible to all. In the context within which we currently operate, where around 20–21 per cent of the school population have SEN and/or disabilities, we therefore need an approach to ensuring that information about SEN is put in the mainstream, rather than sidelined. Thus, 'where SEN and disability information can be provided in a more mainstream and more public place, it should be' (Lamb, 2009: 43).

It is also important to consider ways to make the information more accessible, in terms of the presentation and language/terminology used, to help parents to easily and clearly make sense of the confusing system that currently is the SEN system.

Reflective activity 9.10

■ Where is information about SEN and/or disabilities presented?
■ Is there information available to all, for example, in the school reception or office area?
■ How is information updated and shared with all parents, to ensure that there is understanding that SEN is not a marginal issue?

A number of key issues are central in terms of how and what type of information schools should present for parents:

1   Be aware that parents' 'information needs change over time' (Lamb, 2009: 42). This will therefore include key information about what SEN is, and what the school does once a child is identified with SEN initially, to other information about different services or transition at other times.
2   Information needs to be clearly accessible and available.
3   Information needs to be clearly written.
4   Parents must be informed if their child has been identified as having SEN. At this point, 'they need to know what this means, what they can expect the school to do, what their statutory rights are. They need to know how to complain if things go wrong. They should know what outcomes the school seeks to achieve for disabled children and children with SEN' (Lamb, 2009: 44).
5   There needs to be a school SEN policy, which is reviewed yearly and updated on a three-yearly cycle. Ways to share this in an accessible way, for example, through a shortened parent leaflet, or a link on the school website to make it easily accessible for all parents need to be considered. The information that parents will need from the school SEN policy will include:

- information about the school's policies for the identification, assessment and provision for all pupils with special educational needs;
- the name of the person parents can contact for more information;
- information about outcomes for children with special educational needs;
- how parents can complain about the school's SEN policy or practice;
- information about the local authority's SEN policy and where that is published;
- information about parents' statutory rights.

(Lamb, 2009: 43)

THE STRUCTURED CONVERSATION

In addition to making information available to parents to support them and empower them to become more aware of the SEN system, and ways that they can access relevant support for their child, either in school or from different services, it is also important to consider the need for effective and meaningful face-to-face meetings.

It is, therefore, common practice for schools to meet with parents during formal parent–teacher consultations at different times of the year. It may also be common practice for the SENCO to arrange to meet more regularly to update parents on information about targets and the progress that their child has made, or the support that they may be receiving. For parents of pupils with a statement of SEN, these meetings are then formalised through the Annual Review meeting, which reviews progress in relation to what has been set out in the Statement.

While meetings with parents are therefore commonplace, there is often a focus on teachers and professionals imparting information to the parent: talking at the parent about what targets they have decided on for the child, and what provision they will offer.

There is therefore a need to reconsider the power relationships and the principles of effective communication to develop and embed an approach to communicating effectively with parents, which enables a two-way conversation, and a sharing of expertise, experiences and understandings.

A key component of this new approach is the need to value what the parents say, and for teachers and professionals to develop 'active listening' skills in order to really listen to and respect the unique insights that the parent can bring.

Understanding of the need for this type of approach to communication with parents has become a key component of the *Achievement for All* approach, which has, as one of its three aims, to 'improve parental engagement in their child's education.'

This is achieved through one of the three strands focusing on the introduction and implementation of the structured conversation with parents.

The structured conversation builds on the principles of effective communication outlined previously, with a focus on the 'use of a clear framework for developing an open, ongoing dialogue with parents about their child's learning' (National College, 2010b: 17). It is intended to 'support the greater engagement of parents by enabling them to make their contributions heard and understood by teachers and the wider school' (DCSF, 2009: 4).

Achievement for All therefore sets out the purposes of the structured conversation, which are to:

- Establish an effective relationships between parents and the key teacher.
- Allow the parent an opportunity to share their concerns and, together with the teacher, agree their aspirations for their child.
- Set clear goals and targets for learning and improvement in wider outcomes.
- Determine activities that will contribute to the achievement of those targets.
- Identify the responsibilities of the parent, the pupil and the school.
- Agree the date and time of the next meeting.
- Clarify the most effective means of communication between meetings.

(DCSF, 2009: 4)

This, therefore, clearly sets out a very different purpose to the meeting than typical parent–teacher; parent–SENCO or professional meetings, where the parent is placed in the position of having to listen to the 'expertise' of others. Instead, the structured conversation aims to enable parents to become equal partners in the conversation, jointly agreeing priorities for action, which include the setting of realistic outcomes and aspirations for progress.

In this way:

the conversation is intended to be a mechanism that, once established, will allow teacher and parent to build on their understanding, share strategies, knowledge about the child, and knowledge about the curriculum and how to progress through it. In other words, to become genuinely collaborative in supporting the child's achievement.

(DCSF, 2009: 6)

Reflective activity 9.11

- How could this be achieved in your school setting?
- How would you need to introduce this approach to parents to ensure that they fully understand and engage with the process?
- How will you individualise the ways that you set this up to respond to the differing communication needs of different parents – including offering the meetings at different times of the day, in different settings, including childcare for younger children to enable parents quality time to engage in the discussions?
- Who would participate in the structured conversation? Would it be the SENCO, or the teacher?
- What training would staff require in order to be able to engage in this different approach effectively and fully?
- What impact may this different approach have:

    - On parental engagement?
    - On pupil outcomes?
    - On staff understanding?

PERSONAL BUDGETS

Within the new policy context there is a key focus on supporting and empowering parents so that they are enabled to become active participants in decision making, able to make informed choices, relating to aspects of their own child's education and provision. This has included (as previously discussed) having accessible information in order to enable parents to make informed choices about the type of school that would be best for their child, and what type of support and provision to expect from different settings.

Embedded within current DfE proposals (2011) there is also the new notion of giving individual personal budgets to parents so that 'they can manage the services they receive. . . . [and to] give parents greater choice and control over the support that their families receive' (DfE, 2011: 47).

While currently there is little actual detail about how this will be managed, with a number of pilots due to be implemented and evaluated over the coming years, this is a significant development, and one that both parents and school staff need to be aware of. Thus, by 2014, for those parents of pupils with the new Education, Health and Care Plan, there is the proposal that they will have the option of receiving a personal budget, which will enable the parents themselves to have a 'much greater say in the way their child is supported and give them a clear role in designing a personalised package of support for their child and family' (DfE, 2011: 47).

The aim is (subject to piloting over the coming years) that this will include funding for education and health support and services as well as funding for respite care.

Such a system is a radical move away from the existing system, where parents have little say, and no access to direct funding, to support decision making and planning about the type of support that is required for their child. While the principles behind this approach, around empowerment and valuing the unique expertise that the parents have of their child are to be welcomed, this is a problematic proposal, which may cause tensions that impact on the provision of the most effective support for the individual pupil.

This will therefore require high levels of support so that both parents and professionals understand how this new system will work, and to ensure that all pupils benefit as a result. It is unclear about how a new system where funding is given to parents will be monitored to ensure that all parents are clear about what is available, what would be most helpful and effective for their child, and how to get it. There may be the possibility that some pupils, where parents are not as able or willing to work proactively with services to secure the best support for their child, may be disadvantaged by an approach that will become increasingly dependent on their parent. While for some parents, who have the time, skills and inclination to work proactively to secure the best possible provision and support for their child, this may be a very positive development. But, what about the experience of the pupil who does not have parents who have the time, skills or inclination to engage with the system?

For many parents, we also need to acknowledge the difficulties that they already face on a day-to-day basis battling with the SEN system, and responding on a full-time basis to the complex needs of their child, which can impact significantly on home and family life. For some parents, will the option of the personal budget therefore add another layer of stress to already complicated lives?

At this time, as proposals about the new personal budget are starting to emerge, and pilots are being implemented and evaluated, it is therefore essential that schools immediately start to reconsider the nature and purpose of meetings with parents. Schools therefore need to consider ways that they can start to engage more effectively with parents and families now, in decision-making processes about what type of support is available and how to effectively access it. Parents will need to become more active partners in the decision-making process and relationship between school and home, and this should be seen as a gradual process of development, rather than left until 2014 to suddenly be implemented. This could therefore provide an exciting opportunity for considering new ways to engage meaningfully with parents from now, and it will be interesting to monitor and evaluate the impact of different systems that emerge and develop over the next few years.

ACTION PLANNING

Identify three key points for individual reflection:

1 _____

2 _____

3 _____

Start to consider key issues to be followed up as points of action that have arisen from your reading of this chapter.

This may include:

■ Considering new ways to engage pupils in decision making processes in order to explore and utilise the unique insights that they can bring about their own learning and support needs.

■ Working with others in the school to consider the principles of effective communication, and ways that these are already evidenced in the school, and ways to improve/develop them.

■ Reviewing existing systems for sharing information with parents: is it freely accessible, and placed in the mainstream, rather than marginalised?

■ Setting up parent groups to review the type of information that parents actually require, and how they would like it presented in order to more fully meet their needs, and understand their information requirements from their perspective.

■ Developing and embedding the structured conversation as an approach to effective and meaningful communication with parents.

■ Working with parents to keep up to date about proposals for the new 'personal budget' and start to develop the focus of meetings so that staff and parents become more skilled and able to share decision-making processes relating to how provision and support is prioritised.

■ Others.

ACTION PLANNING TO ENABLE IMPACT

Use the format provided on p. 160 to develop a clear Action Plan for future development of practices for either yourself, or for the school. Make sure that you do not identify too many different actions all at once, have a clear outcome for what you want to achieve in mind, and that you clearly identify the different steps to take to achieve the outcome.

WORKING EFFECTIVELY WITH PUPILS WITH SEN AND/OR DISABILITIES AND THEIR PARENTS: ACTION PLANNING TO ENABLE IMPACT:

Which key issues from the chapter do you want to focus on/ change/develop?	How will you effect this change or development (identify a number of small action steps to achieve your overall goal)?	Who else will need to be involved? How?	What will the outcome be (include timescales)?	Impact:

MOVING FORWARD IN AN ERA OF CHANGE

THIS CHAPTER:

- re-examines the case for change;
- considers the need to celebrate diversity and carefully reflect on conceptualisations of children;
- highlights the importance of an evidence-based practice and an critical inquiry based approach to school development.

THE CASE FOR CHANGE

We are in an exciting era of change: politically, socially and within the education system. It is argued that 'education is a political activity and educational change is a political process' (Reid, 2010: 133). At this current time, we may certainly see it as such: there are many changes and developments in educational policy that are a direct reflection of the new Conservative-led coalition government. However, education cannot and should not just be a political process. Education needs to reflect a values-based approach to working towards an equitable inclusive society for all. In order to achieve this, there is a need for critical, reflective and challenging practitioners who are empowered to take current political policy and interpret it in relation to the impact it will have for the pupils with whom they are working.

At this point in time, as new policy directions emerge, including:

- reducing bureaucracy;
- growth of Academies and Free Schools to increase innovative and individualised approaches to meeting the needs of pupils;
- review of SEN systems;
- increased focus on collaboration between schools, and across different services;
- focus on empowering parents.

We have a 'unique opportunity' to really change practices in order to meet the changing needs of pupils and their families in the twenty-first century.

Yet, change is not easy: it is often messy, problematic, and can cause tensions – unless enough time and effort is put into ensuring that all involved understand the change that is necessary, ways to achieve it and, most importantly, the guiding principles behind the need for change and what we want to achieve.

Throughout the book, the 'Case for Change' has been emphasised. There is a desperate need to critically review and evaluate existing systems and to develop ways to make them more focused on meeting the needs of our most vulnerable pupils and families. How far we accept the challenge, and how radically we do reform the existing systems will be determined, not in the next few months, but over a much longer period. Change takes time to embed, and throughout the changes that we will see over the coming years, there is therefore a need for professionals to take a reflective and values-based approach to understanding and implementing the changes.

As the book has highlighted, the existing SEN and education systems have not fully and effectively addressed the range of barriers to learning and participation experienced by pupils with SEN and/or disability. Pupils with SEN and/or disability are therefore increasingly disadvantaged through inappropriate and inconsistent identification of need, provision and support. The gap between the attainment of pupils with SEN and/or disabilities and their peers is not closing (DCSF, 2010a; DfE, 2011) and pupils with SEN and/or disabilities have increased chances of being permanently excluded from the education system.

In the twenty-first century such facts should not be accepted: they need to be critically challenged and questioned by reflective practitioners; and, as we move into this era of change as a result of new government policy priorities, we need to be strong and brave in ensuring that all the changes that are made are done for the right reasons – with a clear focus on the underlying principles and values for an inclusive and equitable education system and society.

This book has argued and demonstrated throughout that this will not be achieved just through a consideration of how to 'do' new policy directives and education strategies. Rather, it will be achieved through the development of practices that encourage and emphasise criticality, reflection and enquiry, and support a reconnection with the values and principles underpinning approaches and assumptions deeply embedded within existing systems. Meaningful change will therefore only occur when:

> those whose practice is the focus of change are involved in the process of challenging and rethinking the assumptions and theories on which their practice is based. Unless this happens, imposed change in the form of a new 'product' is simply filtered through the lens of established beliefs and practices, and is colonised by that practice. The same things are done but with new labels.
>
> (Reid, 2010: 136)

At this crucial time, we cannot allow this to happen: we must challenge existing practices and support the development of the radical overhaul and reform of existing systems and processes that is required.

The impact-focused approach to development of practice (introduced in Chapter 1 and used to structure the chapters throughout the book), has presented one way to achieve the criticality and reflection required of practitioners in a time of change.

By embedding the approach into whole school approaches to the development of practice, profound understanding and impact can be achieved. The model is based on shared understanding of values and principles, collaborative questioning of existing practices and assumptions impacting on the experiences provided for, and expectations of pupils within the school context, and collective responsibility and ownership of change. The cycle of Review/Reflect/Action/Impact is a simple one – but again supports the development of significant change: change that is meaningful, as a result of the process of reviewing existing practices to understand the issues more clearly, and reflection to collectively create new knowledge of what can and should be achieved to better support the needs of pupils within the school setting. By moving into an approach based on these principles, and away from an approach that is solely based on the Action part of the cycle (where new initiatives are simply introduced and implemented without the critical review of why the change is needed and the impact of the change) deeper change will be possible.

This chapter further supports the reader to engage positively with the notion of change, by providing some further key principles that will effectively support the development of a values-based approach to school development. These include:

- celebrating diversity: conceptualising children;
- embedding evidence-based practice;
- understanding inclusive leadership.

CELEBRATING DIVERSITY: CONCEPTUALISING CHILDREN

Many of the recent strategies and practices embedded in schools have had the effect of emphasising difference: pupils are labelled as having 'SEN' (a term that is not clearly defined and understood as the previous discussions have highlighted). Often pupils have been put into withdrawn intervention groups in order to address their perceived difficulties, and this has the effect of emphasising and highlighting differences between pupils.

As we move into the twenty-first century a different approach is needed: one where difference and diversity is not seen as a problem to be dealt with, and instead an understanding of the individuality and individual strengths of pupils is emphasised and encouraged.

As Barth (1990: cited in Loreman *et al.*, 2010) states:

Differences hold great opportunities for learning. Differences offer a free and abundant renewable resource. I would like to see the compulsion for eliminating differences replaced by an equally compelling focus on making use of these to improve schools. What is important about people and about schools is what is different, not what is the same.

(Barth, 1990: 514–515: cited in Loreman *et al.*, 2010: xv)

For me, this is a key principle underpinning any new approach to reform and development within the education system. At a time where prescription from government is promised to reduce (with the closing of the National Strategies and the review of the National Curriculum to emphasise the skills to be learned rather than how to teach) it is hoped that practitioners will feel able to focus more on nurturing individuality and celebrating and exploring individual learning styles.

Within this development of practice it will, however, be important to critically reflect and consider ways that children are talked about. This is particularly important in the light of the move towards a single school-based category of SEN. As discussed in Chapter 7, while there are positive benefits from such a move, as reflective practitioners we will need to guard against the possibility that this will encourage a move back to a medical model approach to viewing needs: where pupils with SEN are seen in terms of their 'SEN', and the differences between them and peers with 'no SEN' are emphasised.

Loreman *et al.* (2010) therefore discuss the need to move away from a medical model of special education where:

▓ The evidence gathered typically involves assessments [which] take place outside of the context in which the learning takes place.
▓ Professionals suggest alternative solutions.
▓ The solutions may be a programme that is delivered separately from the rest of the student's peers.
▓ The programme is usually not consistent with curriculum models being employed within the school and are therefore unlikely to transfer easily to classrooms and integrate with existing school programmes.

(Loreman *et al.*, 2010: 25)

To a more inclusive model where there is:

▓ understanding that the difficulty is not the child, rather it is the barriers impacting on the child;
▓ a focus on removing barriers to learning and participation;
▓ individualised approaches;
▓ the pupil is involved in discussions and review of progress and provision.

When we are reconsidering ways that systems need to change, we therefore need to retain a clear focus on the pupil as a unique individual, and embed practices that enable celebration of the diversity of pupil experiences, skills, strengths and learning needs, rather than perpetuating a model of practice that expects all pupils to learn, engage and participate in the same ways to uniform learning experiences.

EMBEDDING EVIDENCE-BASED PRACTICE

In a time of change, it is essential that processes and approaches to analysing and reflecting on the impact of change are embedded at all levels of the system: from national, governmental research, to independent research, to local research and evidence, to school-based research and evidence. A rigorous approach to and understanding of key principles of evidence-based practice is therefore essential in order to provide practitioners with the skills and tools to meaningfully reflect on the impact of changes, particularly on the most vulnerable pupils and their families.

This will therefore involve meaningful engagement with research and information about 'what works' provided from a range of sources, and critically reflected on in terms of how it will impact on and fit in with existing practices and systems within the school context. This critical review and reflection about the relevance and potential effective-ness of 'what works' on the individual school context is essential, to ensure approaches are embedded that work for the pupils and staff involved, rather than perpetuating practices that developed through the first decade of the twenty-first century, where the school was overwhelmed with new initiative (or strategy) after new initiative, which were duly implemented without time for meaningful consideration of the impact that they may have.

In this time of change, where there will be less direct prescription from central government about exactly what and how to teach, and, in the current economic climate where there will be an increased focus on schools needing to 'get more and better for less', a critical approach to evidence-based practice: ensuring that there is a clear evidence base that a system or approach works before implementing it; and then critically evaluating outcomes once it has been implemented will be essential. It is therefore accepted that the recent 'dominant model of educational change where educators are excluded from the politics of the political process and expected to simply implement policy and programmes developed by others, is no longer tenable' (Reid, 2010: 137).

The development of collaborative practices that encourage practitioners to work together to review and critically reflect on practices in need of change are therefore essential. Loreman *et al.* (2010) have therefore developed the notion of the 'Professional Learning Community' – which links with the discussions in Chapter 1 about communities of practice. The key characteristics of an effective professional learning community are detailed below, and again reflect the central principles underpinning the approach to school development supported throughout the book.

Characteristics of an effective Professional Learning Community:

- Shared values and vision are understood by all members.
- Focus is on effective teaching for student learning and enquiry.
- High expectations for all students.
- Shared responsibility for student learning.
- Culture of openness, trust and respect.
- Leadership is distributed across the school.
- Contributions are made by support professionals, parents and others from the wider school community.
- Student voices are heard and their input is valued.
- Inquiry is valued and evidence is used to inform and improve teaching and learning.
- Risk-taking, innovation and professional learning are promoted.
- Organisational structures and resources are used to support collaboration.
- Sharing critical reflections and practices is common.

(Loreman *et al.*, 2010: 89)

Thus there will be the need to develop a 'culture of inquiry where systematic investigation and critical reflection are the norm and where everyone participates: teachers, students, parents and other professionals' (Loreman *et al.*, 2010: 88).

This focus on the development of skills to enable that 'culture of inquiry' is therefore central, with Reid (2010) noting that inquiry is 'not a project or the latest fad. It is a way of professional being' (Reid, 2010: 137).

The process of evidence-based practice, involving the principles of reflection, enquiry and criticality is a complex process, including two important dimensions:

> The first – a conceptual dimension – involves educators analysing the reasons for actions taken, such as examining the theory behind their practice and exploring alternatives. And the second – a critical dimension – involves justifying what is done in relation to the moral, ethical and socio-political issues associated with practice and looking at the external forces and broader social conditions that frame it, in order to gain greater understanding.
>
> (Reid, 2010: 138)

Evidence-based practice can be effectively achieved in a number of different ways within the school context, including:

■ collective engagement in wider research and evidence: provided by the DfE, OFSTED, professional bodies or independent organisations – to include critical reflection about the findings and the relevance of those for the development of practice within the particular school setting;

■ collaboration between schools and with other professionals: talking to other schools and professionals about interventions/approaches that they have implemented and how it has worked for them, before implementing it within your own school context;

■ embedding a rigorous evidence-based approach to monitoring, reviewing and evaluating the impact and outcomes of interventions and approaches set up within the school context;

■ school-based action research (Ekins, 2010c);

■ ongoing review and reflection about the school context.

To support these processes of evidence-based practice and review and reflection about existing systems it may also be useful to consider ways to link with professionals external to the school itself, in order to benefit from an objective approach to reviewing and evaluating practices. Recently this role, to an extent, has been fulfilled by the School Improvement Partner. However, with the role of School Improvement Partner now ceasing, and a new focus on encouraging schools to set up their own systems and agenda for school development and review, schools can now consider different and innovative ways to engage professionals working externally to the school in review and evaluation processes to support critical reflection, which challenges embedded practices and assumptions and supports an ongoing dialogue about inclusive school development.

The 'Prompts for SIPs and their Schools' checklist (adapted from DfE guidance, 2010: Appendix 6) may provide a useful starting point for identifying key questions to support the review and reflection process.

The recently revised Index for Inclusion (Booth and Ainscow, 2011) also provides a detailed resource to enable review and evaluation of a wide range of issues impacting on the school. Building on the significant impact of the original edition, the range of dimensions, indicators and questions have been reviewed, developed and updated to reflect even more fully the context of school development in the twenty-first century. The resource therefore provides a tool that can easily be used to support whole school development, with the questions able to stimulate and provoke thinking and reflection about ways in which practices are embedded and used within the school context, and ways that they can be developed. Thus, it is understood and acknowledged that 'if efforts at inclusion are to be sustained then they will need to be integrated into an ordinary approach to school development' (Booth and Ainscow, 2011).

The approach therefore mirrors the central principles running throughout this book: with an understanding of the need to move inclusion and meeting the needs of pupils with SEN and/or disability away from the sideline and into the mainstream. There is also an articulation of how:

> inclusive development can start from a concern to put values into action, a wish to form alliances between principled approaches to development and a concern to minimise barriers and mobilise resources but when we add to these engagement with the indicators and questions of the Index these three approaches are given additional support. [See Figure 10.1 below.]
>
> (Booth and Ainscow, 2011)

These principles are summarised within a diagram that depicts the connections between the three key approaches taken within the Index for Inclusion:

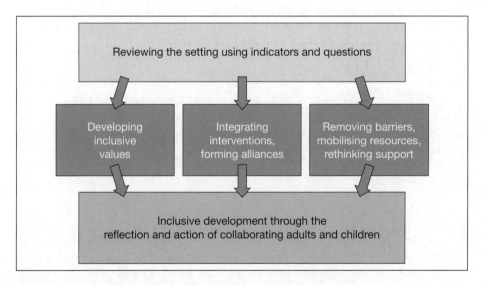

■ **Figure 10.1** The Index for Inclusion (Booth and Ainscow, 2011)

The revised Index for Inclusion continues to embed the importance of close attention and examination of:

■ creating inclusive cultures
■ producing inclusive policies
■ evolving inclusive practices.

but has developed and extended the indicators and questions within each of those key dimensions. Additional ideas for policy development have been included within the 'producing inclusive policies dimension' to include:

■ the school has a participatory development process;
■ the school has an inclusive approach to leadership.

Both of these additions again mirror the principles underpinning the approach taken in this book, and also reflect the emphasis placed through the *Achievement for All* approach on the importance of inclusive leadership (see discussions below).

A further noticeable change, is the addition, within the 'evolving inclusive practices' dimension, of a new section called 'constructing curricula for all' (Booth and Ainscow, 2011).

The approach within the Index is embedded within a 'Framework of Values', with explicit recognition of the importance of values in guiding positive action. Again, this links with the approach developed throughout this book, where action builds on the processes of review and reflection, which enable critical engagement with the values, principles and assumptions underpinning existing practices. There is therefore a need to encourage whole staff groups to consider the values that are underpinning the culture and ethos of the individual school:

■ Are they values about equality, inclusion, creativity, diversity, participation?
■ Or are they values around standards and narrow measures of attainment?
■ How do you know what the values are?
■ How are they explicitly discussed and shared within the staff group, and also with pupils, parents and wider stakeholders in the community?
■ Are the values that are embedded within the school consistent with values that are meaningful within the whole school community?

The *Achievement for All* approach also embeds a whole school approach to inclusive school development. It is therefore clearly acknowledged that to meet the range of aspirations embedded within *Achievement for All*, in terms of improving achievement and progress for all children and young people with SEN and/or disabilities, improving parental engagement and improving wider outcomes requires an approach that implicitly understands that this is:

> not just another task for the SENCO or inclusion manager! School leaders at various levels of leadership and not just headship – will provide the vision, strategic planning, motivation, support, resources, structures and environment for learning that enable staff in schools and other children's services to work with parents and carers to make the very best possible provision for all children and young people.
>
> (National College, 2010b: 3)

The notion of leadership here is important: it is not just about the headteacher, but about shared and 'inclusive leadership', which is built on the key elements of:

■ a shared vision
■ commitment
■ collaboration
■ communication.

As discussed in Chapter 1, these closely reflect the central underpinning principles of the approach to inclusive school development emphasised throughout the book. At this point in the book, as the reader starts to consider ways to practically embed strategies to support inclusive school development within their individual school setting, a range of reflective questions, posed in relation to the development of inclusive leadership within the *Achievement for All* approach is therefore useful. The questions below, while written in relation to the *Achievement for All* approach, closely mirror and reflect a range of questions posed throughout the chapters of this book, and therefore provide a useful resource to review thinking, understanding and practice:

Elements of effective leadership for *Achievement for All*:

A shared vision:

- To what extent is there a shared vision and high expectations for the outcomes for all pupils in your school? How do you know?
- In what ways will the core values in your school underpin the work in each of the three strands of *Achievement for All* (Assessment, tracking and intervention; Structured conversation with parents; Provision for developing wider outcomes)?
- How do children/young people, parents, staff and governors understand and influence those values?
- How do they see those values enacted in the behaviour of leaders and staff in your school?
- What is your vision for the engagement with the school community?
- In what ways will your knowledge of your particular school community influence the work in the three strands?
- How do you ensure that all in your school view each child/family without prejudice and understand individual circumstances?
- How do you value 'pupil voice'? In what ways do children/young people with SEND actively engage in supporting and designing their own learning?
- To what extent is there a shared vision for the engagement of parents and carers in supporting the learning and development of their children? How do you know?
- What does 'SEND' and 'inclusion' mean in your school? Does your school have a common understanding of what makes for effective and inclusive teaching and learning?

(National College, 2010b: 8)

Commitment:

- What evidence of a commitment to the aims of *Achievement for All* is apparent in your school?
- Are expectations of progress high enough across the school? How do you know? Has progression guidance been disseminated to all staff?

---

continued overleaf . . .

▨ What strategies are in place to track children's progress? Is progress good enough? What evidence to you have to support this?

▨ Is there a collective responsibility for the progress of SEND children and young people in your school? How do you know?

▨ In what ways are children with SEND involved in their own learning, target setting and person-centred reviews in your school?

▨ How is the commitment to engaging parents evident in your school?

▨ How do you ensure all staff have the appropriate skills to embed a culture of inclusion in your school?

▨ How high a profile does inclusion have in your school improvement plan?

▨ In what ways are resources appropriately planned to meet the needs of ALL children in school?

(National College, 2010b: 10)

Collaboration:

▨ What evidence is there of effective collaborative leadership within and beyond your school?

▨ How proactive is your school at developing cross-agency partnerships for children and young people identified with SEND? What is the impact of this?

▨ To what extent do you know that your pupils with SEND make an effective transition between classes and between phases and schools?

▨ How do you enable parents to collaborate in their children's learning?

▨ How do you provide parents with up-to-date information about their child's current level of progress and wider achievements in school?

▨ How do you collaborate outside of your school context? Is this external collaboration effective? How do you know?

(National College, 2010b: 12)

Communication:

▨ How do you know there is effective communication between leaders (and between leaders and other staff) in your school? What evidence do you have to support this?

▨ What systems of safeguarding the most vulnerable children does your school have in place? How are these communicated?

▨ How do your communications with parents and carers show that you value the contribution that they can make to support their children's learning? How do you know that the communications are good and work for parents?

▨ What opportunities are provided in your school to set targets with children and young people and with parents/carers? How do you communicate these targets?

▨ In what ways are children and young people involved in your school's decision making processes?

(National College, 2010b: 14)

'Moving to a culture of inquiry will not happen overnight' (Reid, 2010: 142). However, it is hoped that this book has provided deeper understanding of the need for critical reflection and enquiry within a period of change, as well as some practical suggestions and signposts to enable practitioners to engage more effectively with using enquiry to support inclusive school development.

CONCLUDING COMMENTS

As we move through this era of change, there is a need for critical, reflective practitioners who engage fully in asking challenging questions about the values, assumptions and principles underpinning existing and developing practices. Already, we are starting to see the emergence of a new professionalism and professional identity for practitioners, and this is to be welcomed. The DfE (2011) therefore emphasise and recognise the need to enable practitioners (not politicians) to lead the direction of change in our schools. The professional judgement and moral duties of practitioners are therefore acknowledged, recognising that practitioners working in schools will have more understanding of how to best meet the needs of pupils in their particular school context, than policymakers removed from the setting.

Recent legislation has also recently strengthened the status and role of key practitioners (SENCOs) within the school, with a recognition of the pivotal role (DfE, 2011) that they hold in ensuring that the needs of pupils with complex difficulties are fully and effectively met. The requirement for new SENCOs to complete the National Award for SEN Coordination is therefore having the impact of raising the professional status of SENCOs, who are gaining a collective professional identity as a result of their growing knowledge, confidence and skills; and also as a result of increased opportunities to network with other SENCOs through attendance and engagement with the course (Ekins, 2011).

As we embark on this exciting era of change, it is essential that at the heart of our thinking and planning, remains a relentless focus on ensuring positive outcomes (in the broadest sense of the word) for all pupils. Meaningful change, which radically improves systems, processes and outcomes for our most vulnerable pupils and their families is not easy to achieve. It will not be achieved by 'tinkering around the edges' or by simply implementing new initiatives. Instead, it will only be achieved through a rigorous approach to whole school inclusive development, where all changes are embedded within a reflective approach to understanding the values, principles and assumptions underpinning existing practices and the need for change. Meaningful inclusive school development and change therefore requires a collaborative whole school approach. In periods of fast-paced change such as this, it is important for the school to look inwardly to the creation of an agreed culture and ethos (as discussed in Chapter 1, and depicted within Figure 2.1), rather than become fragmented as a result of trying to implement too many new initiatives (Ekins, 2010a).

By doing this, practitioners will lead the development of educational systems that effectively impact on providing improved outcomes for all pupils, including those with SEN and/or disability.

APPENDICES

APPENDIX 1 SUMMARY OF KEY ISSUES IDENTIFIED IN THE DFE (2011) WHITE PAPER 'THE IMPORTANCE OF TEACHING'

Key area of focus	What the coalition government plans to do:	What impact will this have: On the profession/on practice in school/on my own practice/on outcomes for pupils with SEN?
Teaching and leadership	Raise quality of new entrants to the profession: new graduates will need a 2:2 degree to access government funding for initial teacher training; increase in Teach First, and introduction on Teach Next and 'Troops to Teaching'.	
	Reform initial teacher training – with more time spent in the classroom.	
	Develop a network of teaching schools to lead the training and professional development of teachers and headteachers.	
	Sharply reduce the bureaucratic burden on schools.	
	Give schools more freedom to reward good performance and tackle poor performance through more flexible pay structures.	
	Increase the number of local and national leaders of education.	
	Recognise that schools have good pastoral systems and understand the links between educational attainment, safety, physical and mental wellbeing.	
Behaviour	Increase authority of teachers to discipline pupils by strengthening their powers to search pupils, issue same day detentions and use reasonable force where necessary.	

continued overleaf . . . .

	Strengthen headteachers' authority to maintain discipline beyond the school gates.
	Expect headteachers to take a strong stand against bullying.
	Improve and change current exclusion processes and panels: trialling a new approach where schools have new responsibilities for the ongoing education and care of excluded pupils.
	Improve the quality of alternative provision, including through the setting up of Free Schools.
	Ensure that all children being educated in alternative provision get a full-time education.
	Protect teachers from malicious allegations through right to anonymity.
	Focus Ofsted inspections more strongly on behaviour, safety and bullying.
Curriculum, assessment and qualifications	Review the National Curriculum to refocus on core subject knowledge and reduce amount of prescriptive content.
	Ensure that support is available for every school to develop the teaching of systematic synthetic phonics as the best method for teaching reading.
	Review assessment processes: introduce a simple reading test at age 6; review Key Stage 2 testing.
	Introduce the English Baccalaureate.
	Ofqual to ensure that exam standards in this country match the highest standards oversees.
	Reform vocational education so that it supports progression to further and higher education and employment.

Photocopiable resource

■ APPENDIX 1 . . . continued

Key area of focus	What the coalition government plans to do:	What impact will this have: On the profession/on practice in school/on my own practice/on outcomes for pupils with SEN?
	Raise to 17 by 2013 and then 18 by 2015 the age to which all young people are expected to participate in education or training.	
	Obtain an honest view of our national performance by ensuring pupils take part in international tests of literacy, mathematics and science.	
	The new school system Increase freedom and autonomy for all schools, allowing schools to choose for themselves how best to develop.	
	Extend the Academies programme opening it up to all schools.	
	Restoring full freedoms to all Academies, while ensuring a level playing field on admissions particularly in relation to children with SEN.	
	Ensure that the lowest performing schools are considered for conversion to become Academies to effect educational transformation.	
	Increase collaboration through Academy chains, multi-school trusts and federations.	
	Introduce Free Schools.	
	Give local authorities a strong strategic role as champions for parents, families and vulnerable children.	
Accountability	Put more information about a school's performance into the public domain.	

continued overleaf . . .

Place information about expenditure online.

Reform performance tables so that they set out high expectations for progress.

Institute a new measure of how well deprived pupils do and introduce a measure of how young people do when they leave school.

Reform Ofsted inspection so that inspectors spend more time in classrooms and focus on four key areas of performance.

Establish a new 'floor standard' for primary and secondary schools, which sets an escalating minimum expectation for attainment.

Enable more flexible models for school governance, including providing support for governing bodies to benefit from the skills of their local community in holding schools to account.

School Improvement	Make clear that governors, headteachers and teachers have responsibility for improvement: end the requirement for all schools to have a School Improvement Partner and end the current centralised target-setting process.
	Increase the number of national and local leaders of education and develop teaching schools to make sure that every school has access to highly effective professional development support.
	Make it easier for schools to learn from each other through the publication of 'families of schools' data.
	Provide access to evidence of best practice, high quality materials and improvement services that schools can choose to use.
	Free local authorities to provide whatever forms of improvement support they choose.

▉ APPENDIX 1 . . . *continued*

Key area of focus	What the coalition government plans to do:	What impact will this have: On the profession/on practice in school/on my own practice/on outcomes for pupils with SEN?
	Ensure schools below the floor standard receive support, and ensure that those that are seriously failing are transformed through conversion to Academy status.	
	Introduce the new Education Endowment Fund to fund innovative projects to raise attainment of deprive children in underperforming schools.	
	Establish a new collaboration incentive, which financially rewards schools that effectively support weaker schools and demonstrably improve their performance.	
School funding	Introduce the new Pupil Premium that will target resources on the most deprived pupils.	
	Consult on developing and introducing a clear, transparent and fairer national funding formula based on the needs of pupils.	
	Increase the transparency of the current funding system by showing both how much money schools receive and what it is spent on.	
	Devolve the maximum amount of funding to schools, making information and tools available to governors and headteachers to support them in making good spending decisions.	
	End the disparity in funding for 16–18 year olds.	
	Cut bureaucracy from the process of allocating capital funding and securing significantly better value for money.	

APPENDIX 2 'WHEN CHILDREN AND YOUNG PEOPLE WITH SEN LEARN BEST' (BASED ON FINDINGS OF OFSTED, 2010: 47)

Characteristic:	How is this already evidenced within the classroom?	How could it be further developed?
Pupils with SEN looked to the teacher for their main learning and to the support staff for support.		
Assessment was secure, continuous and acted on.		
Teachers planned opportunities for pupils with SEN to collaborate, work things out for themselves and apply what they had learned to different situations.		
Teachers' subject knowledge was good, as was their understanding of pupils' needs and how to help them.		
Lesson structures were clear and familiar but allowed for adaptation and flexibility.		
All aspects of a lesson were well thought out and any adaptations needed were made without fuss to ensure that everyone in class had access.		

continued overleaf . . .

APPENDIX 2 . . . continued

Characteristic:	How is this already evidenced within the classroom?	How could it be further developed?
Teachers presented information in different ways to ensure all pupils with SEN understood.		
Teachers adjusted the pace of the lesson to reflect how children and young people were learning.		
The staff understood clearly the difference between ensuring that children and young people were learning and keeping them occupied.		
Respect for individuals was reflected in high expectations for their achievement.		
The effectiveness of specific types of support was understood and the right support was put in place at the right time.		

▪ What would you identify as key areas to focus on?

▪ Whose support/help could you draw on to help you to develop those areas?

▪ How will you know when you have been successful?

APPENDIX 3 INCLUSIVE TEACHING OBSERVATION CHECKLIST (PRIMARY STRATEGY, 2006)

	Yes/No	Evidence
Has the teacher identified appropriate and differentiated learning objectives for all learners?		
Is there use of multi-sensory teaching approaches (visual, verbal, kinaesthetic)?		
Is there use of interactive strategies, e.g. pupils having cards to hold up or their own whiteboards or coming to the front to take a role?		
Is there use of visual and tangible aids, e.g. real objects, signs or symbols, photographs, computer animations?		
Does the teacher find ways of making abstract concepts concrete, e.g. word problems in mathematics turned into pictures or acted out or modelled with resources?		
Does the teacher use simplified and extended tasks, e.g. short, concrete text used by one group and long, abstract text by another, numbers to 100 by one group or to 20 by another?		
Are tasks made more open or more closed according to pupils' needs?		

continued overleaf . . .

APPENDIX 3 . . . continued

	Yes/No	Evidence
Over time, does the teacher employ a variety of pupil groupings so that pupils are able to draw on each other's strengths and skills?		
Can all pupils see and hear the teacher and any resources in use (e.g. background noise avoided where possible, light source in front of teacher not behind, pupils' seating carefully planned)?		
Is new or difficult vocabulary clarified, written up, displayed, returned to?		
Does the teacher check for understanding of instructions, e.g. by asking a pupil to explain them in their own words?		
Are questions pitched so as to challenge pupils at all levels?		
Is the contribution of all learners valued – is this a secure and supportive learning environment where there is safety to have a go and make mistakes?		
Does the teacher give time and support before responses are required, e.g. personal thinking time, partner talk, persisting with progressively more scaffolding until a pupil can answer correctly?		
Where extra adult support is available for underachieving pupils, is it used in ways that promote independence, protect self-esteem and increase pupils' inclusion within their peer group?		

Does the teacher work directly with underachieving groups as well as with more able groups?				
Are tasks clearly explained or modelled – checks for understanding, task cards or boards as reminders, time available and expected outcomes made clear?				
Are pupils provided with, and regularly reminded of, resources to help them be independent? (e.g. relevant material from whole-class session kept on display, word lists or mats, dictionaries of terms, glossaries, number lines, tables squares.)				
Is scaffolding used (e.g. problem-solving grids, talk and writing frames, clue cards) to support learners?				
Has the teacher made arrangements (buddying, adult support, taping) where necessary to ensure that all children can access written text or instructions?				
Has the teacher planned alternatives to paper-and-pencil tasks, where appropriate?				
Does the teacher make effective use of ICT as an access strategy? (e.g. speech-supported or sign-supported software, on-screen word banks, predictive word processing)				
Is appropriate behaviour noticed and praised or rewarded?				
Are all learners involved in setting their own targets and monitoring their own progress?				

APPENDIX 4 NATIONAL AWARD FOR SEN COORDINATION LEARNING OUTCOMES:

Audit of skills

Date: _____

Name of Student: _____

Type of School (e.g. small/large primary/secondary): _____

Number of years teaching experience: _____

Role(s) within school (eg SENCO/SENCO + CT/SENCO + AHT): _____

Professional context Learning outcome:	Rating and example (if rated 1): 1 = High levels of existing skill/knowledge 4 = No existing knowledge
Statutory and regulatory frameworks and relevant developments at national and local level – training should enable SENCOs to know and understand: – laws and associated guidance on SEN, including the policies and procedures set out in the SEN Code of Practice; their implications for the school, the SENCO and others; and how to put them into practice;	

- laws and associated guidance on disability equality, the actions they require in respect of pupils with disabilities; and how they might best be carried out;

- local interpretations of national guidance;

- relevant guidance on data protection and confidentiality, health and safety;

- the principles and outcomes of *Every Child Matters* and how the school can help pupils with SEN and/or disabilities to achieve those outcomes; and

- the contribution of extended services to improving outcomes for pupils with SEN and/or disabilities.

High incidence SEN and disabilities and how they can affect pupils' participation and learning – training should enable SENCOs to know and understand:

- how children's development can be affected by SEN and/or disabilities and a range of other factors including the physical and social environment in which they are taught;

- causes of under achievement, including those related to SEN and/or disabilities;

- the four areas of need set out in the SEN Code of Practice and the educational implications of these; and

- the high incidence disabilities and the implications of these for teaching and learning and inclusive practice.

Using evidence about learning, teaching and assessment in relation to pupils with SEN to inform practice – training should enable SENCOs to:

- analyse, interpret and evaluate critically, relevant research and inspection evidence about teaching and learning in relation to pupils with SEN and/or disabilities and understand how such evidence can be used to inform personal practice and others' practice, and

continued overleaf . . .

▋APPENDIX 4 . . . continued

Professional context Learning outcome:	Rating and example (if rated 1): 1 = High levels of existing skill/knowledge 4 = No existing knowledge
– identify and develop effective practice in teaching pupils with SEN and/or disabilities, e.g. through small-scale action research based on evaluating methodologies, developing critiques and, where appropriate, developing new hypotheses; – have a critical understanding of teaching, learning and behaviour management strategies and how to select, use and adapt approaches to remove barriers to learning for pupils with SEN and/or disabilities; and – have a critical understanding of approaches, strategies and resources for assessment (including national tests and examinations) and how to select, use and adapt them to personalise provision and remove barriers to assessment for pupils with SEN and/or disabilities.	
Strategic development Learning outcome:	Rating and example (if rated 1): 1 = High levels of existing skill/knowledge 4 = No existing knowledge
Working strategically with senior colleagues and governors – training should enable SENCOs to: – work with senior colleagues and governors to advise on and influence the strategic development of an inclusive ethos, policies, priorities and practices; – work with senior colleagues and governors to ensure the objectives of the school's SEN policy are/can be reflected in the school improvement plan and school self-evaluation form (SEF);	

continued overleaf . . . .

– work with senior colleagues and the governing body to establish appropriate resources to support the teaching of pupils with SEN and/or disabilities, and the means of monitoring their use in terms of value for money, efficiency and effectiveness; and

– develop and provide regular information to the headteacher and governing body on the effectiveness of provision for pupils with SEN and/or disabilities to inform decision making and policy review.

Strategic financial planning, budget management and use of resources in line with best value principles – training should enable SENCOs to know:

– the ways in which funding for pupils with SEN and/or disabilities is provided to schools, including local funding arrangements and, where appropriate, how to seek additional resources to support students with SEN and/or disabilities;

– how funding for pupils with SEN and/or disabilities is used in their school; and

– how to manage and make best use of available financial, human and physical resources, including how to use tools such as provision mapping to plan, evaluate and improve provision for pupils with SEN and/or disabilities, including identifying ineffective or missing provision.

Strategies for improving outcomes for pupils with SEN and/or disabilities – training should enable SENCOs to:

– have a sound understanding of strategies for removing barriers to participation and learning for pupils with SEN and/or disabilities;

– know strategies for addressing stereotyping and bullying related to SEN and disability;

– understand the potential of new technologies to support communication, teaching and learning for pupils with SEN and/or disabilities; and

– draw critically on relevant research and inspection evidence about effective practice in including pupils with SEN and/or disabilities to inform practice in their school.

APPENDIX 4 . . . continued

Coordinating provision Learning outcome:	Rating and example (if rated 1): 1 = High levels of existing skill/knowledge 4 = No existing knowledge
Developing, using, monitoring and evaluating systems – Training should enable SENCOs to develop, monitor, evaluate and review systems for: – identifying pupils who may have SEN and/or disabilities (using classroom observation, data, assessment and other forms of monitoring); – informing all staff about the learning needs, behaviour and achievement of pupils with SEN and/or disabilities; – helping colleagues to have realistic expectations of behaviour for pupils with SEN and/or disabilities and set appropriately challenging targets for them; – planning approaches and interventions to meet the needs of pupils with SEN and/or disabilities, geared to removing or minimising barriers to participation and learning; – recording and reviewing the progress of pupil with SEN and/or disabilities towards learning targets; – assessing the effectiveness of provision for pupils with SEN and/or disabilities; – ensuring appropriate arrangements are put in place (in classroom practice and for the examinations/tests themselves) for pupils sitting national tests and examinations; and – liaising with other schools to promote continuity of support and progression in learning when pupils with SEN and/or disabilities transfer.	

continued overleaf . . .

	Rating and example (if rated 1): 1 = High levels of existing skill/knowledge 4 = No existing knowledge
Using tools for collecting, analysing and using data – training should enable SENCOs to: – know how school, local authority and national data systems work, including RAISEonline; and – analyse and interpret relevant, local, national and school data to inform policy and practices, expectations, targets for improving the learning of pupils with SEN and/or disabilities.	
Deploying staff and managing resources – training should enable SENCOs to: – delegate tasks appropriately, deploy and manage staff effectively to ensure the most efficient use of teaching and other expertise to support pupils with SEN and/or disabilities; – make flexible and innovative use of the available workforce, recognising and utilising particular strengths and expertise.	
Leading, developing and supporting colleagues **Learning outcome:**	
Providing professional direction to the work of others – training should enable SENCOs to: – lead on developing workplace policies and practices concerning pupils with SEN and/or disabilities and promoting collective responsibility for their implementation; – take a leadership role in promoting a whole school culture of best practice in teaching and learning in relation to pupils with SEN and/or disabilities; – promote improvements in teaching and learning, offering examples of good practice for other teachers and support staff in identifying, assessing and meeting the needs of pupils with SEN and/or disabilities;	

189

▓ APPENDIX 4 . . . *continued*

Leading, developing and supporting colleagues Learning outcome:	Rating and example (if rated 1): 1 = High levels of existing skill/knowledge 4 = No existing knowledge	
– encourage all members of staff to recognise and fulfil their statutory responsibilities towards pupils with SEN and/or disabilities; and – help staff to achieve constructive working relationships with pupils with SEN and their parents/carers.		
Leadership and development of staff – Training should enable SENCOs to: – know the range of professional development opportunities available for staff (including support staff and beginner teachers) to improve their practice in working with pupils with SEN and/or disabilities; – give feedback and provide support to teaching and non-teaching colleagues on effective teaching, learning and assessment for pupils with SEN and/or disabilities; – model effective practice and coach and mentor colleagues; – advise on, contribute to, and where appropriate, coordinate the professional development of staff so that they improve their practice in relation to pupils with SEN and/or disabilities; and – support and train trainee and beginner teachers and higher level teaching assistants, where appropriate, in relation to relevant professional standards.		

continued overleaf . . .

Working in partnership with pupils, families and other professionals Learning outcome:	Rating and example (if rated 1): 1 = High levels of existing skill/knowledge 4 = No existing knowledge
Drawing on external sources of support and expertise – training should enable SENCOs to: – know the role and value of families and carers of pupils with SEN and/or disabilities; – know the range of organisations and individuals working with pupils with SEN and/or disabilities and their role in providing information, advice and support; – know the principles of multi-agency working, building a 'team around a child', and the Common Assessment Framework and how to use it, where appropriate, for pupils with SEN and/or disabilities; – know how to draw on specialist support and resources for pupils with SEN and/or disabilities, including from special schools and other specialist services or provision; – can develop effective working partnerships with professionals in other services and agencies, including voluntary organisations, to support a coherent, coordinated and effective approach to supporting pupils with SEN and/or disabilities, including in relation to transition planning for pupils post-16; and – know how to interpret specialist information from other professionals and agencies to support appropriate teaching and learning for pupils with SEN and/or disabilities and support colleagues in making use of such information.	

Photocopiable resource

APPENDIX 4 . . . continued

Working in partnership with pupils, families and other professionals Learning outcome:	Rating and example (if rated 1): 1 = High levels of existing skill/knowledge 4 = No existing knowledge
Consulting, engaging and communicating with colleagues, parents and carers and pupils to enhance pupils' learning and achievement – training should enable SENCOs to: – ensure that pupils with SEN and/or disabilities are involved, whenever appropriate, in planning, agreeing, reviewing and evaluating the provision made for them; and – communicate effectively with parents and carers of pupils with SEN and/or disabilities, taking account of their views and providing them with timely and relevant information about the achievement, targets, progress and well-being of their children.	

APPENDIX 5 WHAT CAN YOUR SCHOOL EVIDENCE IN RELATION TO EFFECTIVE PRACTICES FOR PUPILS WITH SEN, DISABILITIES AND OTHER VULNERABLE GROUPS?

(Adapted from: Special educational needs and/or disabilities in mainstream schools: A briefing paper for section 5 inspectors; January 2011)

The table below provides an overview of the key guidance that OFSTED inspectors are using when inspecting schools under the current framework. It provides an overview of the key questions that will be considered through the inspection, with opportunities for you to engage with your whole staff in review and evaluation of existing practices to ensure that you have the evidence required. It is noted that schools 'should be able to provide all this information easily. If they cannot then this in itself raises concerns' (OFSTED, 2011: 7).

Key issue:	What do we already have in place? Where is the evidence?	How do we need to develop our existing systems/practices/ evidence further?	Who needs to be involved in this?
Picture of identified need: Use Raise-Online and school data to build up a picture of identified needs, progress and provision within the school including: – numbers and proportions of learners identified with special educational needs and/or disabilities throughout the school and by year group;			

continued overleaf . . . .

APPENDIX 5 . . . continued

Key issue:	What do we already have in place? Where is the evidence?	How do we need to develop our existing systems/practices/ evidence further?	Who needs to be involved in this?
– any significant changes of identification between one year and another; – anything disproportionate, for example in identification, exclusions, absence, attainment, progress (these may inform inspection trails); – analysis of value-added scatter plots for progress of pupils with special educational needs; – numbers attending alternative provision.			
Quality of learning for pupils with SEN and/or disabilities and their progress: – Use data (Raise-Online, Progression Guidance data sets and school data) and evidence from lesson observations to show progress for pupils with SEN. – What moderation procedures are in place for teacher assessment (in school moderation processes; local authority/national/partnership moderation processes).			

- Consider the progress being made by pupils alongside the time that pupils have been receiving intervention to analyse progress.

- What is the impact of usual provision (Quality Teaching) alongside any additional and different provision on learning?

- Consider the use of support staff: are they always working directly with pupils with SEN? Are pupils given opportunities to work independently or with their peers?

- What systems are in place to quickly identify any underachievement of pupils?

- What action has been taken for any child not making sufficient progress? What impact has that had on their rate of progress?

- Provide detail about the effectiveness of provision – not just what is provided.

Behaviour:

- Do pupils with SEN feel safe in school (particularly from bullying)?

- What do observations around the school at break and lunchtime show about the way in which pupils treat each other?

- How does the school support its most behaviourally challenging pupils, even where there is a small number?

continued overleaf . . .

▇ APPENDIX 5 . . . continued

Key issue:	What do we already have in place? Where is the evidence?	How do we need to develop our existing systems/practices/ evidence further?	Who needs to be involved in this?
– Are 'reasonable adjustments' made to help pupils with BESD to be included in school (a requirement of the Disability Discrimination Act) or is exclusion the only or main response to their behaviour?			
– In lessons, are all learners engaged well in learning? Where learners need additional support to engage, does this occur?			
– Are learners with emotional and behavioural difficulties given enough support and structure (in lessons and around school) to allow them to engage successfully for a reasonable proportion of the time, and therefore to succeed?			
– Exclusions: look at the breakdown of exclusion data: which pupils are identified as having special educational needs and/or disabilities and at which stage (school action, school			

continued overleaf . . .

action plus, statement of special educational needs) – does this look reasonable or disproportionate? If exclusion is used, does it have an impact? Repeated exclusions indicate that, for that pupil, exclusion is not effective.

- Links between behaviour and low literacy levels: Is there an appropriate focus on literacy in lessons for those pupils who need it?

- Links between behaviour and achievement: look at the school's tracking data – choose a group of frequently excluded pupils or those who have the poorest behaviour records. Look at information about their attainment and progress, and the guidance and support they are receiving for their behaviour. Is this good enough?

- Behaviour in lessons: spend 10 minutes in a series of lessons with bottom sets and groups with a large number of pupils with special educational needs and/or disabilities. How do you recognise and support the vulnerability of some of these pupils who may spend much of their time with those with the most challenging behaviour, and is support appropriate? Are teachers able to manage the most challenging groups?

▎APPENDIX 5 . . . *continued*

Key issue:	What do we already have in place? Where is the evidence?	How do we need to develop our existing systems/practices/ evidence further?	Who needs to be involved in this?
– Vulnerable pupils' experiences: speak to a group of pupils with special educational needs and/or disabilities about their school experiences. – Excluded pupils' experiences: speak to a group of pupils who are frequently excluded.			
Attendance: – Consider attendance of pupils with SEN compared with the rest of the school. – Investigate links between low attendance and levels of progress and attainment as well as the identification of pupils as having special educational needs and/or disabilities. – Are pupils being given the appropriate amount of support and challenge to improve their attendance and is this effective?			

The quality of teaching and the use of assessment to support learning:

- Are pupils with SEN making the same progress in acquiring attitudes and skills leading to greater independence in learning?

- How are pupils' curiosity and persistence promoted by the staff?

- How are pupils with SEN encouraged to use their initiative?

- Do teaching assistants always work with the lowest attaining group? Is this effective? How is the teacher taking responsibility for the progress of those pupils?

- When is the teacher involved in teaching pupils with SEN who are frequently supported by other staff?

- How does the teacher know about the progress that a pupil is making (NB: should not just rely on information from support staff)?

- What interaction does the teacher have with pupils with SEN?

- Do pupils with SEN have an opportunity to work with others or are the majority of interactions adult led?

continued overleaf . . .

■ APPENDIX 5 . . . continued

Key issue:	What do we already have in place? Where is the evidence?	How do we need to develop our existing systems/practices/ evidence further?	Who needs to be involved in this?
– Do support staff have sufficient knowledge to ensure their input and questioning promotes thinking and learning as opposed to task completion?			
– Does the organisation of the lesson and physical environment enable full access regardless of disability?			
– Are teachers and other staff clear about what they want pupils to learn (NB: this may not always be just the subject content)?			
– Compare the books/work of pupils with SEN with others and scrutinise challenge of tasks; evidence of motivation and independence; presentation and marking.			
Curriculum:			
– Does the curriculum raise aspirations and provide realistic opportunities for progression, i.e. not present a 'glass ceiling' for pupils with SEN?			

continued overleaf . . . .

Access and participation: – What is the proportion of pupils with SEN who are participating in additional activities? Is this in line with other groups? – How are 'reasonable adjustments' made to ensure that pupils with disabilities are positively supported to participate?		
Additional intervention/provision: – How are interventions selected? (NB: they should be driven by the pupils' needs as well as a strong evaluation of what works) – Evaluate the impact of the chosen interventions on improving outcomes. – How do the interventions link into other lessons?		
Safeguarding: – What do records show about bullying? Are there disproportionate numbers of pupils with SEN being bullied? What actions have been taken? – Are any pupils with SEN bullying others? What actions has the school taken to 'identify and support the underlying needs of the pupil?		

▪ APPENDIX 5 . . . continued

Key issue:	What do we already have in place? Where is the evidence?	How do we need to develop our existing systems/practices/ evidence further?	Who needs to be involved in this?
– Have relevant safeguarding checks been made for off-site provision?			
– Have relevant safeguarding checks (e.g. risk assessments) been completed for all activities?			
– Do pupils with SEN feel safe?			
– Are all staff aware of safeguarding procedures? How? Review staff training.			
– Observe practices to ensure safety at break and lunchtimes: look at adult supervision; 'safe' spaces in the playground.			

APPENDIX 6 CHECKLIST OF KEY PRINCIPLE PROMPTS FOR SCHOOL IMPROVEMENT PARTNERS AND THEIR SCHOOLS (ADAPTED FROM THE PROGRESSION GUIDANCE, 2010–2011 (DFE, 2010C: 43–44)

Key principles and prompts	Review and reflection on existing practice – including evidence	What more could be done? Action Planning	Impact
Key principle 1: High expectations are key to securing good progress – How do you know that learners are doing as well as they can? – What evidence do you have to show you have sufficient ambition for your learners? – How well are you preparing young people for next steps to full active participation in adult society and how do you know?			
Key principle 2: Accurate assessment is essential for securing and measuring pupil progress How do you know whether: – the school's systems and approaches enable a focus on developing a community of independent, confident learners;			

continued overleaf . . .

APPENDIX 6 . . . continued

Key principles and prompts	Review and reflection on existing practice – including evidence	What more could be done? Action Planning	Impact
– all learners, whatever their prior attainment, have opportunities to know how they are doing, understand what they need to do to improve and how they can do that; get the support they need to be motivated, independent learners continually improving in their learning;			
– teachers are equipped to make well-founded judgements about learners' attainment, based on their age and prior attainment. They understand the concepts and principles of progression and they use a range of information and evidence and know how to use their assessment judgements to forward-plan, particularly for the very lowest-attaining learners;			
– all staff work collaboratively within and across key stages and curriculum areas, enthusiastically sharing their practice and insights. There are high expectations about learning across the school;			
– governors act as critical friends and can contribute to the next steps in the development of secure assessment to support learning;			

- learners play a key role in the assessment process and individual planning;

- assessment and target setting underpin the evidence base for the review process, particularly for learners with a statement of SEN.

Involving parents

- How does the school ensure that parents and carers are provided with key information about how their child is progressing in a parent-friendly format; that they know how their child is doing and what they need to do to improve, and are involved in supporting their child's learning in and outside school?

- How has the school adjusted parent meetings to support more effective listening to parents about their child's learning?

- How does the assessment information and feedback from parents and learners better enable the school to review and negotiate new numerical and curriculum targets?

- What evidence does the school have that conversations with parents, coupled with your assessment knowledge, have improved curriculum delivery and better matched it to the needs of learners?

continued overleaf . . .

APPENDIX 6 . . . continued

Key principles and prompts	Review and reflection on existing practice – including evidence	What more could be done? Action Planning	Impact
– What adjustments have there been to continuing professional development as a result of assessment and moderation processes and conversations with parents?			
Key Principle 3: Age and prior attainment data are the starting points for developing expectations of pupil progress – How does the local authority/school use the age and prior attainment data from the Progression data sets? What other evidence is used to secure judgements on achievement? – How does the data improve the challenge and support from SIPs? – What data does the school share with parents and carers and with the SIP? – How does this inform strategic decisions about planning and commissioning provision and services? – How is the data used to enhance the setting of targets for the lowest attaining learners?			

- What advice does the local authority/region offer to schools, in relation to identification of SEND?

- What evidence is there to show that, as a result, reasonable adjustments have been made and are having a positive impact on learning?

- How closely is the 'Waves' model of intervention aligned with the SEN Code of Practice's 'graduated response?'

- How do you know if the provision being made is making a difference to learners' progress?

- How does the data inform review processes, including statutory reviews?

- How is data used in reviews where learners are in out-of-local authorty provision, for example independent and non-maintained special schools?

REFERENCES

Ainscow, M., Booth, T. and Dyson, A. (2006) *Improving Schools, Developing Inclusion*, Abingdon: Routledge.

Alexander, R. (2001) 'Pedagogy and culture: a perspective in search of a method' in Soler, J., Craft, A. and Burgess, H. (eds) *Teacher Development: Exploring our own practice*, London: Paul Chapman Publishing.

Alexander, R. (ed.) (2010) *Children, Their World, Their Education: Final report and recommendations of the Cambridge Primary Review*, Abingdon: Routledge.

Barton, L. (2010) 'The politics of education for all' in Rix, J., Nind, M., Sheehy, K., Simmons, K., Parry, J. and Kumrai, R. (eds) *Equality, Participation and Inclusion: Diverse perspectives*, Abingdon: Routledge.

Bentley, J. (2010) 'Lessons from the 1%: Children with labels of severe disabilities and their peers as architects of inclusive education' in Rix, J., Nind, M., Sheehy, K., Simmons, K., Parry, J. and Kumrai, R. (eds) *Equality, Participation and Inclusion: Diverse Perspectives*, Abingdon: Routledge.

Bercow, J. (2008) *The Bercow Review: a review of services for children and young people (0–19) with speech, language and communication needs*, London: DCSF.

Blandford, S. (2011) 'Achievement for All': Keynote presentation at 8th Annual SENCO Update Conference, London.

Booth, T. and Ainscow, M. (2002) *Index for Inclusion*, Bristol: CSIE.

Booth, T. and Ainscow, M. (2011) *Index for Inclusion: Developing learning and participation in schools* (3rd edn), Bristol: Centre for Studies on Inclusion in Education.

Bradbury, B., Feeney, A. and Gager, A. (2010) 'Hearing the voice of the child: ensuring authenticity' in Hallett, F. and Hallett, G. (eds) *Transforming the Role of the SENCO: Achieving the National Award for SEN coordination*, Maidenhead: Open University Press.

Cameron, D. and Clegg, N. (2010) 'Foreword' in DfE (2010) *The Importance of Teaching*, London: Crown Copyright.

Corbett, J. (2001) *Supporting Inclusive Education: School Concerns*, London: RoutledgeFalmer.

Dadds, M. (2001) 'Continuing professional development: nurturing the expert within' in Soler, J., Craft, A. and Burgess, H. (eds) *Teacher Development: Exploring our own practice*, London: Paul Chapman Publishing.

Davies, P. and Hattersley, J. (2010) 'Managing financial and physical resources' in Hallett, F. and Hallett, G. (eds) *Transforming the Role of the SENCO: Achieving the National Award for SEN coordination*, Maidenhead: Open University Press.

DCSF (2007) *Primary National Strategy: Pupil Progress Meetings Prompts and Guidance*, London: TSO.

DCSF (2008) *Education (Special Educational Needs Co-ordinators) (England) Regulations 2008: Explanatory note for governing bodies*, London: DCSF.

DCSF (2009) *Achievement for All: the structured conversation – handbook to support training*, London: DCSF.

DCSF (2010a) *Breaking the Link Between Special Educational Needs and Low Attainment: Everyone's business*, London: Crown Copyright.

DCSF (2010b) *Improving Parental Confidence in the SEN system: An implementation plan*, London: Crown Copyright.

DES (1999) *The National Curriculum Key Stage 1 and 2*, London: DES.

DfE (2010a) *The Importance of Teaching*, London: Crown Copyright.

DfE (2010b) *The Case for Change*, London: Crown Copyright.

DfE (2010c) *Progression Guidance 2010–2011: Advice on improving data to raise attainment and maximise the progress of learners with special educational needs*, London: Crown Copyright.

DfE (2011) *Support and Aspiration: A new approach to special educational needs and disability: A consultation*, Norwich: TSO.

DfES (2001) *Special Educational Needs Code of Practice*, London: DfES.

DfES (2002) *Primary National Strategy in England*, London: DfES.

DfES (2003) *Secondary National Strategy in England*, London: DfES.

DfES (2004) *Removing Barriers to Achievement*, London: DfES.

DfES (2004) *Children Act*, London: TSO.

DfES (2005) *Leading on Inclusion*, London: DfES.

Delamont, S. and Atkinson, P. (1995) *Fighting Familiarity: Essays on education and ethnography*, Cresskill, NJ: Hampton Press.

Durrant, J. and Holden, G. (2006) *Teachers Leading Change: Doing research for school improvement*, London: Paul Chapman Publishing.

Ekins, A. (2010a) 'Developing a joined-up approach to strategic whole school approaches' in Hallett, F. and Hallett, G. (eds) *Transforming the Role of the SENCO: Achieving the National Award for SEN coordination*, Maidenhead: open University Press.

Ekins, A. (2010b) 'An Exploration of Developing Inclusive Practices: Case studies of two primary schools', doctoral thesis: University of Kent/Canterbury Christ Church University.

Ekins, A. (2010c) *Understanding and Tackling Underachievement: Whole school strategies to meet the needs of vulnerable children in primary schools*, London: Optimus Publishing.

Ekins, A. (2011 forthcoming) *Impact and implications of the National Award for SEN Coordination for the Professional Identity of SENCOs*.

Ekins, A. and Grimes, P. (2009) *Inclusion: Developing an effective whole school approach*, Maidenhead: Open University Press.

Ellis, S., Tod, J. and Graham-Matheson, L. (2008) *Special Educational Needs and Inclusion: Reflection and renewal*, Birmingham: NASUWT.

Farrell, M. (2010) *Debating Special Education*, Abingdon: Routledge.

Florian, L. (2010) 'The concept of inclusive pedagogy' in Hallett, F. and Hallett, G. (eds) *Transforming the Role of the SENCO: Achieving the National Award for SEN coordination*, Maidenhead: Open University Press.

Hallett, F. and Hallett, G. (2010) *Transforming the role of the SENCO: Achieving the National Award for SEN Coordination*, Maidenhead: Open University Press.

Harris, A. (2006) 'Foreword' in Durrant, J. and Holden, G. (eds) *Teachers Leading Change: Doing research for school improvement*, London: Paul Chapman Publishing.

Hopkins, D. (2007) *Every School a Great School*, Maidenhead: Open University Press.

House of Commons Select Committee (2006) 'Special Educational Needs: Third report of session 2005–2006', London: TSO.

Howes, A., Davies, S.M.B. and Fox, S. (2009) *Improving the Context for Inclusion: Personalising teacher development through collaborative action research*, Abingdon: Routledge.

Kugelmass, J. (2004) *The Inclusive School: Sustaining, equity and standards*, New York: Teachers College Press.

Lamb, B. (2009) *SEN and Parental Confidence*, London: Crown Copyright.

Lave, J., and Wenger, E. (1998) *Communities of Practice: Learning, meaning, and identity*, Cambridge: Cambridge University Press.

Lawson, H. and Nash, T. (2010) 'SENCOs: A partnership role in initial teacher education?' in Hallett, F. and Hallett, G. (eds) *Transforming the Role of the SENCO: Achieving the National Award for SEN coordination*, Maidenhead: Open University Press.

Loreman, T., Deppeler, J. and Harvey, D. (2010) *Inclusive Education: Supporting diversity in the classroom*, Abingdon: Routledge.

MacBeath, J. (1999) *Schools Must Speak for Themselves: The case for school self evaluation*, Abingdon: Routledge.

MacBeath, J., Galton, M., Steward, S., MacBeath, A. and Page, C. (2006) *Costs of Inclusion: A study of inclusion policy and practice in English primary, secondary and special schools*, Cambridge: University of Cambridge; NUT.

MacBeath, J., Gray, J., Cullen, J., Frost, D., Steward, S. and Swaffield, S. (2007) *Schools on the Edge: Responding to challenging circumstances*, London: Paul Chapman Publishing.

McConkey, R. (2010) 'Reciprocal working by education, health and social services: lessons for a less-travelled road' in Rix, J., Nind, M., Sheehy, K., Simmons, K., Parry, J. and Kumrai, R. (eds) *Equality, Participation and Inclusion: Diverse contexts*, Abingdon: Routledge.

Mitchell, D. (2008) *What Really Works in Special and Inclusive Education: Using evidence based teaching strategies*, Abingdon: Routledge.

Nasen (2010) *Policy on the Coordination of SEN and Additional Support Needs*, Birmingham: nasen.

National College (2010a) *A Special Achievement*, Nottingham: National College.

National College (2010b) *Achievement for All: Characteristics of Effective Inclusive Leadership: A discussion document*, Nottingham: National College for Leadership of Schools and Children's Services.

National Strategies (2008) *The Improving Schools Programme (ISP) Strengthening governance: knowing your school*, DCSF.

Nias, J., Southwark, G. and Yeomans, R. (1989) *Staff Relationships in the Primary School*, London: Cassell Education.

Norwich, B. (2010) 'What implications do changing practices and concepts have for the role of the SEN Coordinator?' in Hallett, F. and Hallett, G. (eds) *Transforming the Role of the SENCO: Achieving the National Award for SEN coordination*, Maidenhead: Open University Press.

OFSTED (2000) *Evaluating Educational Inclusion: guidance for inspectors and schools*, London: OFSTED.

OFSTED (2004) *A New Relationship with Schools*, London: OFSTED.

OFSTED (2010) *The special educational needs and disability review: A statement is not enough*, Manchester: Crown Copyright.

OFSTED (2011) Special educational needs and/or disabilities in mainstream schools: A briefing paper for section 5 inspectors, London: OFSTED.

Parry, J., Rix, J., Kumrai, R. and Walsh, C. (2010) 'Introduction: Another Place' in Rix, J., Nind, M., Sheehy, K., Simmons, K., Parry, J. and Kumrai, R. (eds) *Equality, Participation and Inclusion: Diverse contexts*, Abingdon: Routledge.

Pearson, S. (2010) 'The Governing Body: An (untapped) resource' in Hallett, F. and Hallett, G. (eds) *Transforming the Role of the SENCO: Achieving the National Award for SEN coordination*, Maidenhead: Open University Press.

Petersen, L. (2010) 'A national perspective on the training of SENCOs' in Hallett, F. and Hallett, G. (eds) (2010) *Transforming the Role of the SENCO: Achieving the National Award for SEN coordination*, Maidenhead: Open University Press.

Primary Strategy (2006) *Leading on Intervention*, London: DfES.

Reid, A. (2010) 'The politics of educational change' in Arthur, J. and Davies, I. (eds) *Education Studies Textbook*, Abingdon: Routledge.

Rix, J. (2007) 'Labels of opportunity: a response to Carson and Rowley', *Ethical Space*, 4 (3), 25–7.

Rix, J. and Sheehy, K. (2010) 'A collective model of difference' in Rix, J., Nind, M., Sheehy, K., Simmons, K., Parry, J. and Kumrai, R. (eds) *Equality, Participation and Inclusion: Diverse perspectives*, Abingdon: Routledge.

Rix, J., Walsh, C., Parry, J. and Kumrai, R. (2010) 'Introduction: Another point of view' in Rix, J., Nind, M., Sheehy, K., Simmons, K., Parry, J. and Kumrai, R. (eds) *Equality, Participation and Inclusion: Diverse perspectives*, Abingdon: Routledge.

Sakellariadis, A. (2010) 'The challenge of supporting the supporters in the inclusive school' in Hallett, F. and Hallett, G. (eds) *Transforming the Role of the SENCO: Achieving the National Award for SEN coordination*, Maidenhead: Open University Press.

Schön, D. (1983) *The Reflective Practitioner*, New York: Basic Books.

Sergiovanni, T. (2001) *Leadership: What's in it for schools?* Abingdon, RoutledgeFalmer.

Slee, R., Weiner, G. and Tomlinson, S. (eds) (1998) *School Effectiveness for Whom? Challenges to the school effectiveness and school improvement movements*, Abingdon: RoutledgeFalmer.

Stables (2009) 'Schools as imagined community in discursive space: a perspective on the school effectiveness debate' in Daniels, H., Lauder, H. and Porter, J. (eds) *Knowledge, Values and Educational Policy: A critical perspective*, Abingdon: Routledge.

Stoll, L. and Fink, D. (1989) *Changing our Schools*, Maidenhead: Open University Press.

TDA (2009) *The Learning Outcomes for SENCOs Successfully Completing Nationally Approved Training*, London: TDA.

UNESCO (1994) *The Salamanca Statement and Framework for Action on Special Needs Education*, Paris: UNESCO.

Warnock, M. (1978) *Warnock Report: Special Educational Needs, Report of the Committee of Enquiry into the education of handicapped children and young people*, London: HMSO.

Warnock, M. (2005) *Special Educational Needs: a new look*, Salisbury: Philosophy of Education Society of Great Britain.

West, M., Ainscow, M. and Stanford, J. (2005) 'Sustaining improvement in schools in challenging circumstances: a study of successful practice', *School Leadership and Management*, 2 (1) 77–93.

Williams, K. (2011) 'Working with Disabled Children, Young People and their Families': Keynote presentation to 8th Annual SENCO Update Conference, London.

Woods, P., Jeffrey, B., Tronman, G. and Boyle, M. (1997) *Restructuring Schools, Reconstructing Teachers: Responding to change in the primary school*, Buckingham: Open University Press.

Workman, A. and Pickard, J. (2010) 'Professional identity in multi-disciplinary teams: the staff speak' in Rix, J., Nind, M., Sheehy, K., Simmons, K., Parry, J. and Kumrai, R. (eds) *Equality, Participation and Inclusion: Diverse Contexts*, Abingdon: Routledge.

INDEX

Note: page numbers in *italics* indicate a figure.